THE HIDDEN SIDE OF BABEL

Unveiling Cognition, Intelligence and Sense

LAURA E. BERTONE

THE HIDDEN SIDE
OF BABEL

Unveiling Cognition, Intelligence and Sense
through Simultaneous Interpretation

Prefaced by Juan Seguí,
one of the founders of Cognitive Psycholinguistics

First three parts translated by Enrique Robert

EVOLUCION

THE HIDDEN SIDE OF BABEL
is an imprint of Evolución Publishing Division
Esmeralda 1385 C1007ABS, Buenos Aires, Argentina.
http://www.evolucion.com.ar

Translation from Spanish: Enrique Robert.
(*En torno de Babel* by Laura Bertone, Hachette, Buenos Aires,
1989, included in the first three parts of this book).
Chief Editor: Mónica Nosetto.
Interior design: Mónica Nosetto.
Illustrations: Alain Huré (France).
Additional illustrations: Alejandro Barros (Argentina).
Image digitalization: Federico Kuntscher from Arka Digital.
Front cover design: Federico Kuntscher, Mónica Nosetto,
Marianne Costa Picazo.
Cover Illustration: *La Tour Babel* by Lucas van Valckenborch
(before 1535-1597). The Louvre Museum.
Back cover illustration: Alain Huré.
First Edition in Argentina, 2006.

ISBN-10 987-21049-1-3
ISBN-13 978-987-21049-1-7

Bertone, Laura Estela
The Hidden Side of Babel – Unveiling Cognition, Intelligence and Sense
1ª ed. – Buenos Aires: Evolución, 2006.
464 p.; 25x17 cm.
ISBN 987-21049-1-3
1. Psicolingüística. I. Título
CDD 401.9

Fecha de catalogación: 28/09/2006

To my mother,
with Teófilo.

Contents

PART 2
THE FUNCTIONING OF THE INTERPRETER
What the Interpreter Does

PART 3
HOW SIMULTANEOUS INTERPRETING WORKS
Borrowing from other Disciplines to Explain its Functioning

A Word of Thanks

*Between the first publication of part of this book in Spanish (*En torno de Babel – Estrategias de la interpretación simultánea, *Buenos Aires: Hachette, 1989) and this first enlarged edition in English, sixteen years have gone by. There are now a few more people to whom I would like to express my thanks. In the very first place, Enrique Robert, colleague and friend, former UN permanent interpreter whom I met at a conference in Phoenix, Arizona, in 1984 and who took me literally by the arm to the Monterey Institute of International Relations where I would eventually replace him as teacher of translation and interpretation for a whole semester the following year, in what constituted a great personal teaching experience for me. Once back in Chile, his homeland, Enrique took the time and the energy to translate this work into English and always remained confident that it would eventually get published. I want to thank him first for his work, since I had the feeling when reading his translation that I was really reading myself. But I also want to thank him for his trust, respect, and patience. I hope these words transmit my deep appreciation for that infinitely generous flow of letters and mails across the Andes that silently paved the way for this new book. Enrique, thanks!*

Then, Mónica Nosetto who, without special previous experience in the interpreting world, but with a wide and rich experience in the editorial and literary world, proved to be a challenging, passionate and lucid reader. Mónica, thanks! Your help was not only fundamental, our exchanges were also frequently fascinating and fun!

But this work started long before, during Emilio Stevano-vitch's interpreting classes in Buenos Aires towards the end of the sixties. Steve, as we used to call him, unveiled the interpreting world for me, as for so many other interpreters in this part of the world.

I would also like to thank Taddey Pilley, head of the Linguists' Club and one of the leading London interpreters at the time who, after listening to me in a short exam, insisted I should become a member of AIIC, the interpreters' association based in Geneva giving me thus the final thrust for an international career. I should not forget it was my good friend Roberto Devorik who found the connections for me to reach Taddey during a fleeting visit of mine to London.

My appreciation goes as well to Prince Antonin Andronikoff, for years chief Interpreter at the Quai d'Orsay, who welcomed me in his apartment on rue de l'Odéon on a warm summer afternoon of 1976 soon after my arrival in Paris. During what was to me a most fascinating conversation, he suggested my doing research in this field, revealing thus a possibility the existence of which I had ignored till then.

My gratitude goes especially to Gilles Fauconnier (Directeur de Recherche at l'Ecole des Hautes Etudes en Sciences Sociales, and professor at Paris VIII in those days) who became my doctoral tutor.

I would also like to recognize those first readers of my first French manuscripts who had the courage not to discourage me: Jean-Marie Flosch, Ned de Margerie, Jean-Francois Le Ny.

In quite a different period of my life and my research, I am indebted to Charlotte Schuchard Read, a long-life pillar of the Institute of General Semantics who, the first, suggested I should have this book translated into English and made available in the United States.

A special word of thanks to Stuart Jordan, astrophysicist from NASA and great humanist, who took the time and the energy to read a long manuscript and make a most interesting evaluation.

Thanks to my colleagues, especially those who kindly allowed me to record their work, and to all the others – old and young – from whom I always ended up learning something.

My acknowledgments to the authorities and technicians at UNESCO in Paris, and UNISYS in St. Paul de Vence for having permitted me to record some of their meetings.

To Ned de Margerie and Thierry Léfébure for proof reading the French texts. To Douglas Town, Lea Fletcher and Alejandro Parini for proof reading the English texts. Very especially to Alain Huré, and to Alejandro Barros for their illustrations. To Norberto Ruiz Diaz and Francisco Zabala for revising the phonetic transcripts. To Norberto again, to Victoria Massa-Bulit and Susan Presby-Kodish for their comments and suggestions.

The thrust that decided me to embark on this adventure thirty years ago had nothing to do with the desire to develop an academic or a literary career. As if trying to solve a personal puzzle, I was just following an intuition, pulling together pieces that had till then appeared to me as "disconnected". The study of language from different angles and perspectives has been the unifying common thread.

Incredibly enough, the thrust of accepting this challenge in the past proves to be valid still today. I am surprised at my own enthusiasm to update and complete this work in the light of other more recent experiences. In fact, some time after its publication in Spanish, I slowly started shifting my attention and changing activities. It is the result of these other perspectives, and the renewed vision of the old research that I wish to bring to the readers' attention today.

Laura Bertone
Buenos Aires, September, 2006.

Prologue

As many authors have indicated, the cognitive processes that support the production and understanding of language – although taken for granted in everyday life – are extraordinarily subtle and complex. Linguistics, pragmatics, psychology and neuroscience have hardly begun to unravel some of their mysteries. How is it then that the author has had the audacity to write a book about the most sophisticated cognitive-linguistic skill that human beings are capable of – simultaneous interpreting?

No doubt, the answer lies partly in the fact that Laura Bertone does not deal with simultaneous interpreting from the purely academic perspective of a specialist in a certain discipline but draws on her own personal experiences as an interpreter and combines these, in a very coherent and original way, with an excellent understanding of the most recent theoretical and empirical work on language processing.

Laura Bertone's book is wonderfully lively and entertaining. But what I would like to point out here is how the combination of introspective data and experimental results led Laura to formulate an original and important hypothesis on language processing.

I need to go back to our first meeting in the 1980's when Laura was starting her PhD dissertation on linguistics under the direction of Gilles Fauconnier.

Laura told me then that she was convinced it was indispensable for her to learn about the experimental work on language production and understanding in psycholinguistics in order to carry out her thesis on simultaneous interpretation and she asked me for the relevant references. This request surprised me, coming as it did from someone working mostly in pragmatics and who was therefore supposed to be interested in the "higher" cognitive processes. I agreed to her request by inviting her to read some of the latest studies carried out at the laboratory of experimental psychology that I directed at the time. These studies showed very clearly the automatic and irrepressible nature of the basic processes in linguistic calculations, which escape any type of cognitive control.

Laura was very surprised to learn that the presentation of an ambiguous word seemed to activate in the mind of the listener, automatically and unconsciously, not only the meaning appropriate to the context in which it appeared but also its other different meanings. These studies, first conducted by an American colleague, the late David Swinney, also showed that only the meaning appropriate to the context is allowed to emerge into consciousness.

This being so, Laura Bertone sensed that the automatic activation of multiple mental representations was not restricted to the semantic level but was probably a feature of other linguistic levels as well. This made it possible to explain many of the phenomena observed in simultaneous interpreting, as the author shows in the different sections of her book. Recent studies in psycholinguistics clearly confirm Laura's intuition since they unveil the simultaneous activation of multiple representations at other levels of processing (orthography, phonology, morphology, and syntax).

This simple example demonstrates the usefulness of tackling the study of complex cognitive processes using an introspective approach in combination with the latest empirical findings coming from scientific literature. Laura Bertone's book seems to me an excellent example of how fruitful this research strategy can prove to be.

Juan Seguí
Paris, September 22nd, 2006.

My Purpose

One of the aims of this book is to reveal, through the study of simultaneous interpretation, some of our most frequent mental processes so as to get to know and understand them. Those mental processes are at the very core of our behaviours and attitudes, and they will have a direct influence and impact on our inter-personal and inter-cultural relationships on which our welfare and wellbeing depend both as individuals and as nations.

Another goal of this book is to succeed in bringing about a shift in readers' attention, making them focus on certain things or aspects or facets of things they would not normally have taken into consideration – both externally and internally. This, in its turn, may hopefully trigger a re-organization of priorities.

The third purpose is, that upon finishing this book, readers feel not that they know something more, but rather that they know something different.

Last but not least, there is the aim that seeks to reset the study of these complex multidimensional multi-ordinal situations with their enormous complexity within the field not of only one science but at the crossroads of several: the Cognitive Sciences. Linguistics seems today too narrow to embrace perceptions, sensations, feelings, emotions, ideas, thoughts, representations and mental processes associated with language. Embracing them implies bringing not only language in, but also *experience*; it implies taking into account not only the "observable" elements outside, but also some "observable" elements inside and within ourselves.

A Note of Warning

Those who expect this book to be a technical treatise on interpretation subjects should know from the start that it is not. Nor has it been specifically designed for teaching interpretation.

This book is addressed to English-speaking readers, preferably those with some knowledge of Spanish or French. Although all examples have been translated into English, they will be easier to grasp if Spanish or French is understood. Part of this book was published in Spanish in 1989. To the best of my knowledge, it was one of the first books on the subject in the Spanish-speaking world. As Spanish is not one of the main languages of most European interpreters doing research in this area, it has seldom been included in academic bibliographies and reading lists. I hope this new version will help bridge the gap.

I wrote the first part of this work in French. I was then asked to translate it into Spanish. I asked a Chilean colleague and friend of mine, Enrique Robert, to translate the Spanish version into English. I eventually added some paragraphs to the first parts and wrote parts IV and V in English myself. *I did not intend it this way. It just turned out this way.* This accounts for the language chosen for some of the titles in the bibliography. I read the books in the language of the country I was living in at the time of consulting them. I hope English readers will bear with me for this.

There was no gender problem in the eighties in French, nor was there in Spanish when *En Torno de Babel* first came out. Interpreters were referred to by the generic masculine pronouns tacitly encompassing both "he" and "she". I decided to apply the same rule here and to use the plural form as much as possible. Only in a few cases do I introduce the feminine to show I am aware that the constant use of the masculine forms may be annoying. I hope that the sudden shift from one gender to the other does not catch readers off-guard.

A choice had to be made regarding the type of English to be used: British or American – with all the spelling consequences that entailed. I opted for British English simply because one of the first proof-readers was British himself. I hope consistency has been kept throughout. I also opted for the "recognize" version. As shown in a survey on "Establishing Guidelines for English Language" (*See www.tc-forum. org/topicus/ru23resu.htm*) regarding the spelling of *recognize/recognise* for example, the European vote was split almost evenly and there was a clear difference between the Americans and Canadians, who preferred *recognize*, and the Australians and New Zealanders, who preferred *recognise*. These variations show there are more differences than one would expect and no choice can please everybody at the same time. I hope readers will bear with me for this as well.

THE HIDDEN SIDE OF BABEL

Unveiling Cognition, Intelligence and Sense

Introduction

The Fabulous Mystery of Language

Language is that set of tools and rules which enables us humans not only to communicate and transmit at least part of what we perceive, feel, think, believe, know, and do among ourselves. It is also the means to preserve and transmit whatever our ancestors passed on to us and whatever we want to preserve for future generations. But language is not only a communicative "bridge", it is also constitutive "bricks" since it helps us break up and articulate the continuum of "reality out there". Consequently, it helps "create", at least in part, "reality out there". And paradoxically, if language can function as a bridge, it can also act as a barrier; if it can function as *bricks*, it can also function as destructive *gunpowder*.

Although the number of languages in the world is currently estimated at around 6400 (grouped into families and including many dialects and varieties), we know from Chomsky that there is an underlying structure shared by all speakers of all languages beyond the multiple differences from one another.

In this sense, languages are like the human face. No two faces – among the billions the world over – are identical (even if certain similarities allow us to group them in races and families), yet a common basic structure seems to embrace them all.

Similarly, we humans all seem to share the ways in which we process perceptual information, make deductive or inductive inferences, make decisions, construct meaning and knowledge and build mental maps of the world, even if our final conclusions or representations of the world sometimes appear to have little in common.

Using language as our gate of entry, we will be delving into some of these mental processes in the chapters that follow. But language presents, of course, many aspects and so offers many points of access.

As speakers and communicators, writers or journalists, diplomats, politicians or actors, we are trained to become aware of certain aspects of language functioning, mechanisms, styles and effects.

As doctors, psychiatrists, psychologists and psychoanalysts, we are trained to perceive and listen to certain signs, and to be extremely careful of what we say and how.

As consultants and managers, we are – or should be – trained to pay attention to aspects of language use that help convey messages, assign tasks, give instructions, and correct others' mistakes without causing pain, etc.

As language teachers, translators and interpreters, we normally become aware of many other and highly varied aspects and dimensions of language (phonological, morphological, syntactic, semantic, pragmatic rules, etc.).

As researchers in the field of linguistics, we are confronted with other equally fascinating aspects of language; for example, language history, the etymological origin of certain words, the reciprocal influences of two or more languages on one another, the spreading of a language over territories and times, the supremacy of certain languages, the dying out of others.

And yet as human beings, even though it is precisely language which sets the human race apart from other forms of life, we do not seem especially aware of the quality and dimensions, of the potential and boundaries, of the usefulness, the preciousness and the uniqueness of the mysterious set of tools and rules we handle every day.

French writer Edouard Schuré[1] once said that man becomes human the day he understands the link that binds him to his co-existing fellow creatures and the link that binds him to the past and future of his own species. As we go through life, we can

------

1 *Edouard Schuré,* Les Grands Initiés, *Paris, Librairie Académique Perrin, 1960.*

improve and perfect both links, made conscious through language and mostly constituted by language itself, a bit in the same way as members of certain Australian indigenous communities change their own names according to their progress and evolution in life. Thus, *Tool Maker* may eventually become *Tribal Elder; Spirit Woman, Composer,* and eventually *Great Composer.*

In the pages that follow, I will focus on those aspects of language that from one perspective or another (as speaker, or interpreter, or researcher) have often astounded me.

Let us begin our discussion of language, then, at the very beginning. Because it is no simple matter to determine what the basic building blocks of language are (a word, a sentence, a sign, a phoneme, a sound, a letter?) we shall resort to the Ancients. We shall take as our starting point Aristotle's first book of Metaphysics, which describes the world as a fortuitous conjunction of atoms; and Jorge Luis Borges' suggestion that Aristotle's inference requires these atoms to be homogeneous. Differences in the physical world are the result of the different shapes, order and positions, the atoms may adopt, *"much as "A" differs from "N" in shape, "AN" differs from "NA" in order, "Z" differs from 'N" because of its position"*.

As Jorge Luis Borges would have it, languages function like a game: they have a finite number of elements plus a finite number of rules. (We choose to take the written language as a starting point and among its various forms, our Roman alphabet. We shall take letters, not words, as the building blocks.). The number of such elements is not large – letters, spaces, dots – although the number of letters in the alphabet, as well as other symbols such as accents, diaeresis (two dots on a *ü* as in *über* in German), etc., can vary among languages. We can simplify our example by stating that 25 symbols (22 letters, space, dot, and comma) in different combinations are enough to express whatever we want to express in any language (some restrictions and differences granted from the start).

Isn't that fabulous? That the *Old* and the *New Testaments*, the *Coran*, the *Raham Gita* and the worlds of Shakespeare, Herodotus and Aristotle, of Cervantes, Rousseau and Goethe have been conceived, described and conveyed through the *different* combinations of 25 elements (or thereabouts)? Are we fully aware of what this represents?

Are we aware that all those worlds – and many others, including those that use no books like the Egyptian pyramids or those that are yet to be discovered or invented – can be conveyed through the *different* combinations of the *same* set of finite elements? Are we fully aware of what this represents?

Defined as 'a set of tools and rules', language as a game can create an endless number of different worlds. Yet, a definition of language in terms of elements, tools and rules, suggests something relatively static, as structures normally are. A "transversal" general semantics approach, from engineering science rather than from linguistics, may help us shift our focus a little bit and see *language* as something else as well: as a dynamic, permanently changing and creative process. This little addition implies a big change.

Is language, as Borges pretends, an efficient ordering of the abundance of the world? Is language a means for inventing names for our experience of reality?

> "We feel a round shape by touching, we see a heap of light at dawn, some tickling fills our mouth with joy and we melt these three heterogeneous things into what we call an *orange*."[2]

Since Ferdinand de Saussure's groundbreaking work, *Cours de Linguistique Générale*[3] (*Course on General Linguistics*), it has generally been accepted that what connects a chain of sounds to

---

2 *Jorge Luis Borges,* El Tamaño de Mi Esperanza, *Buenos. Aires, Proa, 1926; Seix Barral, 1993. (*The Dimension of Our Hope*)*

3 *Ferdinand de Saussure,* Cours de Linguistique Générale, *Edited by Charles Bally and Albert Séchehaye. Edicion critique préparée par Tulio de Mauro. Paris, Bayot, 1974*

an object is a sign, and that the connection between the two is arbitrary. This idea seems easy to understand today and it could hardly be otherwise, considering the number of languages that exist and consequently the incredibly different ways of referring to, for example, a particular piece of food: *cheese, queso, queijo, fromage, formaggio*, etc. These words do not represent any inherent quality of the processed milk product that they refer to. Likewise, nothing in the word *tree* is inherently related with the object *tree*. Yet, studies of ancient Hebrew and Sanskrit show that the tracing of words originally followed a symbolic path. It will surely be interesting one day to go back our way and find the clues that got lost in time and space.

Language contains other arcane secrets as well. What is the mystery of language that makes it possible for us to say one thing and mean the opposite, as in irony? Or to say one thing and its opposite and rightly claim that both statements are acceptable? What is the mechanism that enables us to create and understand metaphors and similes? How do we normally distinguish humour from aggression in everyday conversation?

These are some of the queries and mysteries of language I shall seek to unveil, if you will bear with me, in the following chapters.

Our "entry point" to the study of language will differ from the ones usually found in academic books on linguistics. It will not be the word, or the phoneme, the grammatical structure, the written letter or any kind of abstraction. It will not be a construct or an example, a sentence taken from everyday life or from a book, a lecture on different theories or a theory of my own. It will be through an intrusion into the "real world" of interaction and exchange at live conferences, where we shall focus on the unusually awkward situation in which somebody is trying to reproduce in another language and in "real time" what somebody else is saying.

Let me finish this introduction by saying that this work aims at giving readers a "feel" of the fabulous jewel they have in their hands.

The World of Conference Interpreting

The world of international summits, conferences and congresses is characterized by the paraphernalia of power as well as by the high degree of organization involved. The participants at such events – usually politicians, economists, scientists, etc. at the top of their professions – come to meet their international counterparts, or even those who oppose or question them, within the symbolic surroundings of palaces, government houses, conference halls or meeting rooms with an often imposing setting. Whether sober or luxurious, ancient or brand new, these are also the venues where international conference interpreters perform and interact daily with people in power, much in the same way as diplomats and journalists do.

Depending on their personality and the different contexts involved, individual interpreters may or may not feel that they belong within this environment. Nonetheless, they learn a lot, consciously or unconsciously, about the sometimes subtle ways in which power is exerted, questioned, counterbalanced and contained.

Because of the nature of their work, interpreters have a rare opportunity to observe and learn. Although they often join the conference delegates between sessions, once they return to the restricted space within their glass booths, which are designed to ensure freedom from distractions as well as sound quality for all concerned, they are effectively isolated from the external world. This distance favours observation.

The Starting Point

If learning a second language invariably makes us aware of certain characteristics of the way we function in our first language, working daily with languages often leads to a deeper reflection about linguistic phenomena. This is especially true for interpreters, who must switch from one language to another instantly and have to contend not so much with different "ways of saying things", as with different "ways of seeing the world" and organizing it.

Rather than being a reflection of some external "reality", language both creates our image of the world and reflects it back like a paradoxical looking glass. Or rather, it is thanks to language that *we* can do this. To use a slightly different metaphor, the starting point for this work was the conviction that the experience of conference interpreting would allow me to isolate some of the mechanisms that make language work, just as a prism breaks light into the different colours of the spectrum.

An Intuitive Approach

When I started my research in Paris in 1977, my initial approach focused on the implicit meanings in speakers' interventions. My intention was to explain what interpreters do to transmit what the speaker does not openly say but which is understood. However this proved to be no simple undertaking. Although the difficulties in conceptualizing and describing this process convinced me of the need to explore other fields apart from linguistics, some of my colleagues were shocked at the time by my interdisciplinary approach. But it was precisely this unusual way of proceeding that enabled me to find some answers, which in turn triggered more questions. Of course I was lucky enough to be stimulated almost daily by the actual practice of conference interpreting in different types of situations. Consequently, I tried to adopt a conscious scientific attitude to my own work, observing, associating, comparing, recording, questioning, drawing conclusions, and checking them again. Some of the intuitions that I could not verbalize then were only to become clear after many years of constant and systematic questioning.

Even in those early days, it was absolutely clear in my mind that some of the insights revealed by this method of research could be of interest beyond the interpreting world itself. Every speaker, every person should know that language provides us with a wonderful set of tools with which we can transform ourselves and thus, the world. But to do so, we need to become aware of the way language works, of its limitations and possible traps as well as its potential, and help one another to use it fairly and creatively. Many years were to elapse before I could find the words to express these intuitions clearly, let alone publish them in a book. In fact, at the end of my first book on this subject, written in Spanish, I was forced to recognize my own limits as well as the road that still lay ahead. Sixteen years and many unexpected turns later, here I am resuming my journey and verbalizing now what I silenced then.

The Research Method

In order to clarify the cognitive, social and linguistic factors that shape the interpreting process, I shall focus on cases in which the interpreter's statements differ somewhat from those of the original speaker. Now, this approach assumes that the study of abnormal cases (where the interpreter seems to say either more or less than the speaker or something different) will allow us to reveal the normal mechanisms used by the interpreter during his or her work. More generally, this approach also assumes that these are the same mechanisms that come into play during normal communication (where no interpreter is required) except that in normal communication they are almost impossible to detect because of their transparency and universality. Working under pressure, compressed by time and cornered by space, the interpreter exaggerates these mechanisms and, thus, makes them easier to detect. Due to this sort of "magnifying lens" we shall be able to reveal the "scaffolding" behind the operations involved.

To this end, I shall draw on the experience of different conference interpreters as well as my own. This experience will be interpreted within a theoretical framework derived from a number of different disciplines.

Theoretical Background

A large part of the theoretical framework for this book comes from the Philosophy of Language, Cognitive Science and Linguistics. In particular, the work of philosophers such as John Austin, John Searle, and H.P. Grice, of cognitive scientists such as Gilles Fauconnier and of the linguist Oswald Ducrot, has been fundamental. With scientific rigour they changed the standard approach to language of their time and opened the way to Pragmatics. In particular, "speech act" theory stands out against the background of the influence, silent or not, of Benveniste, Jakobson, Greimas and Hjemslev. Saussure must also be mentioned for he highlights the problems whose resolution laid the framework for modern Linguistics.

The work of Juan Seguí and Denhière was decisive in the fields of Psycholinguistics and Experimental Psychology while the German Gestalt psychologist Arnheim and the French philosopher Merleau Ponty, working within very different traditions, highlighted the importance of perception. On the other side of the Atlantic, the importance of Bateson and the Palo Alto School of psychotherapy is undeniable for the insights that they give into interpersonal communication, while the work of Canadian sociologist Irving Goffman helps us to understand social roles and their psychological significance. And if Goffman emphasizes the theatrical nature of social interaction, the great Russian director Stanislavski and his great wealth of teachings allows for a permanent comparison with the world of the theatre.

The scant influence of translation theory on this work stresses the difference I see between written and oral language. Although I shall mention here one name, that of humanist Antoine Berman and his work *L'épreuve de L'étranger*.[4] Mention should be

---

4 *Antoine Berman*, L'épreuve de L'étranger, *Paris, Gallimard, 1984.*

made of those interpreters who were among the first to reflect on their own activity such as Jean Herbert, Taddey Pilley, Eva Paneth and Danica Seleskovitch in the Western world. There have been since then many more, some of whom appear in the bibliography.

But throughout these last sixteen years, I have also been exposed to many other influences, most notably, Alfred Korzybski's General Semantics and the practical application of some of his formulations both in everyday life and in different specialist fields, from education to management, from intercultural coaching to crisis prevention. My own experience in some of these new fields – where I started working as consultant – proved a rich and stimulating source of learning. All this led me little by little but with no interruption into the fascinating world of the neurosciences: Jastrow, Schwartz, Hawkins.

It may seem that I have drawn on an excessively wide range of sources and disciplines. But the potential scope of the topic is enormous and a multitude of variables must be taken into account simultaneously. Interpreters must, at different levels, confront the same multiplicity of variables day in and day out. It says much for the profession that, in spite of the complexity of their work, interpreters are usually able to establish solid bridges of communication.

In order to develop a sound theoretical understanding of what interpreters actually do, and how they do it, it is necessary to cross a large number of boundaries. Not only the boundaries between languages or cultures, but between different sciences and disciplines. But before we do this, let us take a look back.

A Little History

S ociety awakens with its first utterances and a faint
inkling of the existence of a divine order. Man becomes human, as Edouard Schuré[5] likes to say, the
day he understands the link that binds him to his fellow beings and the link that binds him to the past and future of his
own species.

From the times of Babylon until the time when, closing
gaps, we achieve "communion" (communion, communication, from the Greek "*koinonia*" and the Latin "*comunicare*",
to be, to have "in common", to be in relationship, to relate
to), the task of overcoming the linguistic barrier became and
remains the task of interpreters.

Hermes, entrusted with the messages sent to the mortals by the
gods, can thus be considered a symbol of interpretation. In the
secret books of the Egyptian Hermes Trimegistes, we can already
perceive the idea, which we will again find in many religions, that
"the Divine Breath is the Word; it is the Word of God".

Interpreters are mentioned for the first time in history in the
texts of Herodotus. They are the interpreters of the pharaohs and
the kings of Persia and are called the hermeneuts, a word derived
from Hermes, the god who speaks on behalf of the other gods so
that mortals can understand. He is the mouth or the "tongue" of
the gods, the Pro-fem in classical Greek, that is, he who speaks to
another, pre-speaks, presays, profetes, prophet. Moses, interpreter

---

5 *Edouard Schuré,* Les grands initiés, *Paris, Librairie Académique Perrin,*
1960.

of Jehovah. Moses uses Aaron, his "mouth" for the Hebrews, whose language he ignores.[6]

Later, in the Europe of the Renaissance "hermeneutics" became the art of understanding and explaining the epics of Homer and the classical texts of the writers of antiquity. It was the art of exegesis, of interpretation. It should be remembered that for centuries knowledge and manuscripts – secret and sacred – had been in the hands of monks, who held knowledge and power; and also that one of the most extraordinary developments of hermeneutics in Renaissance Europe was the interpretation and translation of the Bible.

Undoubtedly, translators and interpreters took their first steps in those centres where power and knowledge concentrated: in the School of Translators in China, the Library at Alexandria, the School of Translators in Toledo; in the monasteries where, at the time, science and religion came hand in hand; in the first universities and the first cloisters. By the end of the Middle Ages it was common for both the courts of monarchs and the palaces of rich traders to employ both translators and interpreters.

The "New World"

The history of interpreting in the New World begins with Columbus' first voyage of discovery. When his expedition set sail in 1492, hoping to find a route to India, it was far from anybody's mind that a whole new continent would stand in their way and Columbus had on board one Don Luis de Torres, an interpreter of Greek, Latin and Hebrew. Needless to say, this scholar was of no use at all during the voyage. During the first landing on Guanahani, in the Lucayan Islands, the Great Navigator decided to take six natives on board to act as guides and interpreters. The most famous of these was christened Diego Colomb. We are therefore able to find in the daily log a num-

----

6 See Mariano García Landa, MML (Mariano's Mailing List), Brussels, 1986.

ber of references to interpreters, at that time called *lenguas* (tongues), *lenguaraces* (talkers) or *farautes*; sometimes we can even find their names. The Faraute, Interpreter or Tongue was synonymous with "counsellor" or "mentor" during the conquest of the vast territories of the River Plate basin. They were guides, knowledgeable and experienced men, entrusted with the responsibility of hazardous enterprises.[7]

Like Columbus, and for identical reasons, the subsequent discoverers constantly had at their service indigenous guides and interpreters. Famous among them – and one of the few women interpreters – was *Doña Marina*, the Aztec Indian princess given as a slave to Hernán Cortés. She was to play an outstanding role in the history of conquest.

In his second letter to Emperor Charles V, dated 1519, Cortés[8] relates how he almost fell into an ambush in Churultecal and how, thanks to Marina, his Indian interpreter and reputedly his mistress, he managed to prevent a massacre and at the same time surprise the enemy. A member of Marina's race had warned her of what was about to happen, thus giving her an opportunity to escape. Marina passed on the information to another interpreter, a Spaniard this time, who in turn informed Cortés. In truth, Marina broke no oath, nor did she lie or unduly use information obtained during her work. However, caught between two cultures and confronted with an extreme situation, she was forced to choose. Indeed, the story of this woman, who helped the Conquistador forge alliances against her own people, shows clearly how minor characters can help change the course of events and how minor history often paves History's way. Since Mexico's independence, *Doña Marina*, or *La Malinche* as she is commonly known, has come to symbolize the betrayal of autochthonous

---

7 *Vicente Arnaud,* Los intérpretes en el descubrimiento, conquista y colonizacción del Río de La Plata, *Buenos Aires, 1950.*

8 *Hernán Cortés,* Cartas y relaciones, *Primera ed., Sevilla, 1522; Buenos Aires, Emecé, 1946.*

values and servile submission to European culture. Todorov[9], however, sees her through an entirely different prism. "She is, in the first place, the first example, and for this reason, the very symbol of the merging of cultures; in this she is a harbinger of the modern state of Mexico, and beyond, she pre-announces our present condition which, if not always bi-lingual, is already and inevitably bi-or tri-cultural."

Continuing with the Conquest of Mexico, however, it is interesting to note that it was because of a mistake in interpretation – certainly not due to the interpreter – that the great Montezuma surrendered without a struggle. Impressed by the god-like appearance of the blond, blue-eyed, white man arriving from the East and by the magnificent stories he told about his sovereign, the Aztec emperor mistakenly concluded that Cortés was the Aztec god Quetzalcoatl and a descendant of Montezuma's own ancestors, the very ones who had once promised to return one day and eventually recover the land. Montezuma's false conclusion and his astounding surrender, which disconcerted both his contemporaries and later historians, may also help to shed some light on a woman's choice and to explain *La Malinche's* so called betrayal.

I have retold these American fragments of universal history at some length not only to honour my own American origins, but also to emphasize that at certain moments in history the intepreter is found upstage along with the main characters.

Indeed, the role of the interpreter has been crucial for exploration, discovery and conquest. When the first contacts with a new culture were made, it became necessary to know who "the others" were and understand how they thought and lived. This was the season for exchange. Once a nation had been defeated, it normally offered less resistance and less interest. The language of the victor was imposed (when his culture was also superior) or became a *lingua franca*. This is, broadly speaking, what happened to Latin in the West during

----

9 *Tzvetan Todorov*, La conquête de l'Amérique. La question de l'autre. *Paris, Seuil, 1982.*

the Roman Empire. Later, the social and political influence of France made French the diplomatic language *par excellence*. After the Second World War Anglo-Saxon economic power and leadership in advanced technologies tipped the scales in favour of English.

The Laws of the Indies

First Attempts at Legislation

On the other hand, the "sun never set" on the Hispano-American empire in the sixteenth century and the endeavour for temporal and divine expansion made the need for exchange one of its main characteristics. The role of the interpreter acquired sufficient importance to become the object of legislation.

Indeed, Title XXIX of the Compilation of *Leyes de India*s, or Laws of the Indies, enacted in 1680, sets down the rules for the work of interpreters and it is one of the profession's oldest and best preserved documents.

The first of the fourteen laws, dating back to 1529, stipulated that interpreters should be of the true faith, Christians and compassionate since they were the instrument through which the Indians were governed, justice was administered, and redress was granted for any harm inflicted. The presidents and *Oidores* of the Audiences should take great care to observe the moral qualities of their interpreters. Before undertaking their profession, interpreters had to take an oath to make good and loyal use of their work, translating impartially without hiding or adding anything, without favour for any of the parties, and with no interest in the trial other than their own fees. They could not accept gifts, donations or promises from the Spaniards or Indians nor any other persons expecting to file lawsuits or do business with them.

If they failed to abide by these conditions, they would be guilty of perjury and would lose their jobs and have to pay costs and damages. Programmes and work schedules were carefully specified, as were remunerations and fines for absences.

The number of interpreters to be employed at any time also changed. At the beginning there was only one but since frauds occurred involving the *lengua*, the simultaneous performance of *two* interpreters was made a requirement. Exactly the same thing happens today at high level intergovernmental meetings, where the presence of two interpreters guarantees mutual control.

In time, the law not only regulated the obligations of interpreters, but extended their services to every corner of the empire. A Royal Order of October, 1656 ordered that all trials held by the King's officers in America should be announced to the Indians in the hinterland, even in the remotest towns, to avail them of the means to ask for justice for any harm done to them. The right of the accused to be heard was already included in the Spanish judicial system. Even Indians and Afroamericans could count, at least in theory, on the assistance of a lawyer and an interpreter.

However, there was still little that the law could do to ensure the quality of the interpreter's work. In their annual reports – or *Cartas Anuas* – the Jesuits describe the difficulties they sometimes had to endure because of interpreters when administering the sacraments, from confessions to Extreme Unctions! Father Burges attributes his initial difficulties among the *mocobies* of Paraguay to the brazenness of the *lengua* who, in order to hide his own ignorance, did not hesitate to affirm flatly that the *mocobies* did not have in their vocabulary the words required, even when they were mere personal pronouns.

From discovery to conquest, from negotiations to peace treaties, including trials and confessions, history is filled with episodes which have required the services of a translator. At different periods of history, interpreters of Greek or Latin, Chinese or Hindustani, Spanish or Quechua, Arabic or Swahili, English or Persian, French and German or Polish and Russian have found themselves required to act as a bridge in the transfer of knowledge, the spreading of a new religion, the exchange of goods or the declaration of peace. It is worth noting that this special space in which the interpreter works is invariably empty and must every time be filled with varying linguistic ingredients. The content that fills this "void" does not depend on *who* occupies it but on those *around* it. If one of the parties decides to cancel the agreement, annul the contract or play deaf, the need for the interpreter disappears. If we know today the names of some "talkers" (*lenguaraces*) of the conquest of America, it is because the life and death of the parties involved hung upon their words.

The 20th Century

But, returning to the question of quality, neither interpreters nor interpreting changed very much until the early decades of the twentieth century. Those who had the luck or the privilege, as well as the ability, to learn another language in depth and share in other cultures helped to extend the frontiers of the profession and give shape to this remarkable skill. Scions of diplomats, military men, *émigrés* and exiled aristocrats were often outstanding in the profession although they lacked any sort of systematic training and their approach was often intuitive.

However, after the horrors of the First World War, the newly-formed League of Nations brought with it the expectation of a better understanding among nations. This was the beginning of the contemporary prestige of the profession of Conference Interpreter. The interpreters of that time were, as a rule, men of great culture who worked "consecutively". Seated on the right of Heads of State, they were given pride of place as, paper and pencil in hand, they first took brief notes of only a few words and then rendered an entire speech of five, ten, and even thirty minutes. This type of interpretation has the great advantage of allowing for better control. The disadvantage is that the time needed to render a speech has to be multiplied by the number of languages.

In November of 1945, at the end of the Second World War, while the International Military Court was being prepared to bring ex Nazi leaders to trial in Nuremberg, the decision was taken to use a new system of interpretation, seldom tried before. In order to cut down on the time needed for communication between the judges and the German defendants, the interpreters would translate *during* the proceedings and not *after* them. This was the birth of simultaneous interpretation.

Eisenhower's interpreter, Colonel Dostert, was responsible for the organization of the interpretation system. It was hard work and it required a very high linguistic level. After preparing the documents and studying the jargon and the terminology beforehand, three teams of interpreters took it in turns to translate. Each team had three monitors and a Chief Interpreter who constantly supervised the versions given. The monitors, outside the booths, controlled the flow of documents and the speed of the speaker, which was not to be more than 100 words per minute[10]. Accuracy was essential to avoid confusion in court and to permit the proper taking of records.

The proceedings were translated into four languages (English, French, Russian and German) and lasted ten months. The entire world was riveted on those trials: lives depended on what was being said there and, as everyone was aware, lessons would be drawn for posterity.

The nervousness of the interpreters during this "world première" was in accordance with the tense atmosphere in the room where the Court strove to reinstate harmony and reason after the folly and destruction that had cost the lives of fifty million people.

The recently created United Nations, whose charter came into force on October 25, 1945, also adopted this new form of communication from the very beginning. The different members of this family of nations use many different languages but the official languages at meetings of the General Assembly are

---

10 *A hundred words per minute according to Ann and John Tusa in* The *Nuremberg Trial, London, Macmillan, 1983; and sixty according to David and Margaret Bowen in* Meta, Vol. 30 *of March 1985. Be it as it may, there is no doubt that much attention was paid to the rhythm at which the orators spoke. For reference, let us note that V. Giscard D'Estaing's speech delivery rate was set at 145 words per minute and F. Mitterrand's at 129 during the 1974 presidential campaign, according to a study made by Cotteret,* 57.744 Mots pour Convaincre, *Paris, PUF, 1975.*

always the same: English, French, Spanish, Chinese and Russian. Because of economic developments, Arabic made a spectacular entrance in some organizations during the sixties.

At first, simultaneous interpretation caused reverence and stupefied the public. In truth, not even the interpreters could explain how they heard and spoke at the same time. For years, simultaneous translation seemed like "magic". "Had they lived in the Middle Ages these interpreters would have gone directly to the scaffold", remarked a UN officer one day, amazed by an interpreter's gesticulations. "He seems to be possessed".

The number of conferences, congresses, symposia, colloquia and meetings has grown enormously in recent years and with them the number of participants, languages and interpreters. What at first was remarkable for its strangeness became part of the scenario and came to be considered just one more "prop".

Simultaneous translation is still, however, a disconcerting factor for many. The fact that yesterday's prowess has become common currency today does not mean that linguistic or communication theories have exploited to the full the lessons to be drawn from instantaneous linguistic conversion. This is precisely what I shall attempt to do in the pages that follow. Multiplicity of exchanges and diversity of patterns are characteristic of the turn of the century. Every daily meeting of the European Union or the European Parliament now requires the conversion of speech into nine or ten other languages at the same time, using one or even two relays[11]. This means that Greek will become French or German before going into Portuguese. In spite of the glass partitions between booths, a dull noise resonating in the background recalls vertiginous Babel.

Let us now delve, through the "simultaneous" work we are ready to examine, into the fabulous mysteries of language.

❖   ❖   ❖

11 Like "pivot", this is an expression from the jargon of the profession for the interpreters whose version will be re-interpreted into a third language.

What the Interpreter Says

"A word is a microcosm of human consciousness."

Lev Vygotsky
(from *Thought and Language*)

Part I

MESSAGES AND

CONTENTS

In this first section, I will try to unveil the mechanisms – and show the wide range of elements – we humans use to make, create and convey meaning.

CHAPTER 1

Language as a Game

Of the definition of "meaning".
The example I bought
the newspaper *is*
analysed in cubist
fashion, from a
variety of standpoints.
Five conclusions on
saying, doing and
interpreting.

Language functions like a game. To see how enjoyable this game can be, let us take a sentence and play with it, transforming its possible meanings right in front of our eyes.

A simple sentence will suffice to illustrate the variety of possible situations, scenarios and plots an utterance can belong to. We shall take our example from Dan Sperber.[1] The sentence **I bought the newspaper,** he argues, is ambiguous and may mean different things. It will also help us to show how complex the construction of meaning can be, even starting from a brief sequence of elements: 1 sentence, 4 words, 15 phonemes, 19 letters.

Let us let our imagination fly. The first scene takes place in New York, sometime last year. **I bought the newspaper,** is what a young yuppy tells his wife as he gets back home after his early morning jogging. We take it to mean that he has bought a copy of *The New York Times, The Washington Post* or *USA Today.* We shall also understand, as pointedly stressed by Sperber, that "it is not worth his wife's while to also buy it".

Let us suppose that his wife, a little deaf for the purposes of this story, could not hear her husband well. While preparing breakfast in the kitchen for her children, she automatically asks them:

– What did he say? I couldn't hear …
– That he's already bought *The New York Times.*
– What?
– That you don't need to buy the paper, mom … Got it?

---

1 *D. Sperber, Rudiments de Rhétorique Cognitive in* Poétique *Nº 23, Paris, Seuil, 1975. Page 385.*

– Oh … he's bought it already, eh? Oh … but today is Friday and I also wanted to buy *Vogue*.

The fact that we normally understand more than we hear is proven by the child's spontaneous replacement of the newspaper by *The New York Times* and by his explanation: *don't need to buy it yourself.*

Let us now pass on to another scenario.

New York, 1929.

Two American tycoons, Mr. Ambrition and Mr. Greedy, had long been more than just business competitors. Business was rather the arena where they fought their battles. Mr. Ambrition has just bought a publishing house, part of a big corporation which has been till now under the control of Mr.

Greedy, his bitterest rival. During a violent argument between the two CEO's and when everything seemed to have come to a dead end, Ambrition pulls an ace out of his sleeve that surprises his rival:

– I bought the newspaper! – he exclaims triumphantly.

Rome, 1952.

A dishonest politician during a rather murky affair, which could seriously jeopardize his career, discusses the matter with one of his advisors.

– What are you planning to do?
  – his advisor asks.
– What shall I do to avoid the
  scandal? I've already done it:
  I bought the newspaper.

There are six basic questions to ask, no matter what the circumstances, in order to reconstruct meaning: who, to whom, when, where, what, what for. They also help delimit the sequence of events, giving it a beginning, a development and an end.

The answers to these questions in the different situations described can give the sentence **I bought the newspaper** three distinct meanings:

1. **I bought a copy,**
2. **I bought the enterprise, and**
3. **I bribed the editor.**

The phonologic and semantic components stay the same but the meaning of the words varies because of the articulation of those components with other elements of a different nature which are grafted onto them at the time of enunciation. Since these elements are different in all three cases, the indirect acts, the implicatures and the implied will *per force* be different since they depend on shared knowledge of situations and contexts; or, as Searle[2] says:

"In *indirect speech acts**, the speaker communicates to the hearer more than he actually says by way of relying on their mutual shared background information, both linguistic and

2 *John Searle.* Indirect Speech Acts in Syntax and Semantics, *Peter Cole, London, Academic Press, 1975.*

non–linguistic together with the general powers of rationality and inference on the part of the hearer".

aɪ bɔːt ðə ˈnjuːzpeɪpə| I bought the newspaper.	1. I bought a copy. 2. I bought the publishing house. 3. I bribed the editor.	**Implied meaning** 1. *It is not worth your while buying another one.* 2. *From now on I am the winner.* 3. *I did the only thing left to do.*

From Words to Acts

Although the meaning varies considerably from one case to the next, the three examples contain only one *direct speech act* (assertion) which in turn entails an indirect act different in each case.

First Case

A young couple in New York at the beginnings of the 21st. century. Every marriage implies an association: its members will avoid duplication of tasks. This couple regularly buys the paper. If one member buys it, it is not necessary for the other one to do so. There would be duplication of tasks with the consequent waste of time and money. When the husband engages in the assertive act he also produces an indirect act of warning: *it is not worth your while to buy it* – or of kindness: *you will not have to do it since I have already done it for you.*

Second Case

Messrs. Ambrition and Greedy in New York in 1929. When Ambrition plays the ace he had up his sleeve and produces a *direct act of assertion* he provokes a second similar act, indirect this time, for when stating that he has just bought the newspaper, what he is saying is that from then on he has got the upper hand. This is what both understand in view of what they know about their respective spheres of influence, their enterprises, the power of the press and the precarious situation during that unhappy year of 1929. If the card *I bought the newspaper* has the value of an ace in the hands of Ambrition, it is not so much because of the contents of the statement itself but rather because of what can be inferred from it. Indeed, it is the manifestation of the power of Ambrition as reflected in the statement that puts Greedy out of the picture.

Third Case

Rome, 1952. When the tinpot politician answers, overwhelmed, that he bribed the editor of a newspaper, he produces a direct act of assertion. The tone of his voice, however, conveys the image of a man at the end of his tether. The statement carries in this case an indirect act expressing weariness, bitterness and desperation.

Direct Act	Indirect Acts
	Of warning or kindness It is not worth while for you to also buy the newspaper.
Assertion *I bought the newspaper.*	*Of Assertion of power* From now on, I am the winner.
	Of bitterness (assertion of impotence) I did the only thing left for me to do.

Let us go back to Dan Sperber's example and our initial situation of a couple in New York and see that it suffices for one element to change in the situation – the time of day, for instance – to understand something different: The *XXX* instead of *The New York Times*. This brings up a long existing problem in linguistics: that of reference. Reference can be modified not only by a change in the time of day but also by the socio-economic situation, the educational level or place of residence of the couple. If the scene had taken place in the United Kingdom, we would have thought of *The Observer*, *The Times*, *The Evening Standard* or any other British paper. In France the reference would become *Le Monde* or *Le Figaro* and in Argentina it might be *Clarín* or *La Nación*.

Of yet greater interest is to see that even without changing any parameters of the initial situation and without modifying the references at all, the addition of just one detail or the transformation of the relations between the various elements can also produce substantial changes in meaning:

A couple in crisis after 20 years of married life. When the wife is about to leave to go shopping, her husband says, in an unpleasant mood:

– I bought the newspaper ...

The meaning of the sentence remains the same (I bought a copy) as does the implication (I bought *The NYTimes*) but the innuendo *it is not worth while for you to also buy it* is no longer there. Rather, the implied message is *you would have forgotten, as usual*.

How very different from:

– I bought the newspaper, eggs, croissants and oranges and we shall now prepare breakfast and have it in bed.

These two acts, one of aggression and the other of love, are made out of the same *phonetic, phatic and rhetic*[*3] material. Why then is there a difference? Because of the *illocutionary force** of the utterance, which is responsible for the innuendoes, the implied meanings and subtexts and which depends directly on the intention of the speaker.

> "*Ce qui crève les yeux* – says Gilles Fauconnier[4] – *c'est qu' une phrase lexicalement et grammaticalement banale peut s'employer avec une gamme très riche de valeurs illocutoires.*" ("What leaves me astounded is that a trivial phrase from the lexical and grammatical viewpoints, can be used with a tremendously rich variety of illocutory values").

Why, then, do we think we understand approximately the same thing as other people in everyday communication?

If in our daily exchanges, several or many people come to understand approximately the same thing, it is because they share certain knowledge and often a common frame of reference or because they can infer or imagine them. If one of those persons has additional information – as for instance "this couple is going through a crisis"– that person will understand the statements in a somewhat different light from others for whom only the tone of voice or the intonation hint that something is not as right as it should be.

From what has gone before, we can draw the following conclusions:

1. The way in which something is said can alter its meaning.
1'. In order to interpret, we must take into account not only what the speaker says but also the way in which he says it.

----

3 The asterisk (*) indicates the terms are explained in the glossary. See page 415.

4 Gilles Fauconnier, "Comment Contrôler la Verité. Remarques Illustrées par des Assertions Dangereuses et Pernicieuses en Tout Genre", in Actes de la Recherche de Sciences Sociales, *Paris, Service de Publications de la Maison des Sciences de l'Homme, Minuit, January 1979. Page 5.*

2. By saying something in a certain way, we can do something different (even the opposite) from what we say.

2'. In order to interpret, we must simultaneously take into account what the speaker says and what the speaker does when saying what he says in the way he does.

3. For two or more people to understand approximately the same thing, they need to establish the same relationships between the same elements.

3'. The more the interpreter knows about the situation of the enunciation the better he will be able to interpret since he will be more likely to know the elements the speaker knows and to establish similar relationships.

4. We understand by "meaning" the dynamic result of the relationship between what someone says and the fact of saying it in a certain way under the present circunstances, and with the fact of doing what he is doing when saying what he is saying.

4'. To interpret implies recreating and conveying the meaning of what is said and done by the speaker; it implies saying what the speaker says in the same way so as to produce similar effects.

5. A shift of perspective that reveals a new variable, or a discovery that makes it possible to shed a different light on a subject, or the consideration of some facts, already present but not perceived before, may alter and transform the understanding – or the meaning – of an utterance or of any other observable phenomenon. We infer from this the dynamic and relative nature of meaning.[5]

---

5 "Any message or fragment thereof is like the formula or equation that the mathematician puts in brackets: – its value can be totally modified by a multiplier outside the bracket which can be added at any moment, even many years later." G. Bateson. Vers une ecologie de l'esprit. Vol. II, Paris, Seuil, 1980, Page 54. (Steps to an Ecology of Mind, Chicago: The University of Chicago Press).

Stereotyping

Reflecting on what we did

In order to drastically change scenarios and help picture a situation completely different from previous ones, what I did to rapidly assign new meanings to the phrase *I bought the newspaper* was use stereotypes. Thus, an image, an idea, a character may have become commonplace, fixed, standardized in a conventional form, like the corrupt Italian politicians in the 50's, or the powerful American tycoons in the 20th century.

Standardized elements or stereotypes prove extremely useful for transmitting something quickly. One stereotyped character may trigger others and even a stereotyped plot. We can rapidly evoke a familiar situation or a situation which evokes something easily recognizable for the audience.

Stereotyped characters, or situations may function as *invariant representations*, which may prove useful for describing, in their turn, novel situations.[6]

We should not forget, though, that what we gain in speed thanks to *stereotypes*, we may lose in precision, in details and in uniqueness.

References, the syntheses of past experiences or of what we call "a shared culture" are important. Instead of identifying ourselves with them, we should always be on the look out for the distinctive feature, in search of subtle differences, nuances, the unknown elements and the surprise!

There is nothing intrinsically wrong with stereotyping provided we stay fully aware of what we are doing and why.

---

6 *"To make predictions you need to have memorised sequences of events", Jeff Hawkins in* On Intelligence, *New York, Henry Holt and Company, 2004. "To make predictions of novel events you should resort to invariant representations".*

Context

So far, we have played with the variables of situations and contexts so as to show how one and the same sentence can be understood in an array of different ways. This has enabled us to: 1) detect the variables; 2) follow the flow of the relationships underlying each situation and 3) to lay bare – under the scaffolding of the actual words – the social structure supporting the utterance.

We will now see that what is true regarding words or sentences can also apply for things we see.

 Perceiving the ambiguity of an element implies detaching it from its context in order to grasp only its structural features and submitting it to momentary and forced isolation. Depending on what we take for figure or for ground, we spontaneously organize the shapes we see here as those of a vase or those of two profiles.

Talking about colours, *red* must surely produce the same type of vibrations on different occasions, but the sensorial effects produced by this colour will vary as a function of the colours surrounding it. The *same* colour will seem different if it is supposed to evoke a face, a horse, a tree or a bloodstain, for in each case an implicit comparison will be made with the normal colour of the object in question.

A similar marble cube will be perceived as the head of a woman in the cubist sculptures by Lipschitz or Curatella Manes and as a block of stone in a sculpture by Rodin.

The single unique object is unapproachable. To perceive it, it must at least be detached from a background; but as soon as a new element is included the perception of the whole changes, reciprocal influence becomes apparent and context comes into action.

The mere inversion of the short lines produces an apparent change in the size of the main element.

Any figure, however familiar, can remain hidden in certain environments.

Like new objects coming into our visual field, new data are regularly and systematically integrated by our nervous systems.

However, the incorporation of a new element can sometimes pose a problem: it may require total, often painful, restructuring of the entire object or of the whole organization through the restructuring of the subject's mental framework.

Faced with "unbearable" information, the subject may, little by little and in spite of his difficulties, succeed in modifying the whole; but he can also end up rejecting or denying the new information to protect his existing vision of reality or he can deny the entire whole. According to Watzlawick, this last instance reflects the very essence of madness.

Following J. Samuel Bois,[7] in a demonstration derived from Gestalt theory, let us see some of the multiple possibilities of arrangement of twelve simple straight lines of equal length.

----

7 *J. Samuel Bois,* Explorations in Awareness, *Viewpoints Institute, USA .* *Institute of General Semantics.*

Each line can be considered as a part, or an element of the total picture. The elements may be grouped in fours, in threes, etc.; the total picture will remain linear and one-dimensional in its arrangement.

Now if we place these elements differently, we may have a picture that represents surfaces instead of lines, creating a two-dimensional whole.

The arrangement is of a different order. The elements are the same as before; the whole is different. It is a square, an area.

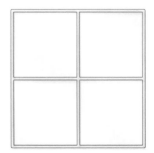

The next jump is more spectacular. By re-arranging the elements, we obtain a different structure.

We have a cube !

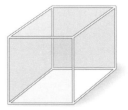

The organizational change which brings about the new type of structure integrates the lines in a somewhat new manner: integration is so strong that something new and unexpected occurs: a square in one case, a cube in the other. This semantic jump implies both the perceptive jump closing the structure (by integrating the otherwise isolated elements) and a new designation for it.

Now, what happens if we want to add another line – a thirteenth element? We would not have much problem in the first case where the lines were parallel, we could simply have started a new subdivision. But in the latter cases, the dismantling of the whole is necessary in order to integrate new elements.

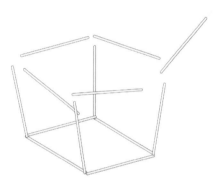

And this is no easy step. Letting go of a well-known structure, allowing for its de-structuring often triggers fear; courage is required to take this step. When we dare take it, creativity can help us find more and more beautiful and complex structures.

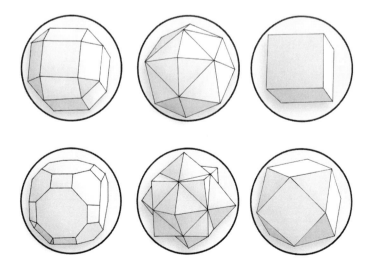

Point of View

We can see things from different points of view but not *at the same time*. Even with figures that lend themselves especially well to dual interpretation, it is not possible to see both figures simultaneously. Our perception, as K.Lorenz[8] quite rightly points out, chooses only one of the possible interpretations and communicates it to us as being the "only one". Subsequent work of re-accommodation becomes necessary to apprehend all other readings as the following examples show.

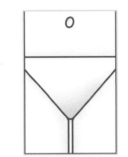

In this image you can integrate the line, the point and the triangle and "see" an olive falling into a glass (enjoy your Martini!) or a modern painting of a young lady in a bikini.

Ambiguities of this type occur in language, too. The delegate who understood *l'Afrique n'érigera plus des autels aux Dieux* ("Africa will no longer build altars to the gods") as *l'Afrique n'érigera plus des hotels odieux* (Africa will no longer build awful hotels) was no doubt influenced by his extremely uncomfortable lodgings at the time.

---

8 *K. Lorenz,* Consideraciones Sobre la Conducta Animal y Humana, *Barcelona, Plaza y Janés, 1976. Original title:* Studies in Animal and Human Behavior, *Volume I (1970).* Studies in Animal and Human Behavior, *Volume II (1971).*

Our perception decides, before we do, how to outline the image. A little training lets us integrate the elements in different ways and go quickly from one perceptual organization to the next; it is not possible to see them both simultaneously.

These unconscious decisions occur at different levels with both visual and auditory perceptions: with lines, colours, shapes, structures, patterns as well as with phonemes, words, grammatical structures, etc.

Can you perceive several possibilities of interpreting this picture?

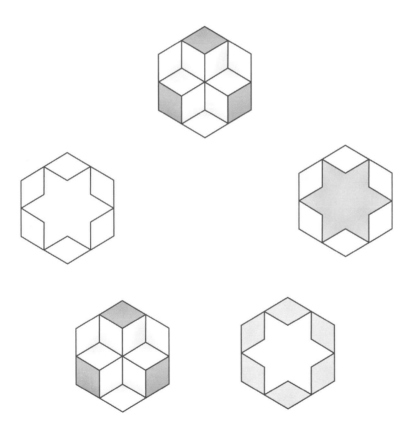

They can also be found in the attitude or point of view adopted for telling a story or describing an event.

Michelangelo's Pietà in the Vatican shows a mother holding her dying son or a man abandoning his mother.

Ordering sequences in one sense or another creates different views or "realities".

As a humorist reports: A man dies, goes to Heaven and finds there an old friend with a beautiful young woman sitting on his lap: "Heavens!" – exclaims the new arrival – "is she your reward?" The old man answers, sadly: "No. I am her punishment."

As all games, in form of play or sport, language has its rules. But language also has its own little games that I will soon attempt to unveil, always playing though, a fair game.

❖　　❖　　❖

CHAPTER 2

This Side of Words and Beyond Them

Of the importance of the speaker's identity and the interpreter's presence.

Tell me who says it and I will tell you what it means.

Stanislavski and the fundamental questions an actor must ask himself.

An out of the ordinary invitation

I will now invite the reader to briefly occupy the position of the interpreter: that curious space from where one might say one has a double vision, from where two speeches can be simultaneously perceived: the one given by the speaker and the version of it provided by the interpreter in real time in another language.

The space feels a little awkward and the sensation it gives can be compared to that experienced by cinema goers having some knowledge of a foreign language. In the darkness of the cinema, they can have glimpses of an insight when, making a generally involuntary comparison between what they hear and what they read in the subtitles, they feel the sensation, sometimes, of *discovering* something, a fleeting gap, a difference, some unexpected revelation, a loss in meaning, a misinterpretation, an error, or something new to learn.

Our working method will consist in the confrontation, comparison and analysis of two fragments of speech recorded simultaneously: the one delivered by the speaker and the simultaneous version of it provided by the interpreter. But we will let words and meanings flow until something draws our attention precisely because we have detected a deviation, a difference or a gap. It is the detection of "abnormalities" that will enable us to reveal the hidden mechanisms used in normal interaction.

We therefore enter the dual, or twofold, world of the interpreter. In the next five chapters a comparison between both parts of an interpreted *speech act*[1] will allow us, as we go along, to detect the fundamental discursive dimensions and the indispensable ingredients of communication.

Anyone with an elementary knowledge of English and Spanish will probably take for granted that "one" and "*uno*" (or "*una*") are always equivalent and would probably be taken aback if asked to translate "*uno*" as something other than "one". **One** and *uno* can be considered equivalent "in abstracto" at the level of *language**; however, we can also find other possibilities, depending on situation and context, at the level of *speech**".

During a Conference on International Standardization of Statistics held at UNESCO's Headquarters in Paris in June 1978, after nine amendments to the initial by-laws had been debated and voted, the chairman of the meeting said:

Speaker's words	Interpreter's words	
Amendment number ten ... eh ... eh ... deals with the first paragraph ... ... ⟨... one ...⟩	*Eh ... eh ... la enmienda diez se refiere al ... ... primer párrafo ... al ...* ⟨*primer inciso*⟩	Eh ... eh ... amendment number ten refers to the ... ... first paragraph ... ... ⟨... the ... first inset⟩

first inset   In this case, *one* was translated as *primer inciso*. Since nothing the speaker had said could justify this transformation, only unsaid or extra-discursive elements could have permitted this change while preserving equivalence.

Let us analyse the situation. The tone of voice here played a predominant role: the speaker's uttering of the word "one" after saying *first paragraph* may have been considered a slip

---

1 *The asterisk refers the reader to the glossary at the end of the book where technical terms are explained.*

of the tongue. The interpreter heard "one" but said nothing. It was not until he *saw* that the paragraph in the text of the amendment had a number of sub-paragraphs that he said *primer inciso*. Thus we see a deliberate search on the part of the interpreter for extra-linguistic elements to help clarify the meaning.

first inset

In this case, it is the *relationship* between what is heard and what is seen that explains what has been said. It is as if the interpreter were using an early warning system to scan for signs and signals of all sorts that may facilitate and speed up understanding.

Only the *physical presence* of the interpreter can explain the shift from one to *primer inciso*. It should be stressed here that it is the simultaneous presence of the speaker and the interpreter in time and space which allows the conference interpreter to sense and process a series of data which can potentially but not necessarily be made explicit. Indeed, a speaker does not normally describe himself during a speech nor does he describe his listeners or the place where they are. It would be irrelevant, even ridiculous, to do so since this information is already shared by everybody present.[2]

The mere fact that the interpreter finds himself where the words are uttered puts at his disposal a number of important elements: who (the speaker), to whom (the listener), where, when, and often, why (the motive). As we shall see, one of the first tasks of the interpreter is inferring the parameters he does not possess.

Let us imagine the following scenes.

---

2 *The difficulties that children have in learning to write descriptions show the depth to which Grice's Principle of Relevance is rooted in the world of speakers. We all remember agonizing over essay titles such as "Our classroom", "My school", etc. Our readers —schoolmates or teachers— already knew what we were asked to describe, so why do so? We did not know then that we were supposed to write for an imaginary reader who might be interested in our descriptions, or for schoolmates and teachers but in such a way as to awaken their interest.*

The bell rings at the Jones'. It is a telegram from Joe saying: **I am OK.** His parents learn that everything is going according to schedule. Joe has arrived in Lima (Peru) in the first week of December, so completing the second leg of his motorcycle trip.

In May 2004 Mr. and Mrs. Oliver receive a telegram from their eldest son, Robert, saying, **I am OK.** They fall in each other's arms; moved and relieved at recovering the peace of mind they had lost over the last few days. Robert Oliver had appeared on a list of soldiers supposedly killed by Iraqi rebels during an attack in Baghdad.

The contents of both telegrams were identical but what a difference one of them made for the Olivers!

Two groups of students at Columbia University were asked to write an essay on the subject "The Revolution is on". A demanding and experienced jury corrected and compared the papers. There were huge differences between the two groups; they did not seem to be writing about the same subject at all. And they were not. The first group had been told that the title was a quotation from Thomas Jefferson while the second group was made to believe it was from Karl Marx!

However, knowing the name of the speaker and the place and time of his speech may not always be enough. Let us listen to what Danica Seleskovich, interpreter and one of the first researchers in this field has to say:[3]

----

3 *Danica Seleskovich,* The Interpreter in International Conferences, *Paris. Minard. 1968. Page 62.*

"I remember, some years ago during the General Assembly of the Council of Europe, having to interpret, without any preparation whatsoever, a speaker whose name and nationality I did not know. He spoke perfect English, interspersing very British 'hem … hems …' from time to time, gave remarkable evidence of undue modesty and had started his speech with a standing joke among the British. Convinced that he was an Englishman, probably a conservative to judge by his accent, I understood nothing of his plea for a European free exchange zone of agricultural products. After having massacred his speech, toning down everything that was mordant and obviating ambiguities, I found out that the man in question was Danish and understood, somewhat belatedly…"

Knowing the identity of the speaker means recognizing those aspects of his personality or function relevant to the situation. Knowing that Brown is the name of the man in the grey suit who has just taken the floor is perhaps not enough. It is also of vital importance to know which organization or institution he represents and what his role or function is *vis-à-vis* the other groups or interests represented at the meeting.

The comparison of a fragment of speech with its simultaneous interpretation stresses the importance of the co–presence of the interpreter during the process and of keeping in mind certain unmentioned parameters from which the meaning of what is said can be reconstructed. Looking at the problem from another angle, Stanislavski used to tell his students that if actors wanted to make sense onstage, they first needed to find very precise answers to the basic questions posed by their characters: Who am I? Where am I? What is my position here? Where am I going? And for what reason?[4]

---

4 *Constantin Stanislavski, El trabajo del actor sobre sí mismo, Buenos Aires. Quetzal, 1962, chapter IV. (An Actor Prepares, Routledge, Reprint Edition, 1989). In the management world, it is this set of basic questions all members of a team should ask themselves before a meeting, or anybody taking part in a negotiation or any of us in our daily interactions.*

Interestingly, this set of basic questions (who, to whom, where, when and on what subject) has been challenged by the new modes of communication: cell phones and the internet. The set is still valid; it is the relative priority of some parameters which can vary. When calling a cell phone, the first question is no longer: who is it? But rather: where are you? Can you talk?

In virtual conversations on the net, the range of possibilities depends only on the imaginative capabilities of those who communicate: They can invent new "who's" and "where's" and "why's".

The physical weight of words

first inset

Like a small wedge maintaining two things separate, *primer inciso* marks the presence of the interpreter and his intrusion, in this case successful. But in their search for greater clarity interpreters can also complicate matters and even trigger a diplomatic incident; this is what reportedly happened in August 1954 during the delicate negotiations between representatives of China and Russia (in favour of North Korea) and a United Nations delegation conducted by Paul Henri Spaak[5] basically in favour of South Koreans. Those were the days of the Cold War and the East-West confrontation.

Apart from the interpreters, probably the only other person who understood the origin of the confusion was Colonel Robert B.Ekvall, who spoke all the languages used at the conference and amused himself by comparing the various versions. In fact, he had often acted as an interpreter himself. He tells us what happened[6] that day:

....

5 *Paul Henri Spaak (1899-1972) was the most outstanding Belgian statesman during the decades following Second World War.*

6 *Robert B.Ekvall,* Faithful Echo, *New York. Twayne, 1960. Also Quoted by P. Watzlavick in* La réalité dans la réalité, *Paris: Seuil, 1978.*

"The language line of communication between Paul Henri Spaak, then Belgian Prime Minister and Chou En-lai, Premier of the Peoples' Republic of China, the two protagonists of the drama which was about to unfold, was French to English to Chinese and Chinese to English to French. There was consecutive interpretation in French on the floor and simultaneous interpretation into English and Chinese from the booths. Another irregularity in the set-up was that Chou En-lai, the Chinese delegate, was using his own interpreter into English."

Spaak said in French:

"The scope and authenticity of the proposal offered by the United Nations rendered superfluous the consideration of any other proposal." And he concluded with the following statement: "*Votre déclaration est contenue dans notre texte*" (This declaration (yours) is included in our text).

However, the simultaneous English version Ekvall heard through his earphones was: "this statement is contained in the text of the armistice agreement".

To the ears of Chou En-lai, Spaak had said that the Chinese proposal was contained in the text of the armistice agreement, when in truth it had nothing to do with the armistice agreement.

It was later determined that the interpreter had heard "*dans l'autre texte*" instead of "*dans notre texte*" and feeling that *l'autre* was vague and required an explanation he had added his own clarification: *of the armistice agreement*.

Erkvall goes on:

in **our** text

in **the other** text

"From then on things got worse. Chou En-lai accused Spaak of having made an unsound statement and proved that – contrary to what had been said – the proposal of the delegation from the Peoples' Republic of China was not part of the armistice agreement. The delegates who had listened to Spaak in French were confused by Chou En-lai's reaction whereas those who only had the supposedly improved Anglo-Chinese translation found that the indignation in Chou En-lai's reply was out of place. Spaak managed to prove he had never uttered the fatal words of the armistice agreement, but the tone of the meeting had been poisoned and the misunderstandings continued. In the heat of the debate that followed, Chou's interpreter made another mistake, by omission, and not by commission this time, of certain words which softened and restrained the scope of the declaration. Confusion and misunderstanding reigned once again. Delegates spoke at cross-purposes, in bewilderment and even anger for about three quarters of an hour.

(…) "It was perfectly obvious at what instant Chou En-lai heard that amazing statement – so contrary to fact – for he started as though a bee had stung him and began signalling the chairman, Sir Anthony Eden, for the floor … He had caught the great and famous spokesman for the West in a clumsy mistake. 'I am surprised to find there is so little understanding and that I am so greatly misunderstood … this assertion is groundless', said he."

If communication had been the only aim and purpose of the exchange, the interpreter might have been bold enough to put an end to the dispute, explaining his own mistake and clarifying the misunderstanding. But often communication rules depend on wider power structures and it may be difficult for somebody in a secondary role to interfere in the play of the protagonists, even for the sake of clarification.

With the exception of recent computer-synthesized voices – and not-so-recent Biblical voices – we cannot conceive of the spoken word without a human source. Spoken words always carry a visual subtext and so the normal tendency is to look at the person who is speaking. Simultaneous interpretation modifies the rules of the game and organizes, as it were, a new space: the listeners hear the interpreter but look at the speaker. The interpreter is simultaneously perceived as someone who is not there and as someone who is everywhere.

On the other hand, when the interpreter sits next to the speaker to work "consecutively", the speaker's physical presence can be as important as his or her voice. In this case, spatial organization becomes crucial.[7]

Body, voice and gestures in consecutive interpreting are as important as translation itself. Metaphorically, the image of the interpreter can become the image of a group, of a country's authorities or of a trademark. This presence is humorously revealed by Mafalda in a comic strip.[8]

The abrupt change from words to acts – from insults to sports – matches the other equally abrupt change from a dream of international understanding to a somewhat more violent

---

7 *We know today that organization in space reveals relations and that the distance between persons varies from one culture to another. See studies on proxemics by R. Birdwhistell and E. Hall in* La nouvelle communication. *Paris, Seuil, 1981.*

8 *Quino,* Mafalda & friends, Nº 2, *Edición de la Flor, Buenos Aires, 2004.* © *Joaquín S. Lavado - Quino. Reproduced with the copyright holder consent.*

reality. Mafalda shows, intuitively, that she can, beyond two tongues, find the equivalence between different codes.

Communication is, above all, action. We may attack or defend, invade or protect, struggle, oppose or seduce through a variety of gestures and language codes.

❖   ❖   ❖

CHAPTER 3

The Implied

Of how a speech creates dimensions it does not contain. Appearances are sometimes misleading. Tell me how it was said and I'll tell you what it means. The importance of tone. Hand in hand with Ducrot down the path of implicitness. Examples: Chaplin, prostitutes and a good friend. Stanislavski and the sub-text.

S ometime in the sixties, during a session of the United Nations General Assembly, a high ranking Soviet officer (some allege it was Nikita Khrushchev himself) showed his disagreement and anger by banging on the podium as he repeated:

" `*Njet …* `*njet …* `*njet.*"

One of the two interpreters in the English booth translated, unperturbed, as

" ˌ*no …* ˌ*no …* ˌ*no.*"[1]

The case here is the opposite of the one presented in the previous chapter (one / primer inciso) where, inde one/first inset pendently of the pre-established equivalence of words, the interpreter had transformed the textual surface of what was "said" to protect the equivalence of the message. In this case, however, the interpreter maintains the

---

1 *The prosodic notation used here indicates:* ` *"descending curve of the voice" or "High fall" and* ˌ *"small descending curve of the voice" or "Low fall".*

semantic equivalence of the terms "njet" and "no" but by changing the tone of voice he changes the message. As these two examples show, sometimes equivalence can only be kept by changing the textual surface, but sometimes equivalence can only be kept by preserving it.[2]

What is clear from all this is that *the pre-established equivalence of words being used does not necessarily ensure the equivalence of the message.*

We have confronted two examples, each made up of two parts: the speaker's version and the interpreter's version. This duality which seems to characterize the space occupied by the interpreter led us to the already mentioned conclusion: *equivalence in form does not guarantee equivalence of content or equivalence of effect.*

If we can manage to determine the *equivalence* of the message in two fragments which differ in form (*one = primer inciso*) and, at the same time, determine the *non equivalence* of two messages conveyed by two corresponding terms (njet = no), it is because there must be dimensions in speech which are not necessarily included in the words themselves.

The interpreter's perspective, entailing unfolding and duplication at different levels, facilitates comparisons that are useful for finding discursive dimensions usually hidden in our everyday use of language.

When the Soviet delegate shouted: `Njet ... `Niet ... `Njet and the English counterpart whispered: ˌno ... ˌno ... ˌno, the most meaningful elements of those utterances were implied rather than stated openly.

one/first inset

---

2 *It can be incongruent or grossly mistaken, at certain levels, to speak of "equivalence in what has been said" or "equivalence of the textual surface" in the case of an operation – translation – which by definition implies the complete transformation of the textual surface (Italian into Portuguese, Portuguese into Chinese, etc.) However, by "equivalence in what has been said or on the textual surface" we mean the equivalence of meanings and structures at the language level* between two languages. We assume that people knowing two languages very well will be able to recognize the interlinguistic equivalence of words and structures. For instance: "Je veux que tu viennes" = "I want you to come" = "Quiero que vengas".*

The Soviet delegate in our story was ardently defending his government's position. He was perhaps rejecting a proposal, a recommendation, an accusation or an amendment. It is not important. What we do know and what matters, is that he was furious; his tone of voice and his gesticulations proved it. The English-speaking representatives who were following the interpreter's version through their earphones found some discordant elements between what they saw and what they heard. The tone of voice of the interpreter did not correspond to the excitement of the speaker or to the banging of his fists or shoe on his desk, even when taking into account the different ways of expressing anger in two different cultures.

The interpreter could have used a neutral tone: ˌno ... ˌno ... ˎno ... knowing, as he did, that most delegates present could see the Soviet representative gesticulating at the podium. Had he done so his listeners would have completed the oral information they were getting over the earphones with the visual data, which would have reconciled the *perlocutionary* effect* of the speaker with that of the interpreter. But the interpreter did not state the negative in a neutral tone; he used the intonation normally used in English in an enumeration to encourage the speaker to continue or show his disposition towards a reconciliation.

To express anger and produce a similar *illocutionary act,* the interpreter should have used a descending tone in his voice when saying ˋno or completely change the textual surface, saying, for instance: *Of ˋcourse ˋnot! ˋNo, 'absolutely ˋnot!*

ˋnjet ... ˋnjet ... ˋnjet	=	ˋno ... ˋno ... ˋno
ˋnjet ... ˋnjet ... ˋnjet	=	Of ˋcourse not!
		ˋNo, |'absolutely ˋnot!
		I 'can't ˇstand | and I
		'won't acˋcept that. |

By expressing `njet ... `njet ... `njet as ˌno... ˌno ... ˌno ... the interpreter reproduced the *direct* act* of negation but transformed the *indirect* act* of rejection into something almost conciliatory. Using Searle's terminology we could say that the *secondary* illocutionary act* was respected – the negation – but not so the *primary* illocutionary act* – the rejection. The interpreter did not seem to adopt the point of view of the speaker or to side with him. Rather, he maintained a certain distance, as apparent in his tone of voice, which seems to suggest: "There is no point in losing one's temper..." or "How uncivilized to get this angry!". The content implicit in the speaker's words *cannot* have been the same. The interpreter therefore betrayed the implied contract of complicity between himself and the speaker and in so doing made his interpretation misleading, not because of the words he used but because of the way in which he used them. In other words, he falsified his translation by betraying the implicit.

If his purpose was to make an amused wink to the Anglo-Saxon listeners, there is no doubt that he achieved it. Regrettably, the situation swiftly turned against him like a boomerang, since the laughter in the audience reportedly increased the anger of the delegate, who harshly denounced errors in the translation: the effect of his speech was far from being the same as that produced by the English version of it. The grapevine has it that maximum sanctions were applied to the interpreter.

This case revealed a remarkable facet of speech: *the possibility of saying something other than what is stated.* This being an ambiguous slippery domain by definition, we will now turn to a careful classification of *implicatures*3* proposed by French semiologist Oswald Ducrot in the 1970s in *Dire et ne pas dire*[4]

----

3 An implicature is anything that is inferred from an utterance but that is not a condition for the truth of the utterance.

4 See Ducrot in Dire et ne pas dire. *Paris. Hermann. 1972.*

(*Saying and not Saying*), showing how it can be relevant to our field of interest.

Ducrot proposes a logical and a psychological classification of implicatures. Within the first group, he distinguishes two types of logical implicatures:

1. the implicature in the utterance (in whatever is being said) and
2. the implicature in the act of enunciation (i.e. in the act of making an utterance).

Within the second group, which Ducrot calls "psychological implicatures" for want of a better word, he distinguishes four types:

1. the implied as an involuntary manifestation;
2. stylistic manoeuvres;
3. connotative rhetoric and
4. proven implied meaning as an intermediate stage between 2 and 3 which we will not discuss here.

Let us start then with logical implicatures.

The Implicature in the Utterance

A simple procedure for disclosing facts that we do not want to mention explicitly consists of submitting in their stead other facts which appear to be the cause or the consequence of these facts. We say that the weather is good to let it be known that we are going out; we speak of what we saw in the streets to make it known that we did go out. There are *syllogisms*: "So–and–so came to see me; he must be having problems"; and also less formal reasoning as in "Do not ask me for my opinion for if you do, I will give it to you" where the missing sentence "*you are not going to like my answer*" is the real content of the entire phrase.

If somebody says "It´s a beautiful day" with the implicit load of "I am going out" and if an interpreter transforms and turns it into "Here I am, locked up in this booth all day!" it is of little importance whether he has kept or not the textual surface when saying in Spanish: "¡Está lindo!" "El tiempo está espléndido." "¡Qué lindo clima!" or "¡Está tan cálido y soleado!" since he will not have respected the point of view of the speaker. He will have produced an equivalent *direct act* (assertion) and a different *indirect act* (speaker's assertion, interpreter's complaint).

– The sun is shining.
– What wonderful weather!
– It´s so warm and nice!

If we accept the idea that the implied meaning is like a kind of thread running through the warp of speech, comparable to what Stanislavski called "sub–text" in the theatre, we also have to admit that changing the latter is tantamount to transforming the original communication.

We could use this concept to explain the difference in meaning between the two telegrams in one of the examples of the preceding chapter where "I am OK" could translate as "as scheduled" in one case and as "I am alive" in the other.

Professional interpreters will maintain – quite rightly – that at a meeting discussing enamelled bathtubs or the toxicological effects of aminoglucose it is difficult to follow the course of implied meanings. It is precisely for this reason that computerised translation achieved its first success with technical and scientific texts, where the semantic content of the terms used had been unequivocally codified beforehand and where the implicit dimension practically ceases to exist.

In oral communication the tone, the accent and gestures suggest what is implied; and the implication is used as a bridge to reconstruct the meaning.

Let us look at a very simple example: *'give me `your book.|* The accent on *your* indicates that there are other books belonging to other persons but that they are not of interest to the speaker. (It's *your* book, not his or hers).

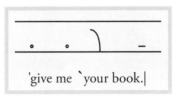

'give me `your book.|

Let us compare this with: *'give me your `book.|*, where the book is compared, tacitly, with other objects. (Give me your *book*, not your pen or your folder).

'give me your `book.|

Oral mode is not, however, the exclusive field of implied meanings. The following example has been taken from a newspaper article:

After the death of Charles Chaplin in December 1977, the Argentine newspaper *La Nación* devoted several pages to his life and art. A picture from one of his films showed him in his most famous role as the tramp, embracing the woman he loved, and beneath it was the caption: *"Poverty does not preclude great feelings"*. Although one might agree with the sentiment, there was something disturbing about this phrase that was difficult to pinpoint at first. Then, suddenly, it becomes obvious that the disturbing element is not the phrase itself but rather what it silenced: *"Wealth favours them"*.

The caption served as a timely reminder that to enter a discussion without making explicit, or without at least becoming aware of whatever is implicit, is to surrender from the outset, since it implies accepting unwittingly the adversaries' rules of the game.

Recapitulating:

> **A:** Poverty does not preclude great feelings.　　**TRUE**
> **B:** Wealth favours them.　　**FALSE**

"Poverty does not preclude great feelings", a proposition we shall call "A" is, in our mind, true. It does, however, invite the inference we shall call "B" which seems false to us. If somebody mentions "A" and "A" implies "B" we cannot accept "A" without accepting "B" at the same time, unless we state our explicit agreement with one and our explicit disagreement with the other.

If we now interchange the terms, we shall get the following:

> **A':** Wealth does not preclude great feelings.　　**TRUE**
> **B':** Poverty favours them.　　**FALSE**

If "A" and "A'" are true and contradictory statements at the same time; and "B" and "B'" expressing opposite views turn out to be both false, it is the connection between A and "A'" and "B" and "B'" which seems erroneous. In other words, the cause–effect relationship which the author establishes between money and feelings seems to be out of place, and its effects are all the more irritating since they are surreptitious. As stated by Grice,[5] the implicature is not conveyed by *what is said* but rather by the mere fact of stating something or by saying something in a certain way. What is stated may be true

---

5 H. P. Grice. *Logic and Conversation in* Syntax and Semantics. Pragmatics, *Nº 3, Peter Cole, London Academic Press.*

and what is implied may be false. It is better to know this to avoid pitfalls.

A child who is told:

1. *If you come back after ten, you will be punished* will be surprised, as rightly pointed out by G. Fauconnier,[6] to find himself punished if he returns by nine. This situation belonged logically in [1] which said nothing about returning at nine but did insistently invite the inference:
2. *If you come back before ten you shall not be punished*, an inference which is uncertain or, at the very least, incomplete:
3. *If you return before ten you will not be punished for being late.*

The Implicature in Enunciation

The implied meaning in what we are saying, says Ducrot, is no longer in question here; what is in question is rather the very fact that at some precise place and time we have chosen to open our mouth to say something. It is a question of what is implicit when we speak at any given moment.

"The implied here should not be sought at the level of enunciation as an extension or complement of what is explicited, but rather at a deeper level as a condition for the existence of the act of enunciation."[7]

From this standpoint we agree with Ducrot that:

"Mentioning subject X to interlocutor Y can, in certain circumstances, mean tacitly that Y is 'interested in X' or rather that the speaker believes he is; that giving an order

---

6 *G. Fauconnier, Questions et Acts Indirects*, Langue Francaise, *N° 52, Paris. Larousse, December 1981, Page 9.*

7 *O. Ducrot,* Dire et ne pas dire, *Paris, Hermann, 1972*

normally requires a certain hierarchical relationship between the giver and the receiver and that not everyone is allowed to ask just any question. Among its functions the act of questioning (or interrogating) includes that of affirming, in an implicit way, the right to interrogate".

These considerations imply that if we know speaker "L" and his opposite number "Y", we can predict, for instance, that subject "X" will not be broached. This in turn shows that, to a certain extent, the interpreter knows the probable statements of the speakers as far as substance and form are concerned.

If I am at a meeting of the International Sugar Organization in London (May 1980) I will be ready to hear exporters and importers speak of trigger prices, export tonnage, quotas, buffer stock financing, etc. And if Cuba asks for the floor after a statement by the USA I will get ready to hear a debate on the delay of the American Congress in ratifying the Sugar Agreement and not an exchange on the Bay of Pigs invasion of 1962. I will also have set my frequencies to a certain discursive style, vocabulary and *register*.*

A state of alertness *must* be maintained, however, for whoever has the floor may surprise us at any time. How? By the use of certain words and possible lack of reverence for certain implicit rules that govern social behaviour. Any speaker can, after all, break the silence surrounding certain subjects and say what others do not dare to state.

To show the extent to which an interpreter can be blocked by the framework of probabilities of expressions he may have assigned to the speakers, I will describe a personal experience during an Interamerican Bishops' Conference held in Mar del Plata a few years ago. A Canadian Bishop was speaking and I was interpreting into Spanish when, all of a sudden, in the middle of a statement proceeding normally I heard, literally, a noise. I realised that it corresponded to a word I had missed. Its absence was not noticeable in my delivery but I began to worry because I was no longer making much sense of what I was hearing. The same thing happened a few seconds later. In a split second I turned off my microphone and anxiously asked my colleague: "What's he saying for heaven's sake?" The answer, quiet and surprised, was *prostitutes*. As in a film going backwards, immediately the pieces of the puzzle fell into place and I understood the meaning of the previous sentences. Reassured, I continued working realizing at the same time that my *deafness* had been due

to an idiotic prejudice, which prevented me from putting the word *prostitute* in the mouth of a prelate. I was simply denying him the possibility of discussing such a subject in such a context. This is closely connected to a field about which there is much yet to be discovered: perception. Everything seems to indicate in this example that I had properly heard the term but that a *prejudice* had managed to disintegrate it into unintelligible noise and had done so at the speed of light!

We know[8] that when hearing somebody speak, the recognition of the word is the result of an analysis of sounds and context.

> "… words in fluent speech are partially specified by their acoustic structure and partially specified by the context in which they occur."[9]

---

8 *Bagley (1900), Polack and Picket (1963), Cole and Jakimik (1978) and Warren (1970).*

9 *Cole and Perfetti (1980).*

To be more specific, recognition of a word requires the active use of various sources of knowledge: phonological, prosodic, lexical, syntactic, semantic and pragmatic.

In the example given above there was no technical failure; both the public and my colleagues had heard the word correctly; I had not been having a fit of coughing and had not even so much as sneezed. The phenomenon occurred twice. It would seem then that not only had I heard the word *"prostitute"* – and that I had processed it correctly at all levels – phonological, prosodic, lexical, syntactic and even semantic – but that I rejected it precisely because I understood it. The speed of the response is staggering. All this suggests that there is a processing of information at a deep level, which happens *simultaneously* with acoustic processing and other operations.

This suggests the existence of a sort of *scanning mechanism* with very rapid to-and-fro or up-and-down movements between the various levels. It is when something does NOT work that this spontaneous scanning mechanism becomes visible.

The web of hypotheses I had built around the participants, their interests and intentions acted as a dam against which the word *prostitute* crashed like a wave. The shock produced "noise", the only thing I was able to hear consciously. When my colleague came to my rescue and repeated the word, not only did he shed light on the meaning of what I had been hearing but also brought about a restructuring of the web of hypotheses, now enlarged to include "prostitution" and everything the word entails: subjects such as alcoholism, drugs, gambling and homosexuality. All that gave new shape to my reference framework thanks to what we may call a *"dynamic restructuring"* of the knowledge web.

Another example comes to mind. When we are abroad and somebody asks us a question in a language which is not the one spoken in that country, *even if it is our own mother tongue*, we often have to ask them to repeat the question. It is as if the initial surprise acts as an obstacle to understanding: we didn't expect it. In other words, that somebody might speak to us in language "x" instead of in language "y" was not part of our initial hypothesis.[10]

Like actors, interpreters must, before starting work, recover *point zero* as Stanislavski would say, if they are to make themselves open to all possibilities and all shades of meaning.

Before going on to consider the second part of Ducrot's classification – psychological implicatures – it seems appropriate here to stress, with Ducrot, that:

> "… what is important for us is that in all cases the implicit meaning (IM) is something added to another meaning which we shall call literal (LM). To better define the nature of the addition, or value added, it will be observed that IM always allows for the existence of LM side by side."

If it is true that announcing the time of day can hold the IM "it is time for you to go", it is also true that even in this case, the literal meaning still holds good: "It's 4 o'clock". And the listener will always have the possibility of answering in accordance with a literal interpretation.

The analysis of an example given by Grice will show that the problem can be extremely complex:

> "X" who has until now been a great friend of "A" has recently betrayed him by selling a secret to his main competitor. "A" and his listeners know the fact and this allows them to understand: *"X" is a great friend* as an irony which means exactly the opposite.

---

10 *To verify the hypothesis that simultaneous translation presupposes the existence of probabilistic prediction, Chernov (1979) changes a speech, systematically introducing in it semantically correct sentences of an unexpected nature instead of highly predictable phrases. The results of his experiments were the following: in 24% of the cases studied, translation is accurate; in 38% of cases there is a "wrong" interpretation suggested by the context and in 38% of cases no translation is given.*

Let us assume for a moment that among "A"'s opposite numbers we find "B" who is also a great friend of "X" but is not aware of his betrayal.

Let us imagine the following dialogue:

> A: – X is a great friend.
> B (*after a pause and in a serious tone*): – Of course!
> A: – We agree. It is exactly what I have just said.
> B: – It is exactly what you have just said but it is exactly the opposite of what you wanted to say.

When "B" replies *of course!* in a serious tone he reveals that he has understood the irony in the previous comment. By acknowledging reception of the *indirect act** (denial of assertion of the direct act) "B" counters to defend his friend by repeating and insisting on the literal meaning. This insistence is his weapon against irony (in other words, against the indirect act with which "B" does not agree).

Let us now analyse the case in depth:

> "A" said "p" but meant "q" and "p" is the opposite of "q" (p ≠ q).
>
> "A"'s interlocutors know condition "d" and certain linguistic procedures which can allow them to understand "q" when hearing "p" (even in cases where "q" is exactly the opposite of "p").
>
> "B" ignores condition "d" but does know certain linguistic procedures allowing him to infer "q" when hearing "p". "B" does not agree with "q" but does agree with "p".
>
> When stating his agreement with "p", *having understood* "q", he *tacitly* expresses his disagreement with "q".
>
> This veiled feint could have ended there. But "A" decides to go ahead and insist on literalness, shielding himself with it:
>
> A: –"We agree. It is exactly what I have just said."

This is where matters begin to get complicated because – as mentioned by Ducrot:

> "Even though we always have the possibility of an answer only referring to the literal meaning, to do so in certain cases, such as the one at hand, brings to the surface the concept of lying and with it the problem of truth itself."

Superficially, "A" is telling the truth; he has just said: "'X' is a great friend". But "A" does know that certain linguistic procedures permit understanding the opposite of what is said; he knows that his listeners know them too. He knows he shares with them the knowledge of condition "d" (the betrayal he was victim of). He knows that there is incompatibility between knowledge of condition "d" and the statement "'X' is a great friend".

His listeners can only infer the opposite, that is: "'X' is a bad friend".

He then knows that when saying "'X' is a great friend" he meant the contrary, which is what everybody else understood. He has, therefore, lied.

If dealing with stage work, instructions would be:

A (*cynically*): – "We agree. He is…"

Such bad faith angers "B" and makes him bring the conflict[11] openly to the surface explaining what happened.

B: – It is **exactly** what you have said but also exactly the **opposite** of what you wanted to say.

---

11 A careful reading of Jorge Luis Borges' El informe de Brodie *and his masterly treatment of the subject of "duels" allows to interpret this one as yet another of the many duels we can engage in daily fashion.*

By revealing the duplicity of "A"'s manoeuvre, "B" comes out as the winner in the exchange.[12]

The example at the beginning of this chapter, "njet, njet, njet/no, no, no", also shows that the interpreter's reasons for defending the literal meaning were not enough. By changing what had been implied, he ended up changing the meaning. The implicit dimension acquires autonomy.

As mentioned above, Ducrot termed the second classification of implicatures as *psychological* for lack of a better word. Let us look at the first three cases in turn:

a. the implied as an involuntary manifestation;
b. stylistic manoeuvres;
c. connotative rhetoric and
d. proven implied meaning as an intermediate stage between (b) and (c) which we will not discuss.

a) The implied as an involuntary manifestation.

"The discursive process which clarifies the implicit meaning often seems not to have been foreseen by the speaker and to appear more connected to a critical reflection than to mere decoding. It is impossible therefore to assign to the speaker the conscious intent of the meaning involved and the implicit will then be considered related to a certain depth of the message unknown to the author himself"[13].

For instance, it is possible to seek in any text the implied reflection of the beliefs of the time. But this is also the domain of *lapsus linguae* or slips of the tongue.

---

12 *In fact, we consider "A's" second statement cynical and not ironic for, as "B" did not join in the complicity of the ironic game, "A" should have either explained it or put an end to the exchange. Once complicity is broken, by insisting on the same procedure "A" goes from irony, intended as humour, to cynicism and mendacity both trying to confuse perception.*

13 *O. Ducrot.* Dire et ne pas Dire, *Paris: Hermann, 1972.*

Sigmund Freud himself offers us an example taken from the conference world.[14] During the inaugural meeting of a Session of the Austrian House of Representatives the President made the following announcement: "Honourable Representatives, after having counted the number of those present, I declare the session *adjourned*." We have here a typical case of mistaken substitution of one word for another with an opposite meaning.

The explanation, as offered by Meringer and shared by Freud, is that the President wanted to adjourn as soon as possible a meeting from which he expected no good; his wish would have followed its course at least partially, and the result was the slip of the tongue which made him replace *I declare the session open* with *I declare the session adjourned*.[15]

What should an interpreter do in such cases? Must he ignore the lapsus? Must he make room for it in his delivery or should he explain it? In a case like this one, it is preferable, to my mind, to reflect it for two reasons: 1) firstly because the reaction of the listeners to the original speech would have

_14 In_ Psicopatología de la vida cotidiana _Madrid, Alianza Editorial, 1970, Pages 71 and 72, where he quotes an article by Meringer published in_ Neue Freie Presses _in 1900 entitled "How We Can Make mistakes". (_Psychopathology of Everyday Life, _Modern Library, 1995._

15 When proofreading the final version of these pages I found in La Nación _a report of the same mistake committed conversely by Vice President Victor Martínez after the Presidential address of May 1st. 1988 when he said: "Having achieved the objectives of this Legislative Assembly I now declare the meeting open". The confused looks exchanged by those present and some murmuring made him notice his mistake. "I declare the meeting adjourned", he corrected himself._

told those needing a translation that something awkward had occurred and they would have certainly wanted to know the reason for such hilarity, and 2) because if Freud and Meringer had been present and depending on the interpretation, they would certainly have wanted to know what had happened since *slips of the tongue* were full of meaning to them.

Since a *lapsus linguae* reveals the most intimate trains of thought, its effects and consequences will depend on the situation, the context and the relationship between the participants.[16] The decision to translate it, explain it or omit it will ultimately depend on its relevance within the general framework. And the array of different situations can indeed be wide (a technical meeting on peas, a hard negotiation between Heads of State, the deposition of a defendant before the judge, among so many others).

b) Stylistic manoeuvres.

Stylistic manoeuvres are almost the opposite of involuntary manifestations. They are the set of means available to the speaker to obtain a desired effect.

> "They allow the speaker to awaken certain opinions in his listeners without having to run the risk of verbalizing them. They therefore let something be believed without having actually said it. Frequently however, these manoeuvres work more actively: it is not only a question of allowing something to be believed, it is question of sending a message without having stated it".

What does an interpreter do to say without saying what the speaker has said without saying? He must preserve the delicate balance between substance and form (figure and ground) and try to reproduce the same direct and indirect

---

16 *See chapter 17 on "Interference", page 273.*

effects sought by the speaker. A spontaneous translation of the aforementioned dialogue shows that a clear understanding of what is going on produces the appropriate intonation pattern and thus an equivalent meaning.

From a theoretical point of view, the ability and competence of the interpreter consist precisely in finding a very fine

A: – X es un gran amigo … B: – ¡Por supuesto que sí! A: – Estamos de acuerdo. Es exactamente lo que acabo de decir. B: – Es exactamente lo que acaba de decir pero exactamente *lo contrario de lo que quiso decir.*	A (*ironically*): – X is a very good friend … B (*after a pause*): – Of course he is! A (*cynically*): – We agree. That's exactly what I've just said. B (*indignantly*): – That's exactly what you said but exactly the *opposite of what you meant.*

distinction among the various types of implicatures and contextual information so that he can build the adequate framework to interpret what has been said and say it again in another language respecting the implicatures and transmitting the explicit contextual information.

c) Connotative rhetoric.

"Even though in its origin the stylistic manoeuvre can be seen as similar to a stratagem through which a causal action tries to produce certain beliefs in the listeners, it (the manoeuvre) tends constantly to institutionalization and thereby originates a second code which is superimposed on the language as described in grammars and dictionaries. This second code is at least an important part – and perhaps even the entirety – of what has been called rhetoric".

"When Stendhal uses an Italian word it is not only – or even necessarily – due to the very meaning of the word (or because a French term could not render the meaning just as precisely); rather, it is to make it "sound" Italian, to make it sound "peninsular" so as to introduce at that point in the text the full array of feelings that Italy evokes in him ... What is significant in a text by Stendhal is, indissolubly, the intention and the meaning of the Italian language. We could say the same about certain technical terms – directed at giving the impression of something technical – to imply technical knowledge. It is difficult in this case to speak of implied meaning; once again we have before us a case of explicit meaning although explicated in another language".[17]

The interpreter should perceive those "second codes" – slight "jumps" from one register to another – so as to try to produce equivalent semantic effects in his own discourse.

The comparison of a fragment of speech with its simultaneous interpretation revealed one dimension, the implied, which is often manifested in speech by the tone of voice, stress and intonation.

Stanislavski's theory of theatre proves he was fully aware of the various discursive dimensions. He proposed certain exercises where students were made by force of the dramatic situation to say NO - for example - with an incredibly open array of sub-texts: 1) I don't; 2) I don't know ; 3) Perhaps; 4) I love you; 5) Yes.

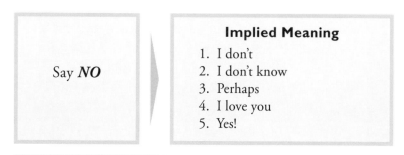

Say **NO**	**Implied Meaning**
	1. I don't
	2. I don't know
	3. Perhaps
	4. I love you
	5. Yes!

17 O. Ducrot, Dire et ne pas dire. *Paris. Hermann, 1972. Pages 16 and 17.*

The Melody in Words

I remember a scene in an old American film by Sidney Lumet where the President of the USA reveals his awareness of the importance the slightest changes in pitch, the subtlest changes in breathing and intonation can have for the outcome of a dramatic situation. The film was called *Fail Safe* and here is its summary (from *www.rottentomatoes.com/m/fail-safe/about*).

> "Taking place over the course of a single day, the film follows government and army officials in New York and Washington, as they go about their day supervising, examining, and speculating on the fragile state of affairs engendered by the tense nuclear standoff between the U.S. and Russia. When an off-course commercial airplane triggers the Pentagon's complex fail-safe maneuver, leaving an arsenal of nuclear-bomb-carrying jet fighters at the ready, a mechanical error puts the entire world in danger of destruction. Henry Fonda plays the American president who must navigate the complex and urgent political trauma and prevent total destruction, even at an unthinkable price".

There is a particularly dramatic scene where Henry Fonda, the American President, has to decide whether or not to press the button for a nuclear attack while on the telephone with his Soviet counterpart. Tension is at its peak. The American President asks his interpreter to translate *everything*: he must decide what to do on the basis of how much he trusts his adversary and this will largely depend on what he perceives on the telephone. In this nerve-wracking scene, the President attempts to detect both what the other is saying and what he may be hiding. The slightest pause, the most imperceptible muttering, an infinitesimal change in breathing could reveal a doubt, a second thought, a change of mind that, correctly interpreted, might end up sparing thousands of human lives. Aware of the importance of the subtlest elements, the president and his interpreter wisely managed to avoid that risky point of no return.

One of the key elements in interpreting the meaning of spoken utterances is word stress, which guides us like a pointed finger, as Stanislavski liked to say. A change in stress transforms meaning under our eyes.

Emphasis changes and with it meaning.

- Did **you** come yesterday?
  *... we expected **your associate** to come.*
- Did you **come** yesterday?
  *... we thought you would **telephone** first.*
- Did you come **yesterday**?
  *... we expected you **today**.*

Stress and emphasis unveil implied meanings. But stress and emphasis go beyond: they reveal emotions and hidden feelings.

Not only is it possible to ask the *same question* with any of those *different meanings*. It is also possible to ask the same question expressing a wide range of *different emotions*, from astonishment to indifference, curiosity or rage.

The Hidden Side of Words

From the moment two people know they share a set of data they can communicate more (or less, or something else) than what they actually say. "Implicatures" and underlying meanings are thus born from this store of shared knowledge.

A: – The meeting is adjourned till Friday.
B: – There is a general strike announced for Friday.

> *Implied meaning: "... better adjourn till Monday"*

A: – We haven't seen each other for ages.
B: – I'll phone you next week.

> *Possible implied meanings:*
>
> *"...I am in a great hurry."*
> *"... I will explain my silence then."*
> *"... I apologize for not doing so before."*
> *"... It has been ages and will be some more! You can take a seat and wait."*
> *"... I must first look at my appointment book."*
> *"... Don't call me. I will call you."*

Much more is communicated than said by using the resources of logic, inference and common sense available to us – as human beings.

It is precisely these implied cognitive mechanisms that we are trying to reveal.

A: "I'll come by and see you this afternoon."
B: "I won't be home"

> *Implied meaning: "... Do not therefore come."*

The Slippery Notion of Truth in Language

If someone told us that it is possible to assert something and then its opposite and yet pretend that both statements can be considered *true* – or valid – we would most probably refuse to admit it. Logic rejects that kind of contradiction and these implicit rules seem to safeguard the realms and boundaries of sanity. And yet …

Let's consider the following example. Klebnikov (quoted by George Steiner in *After Babel. Aspects of Language and Translation*[18]) used to say that the sun obeyed his syntax. How come, one might argue at first? Well, the sun obeyed his syntax since he could make it sneak in through the window or slip under the door. He could also turn it into a football to play a match with or borrow one of its rays to explore outer space. We can make the sun's rays light up a scene in the woods, or project colourful spots on the walls of a child's bedroom. We can visualize planets turning around it in a cosmic carrousel …

We also know though, from observation, research and inference, that the sun obeys certain laws over which we have no control and that, consequently, "the sun does not obey our syntax". The *sun* has been out there for much longer than we can remember and it will still be there much longer after our passing away … We also know that life on earth depends on it and that we, humans, seem to have little impact on it. How pretentious – and unrealistic then to say that "the sun obeys our syntax". In fact, even a child knows that it does not.

Klebnikov seems, then, to be right and not right at the same time. It is therefore possible to say one thing in a certain context and even its opposite in another, without in any way jeopardizing the *truth*. We can easily slide from a realistic level of language use to a metaphorical one without as much as a warning to our counterparts, assuming they will sense the switch.

---

18 *George Steiner,* After Babel. Aspects of Language and translation. *Oxford University Press. London. 1975.*

What mysterious mechanisms in language allow for this? How come two contradictory statements can both be *true*? In what context? In reference to what parameters? Can a sentence be considered *true* in isolation? When contrasted to what cultural, or scientific parameters? Or within which code of values or beliefs?.

We may say then that the truth of a statement does not depend exclusively on what it says; it also depends on what it implies for speaker "A" when facing his listener "B" at a given place "x" and a time "T".

Let us now consider the validity of another example.

$$A = A$$

If you were told that "A" equals "A", you would normally agree. No problem there.

But once again, what appears clear-cut and easy at first sight may turn out not quite so simple on second thoughts … If both elements: first "A" and second "A" point to an abstract third entity "A" (opposed to B, C, D, E, F, etc.), we can easily accept the validity of the identity. It seems also unquestionable, though, that the first "A" cannot be considered identical to the second one if we take into account their positioning regarding the symbol "=", since one appears before and the other after it.

| $A = A$ | "The sun obeys my syntax." |
| $A \neq A$ | "The sun does not obey my syntax." |

Nothing in the words themselves – or in their alignment – either in English or in any other language, seems to justify or explain the adjustment we make in our minds so as to produce such a semantic jump that enables us to interpret each one of these statements in completely different ways.

It is the listener or the speaker who operates the internal reorganization of meanings. It is this restructuring that allows us to state that both contradictory statements are true to life, and still *feel* sane.

Truth or mendacity in ordinary life cannot be contained in an isolated sentence. To grasp them, it is necessary to start from a situation, a context and an entire web of words, people and actions.

A set of symbols (22 or 25 or 28, etc. letters according to the language, space, dot and comma) in different combinations are enough to express whatever we want to express in any language but even if we combine the *same* symbols in the *same* manner, we can produce *different* meanings and consequently *different* effects. Billions of humans the world over, using different languages, have for the most part got used to this wonderful set of tools and have eventually taken them for granted. Familiarity tends to distract us and repetition puts many players to sleep but the mystery of the language game is not only still intact, it even seems to increase as we play.

Language functions as a curious tool: depending on how we use it and on how aware we are of its array of possibilities, it can help understanding or block it altogether; it can dispel confusion or increase it; it can help build bridges or become an isolating barrier. Some people with special language training – like journalists, academics, etc. – are normally well aware of the fact that they can develop a rational solid argument for or against the same position. Or as someone once put it irreverently: you want me to write an article on God … for or against Him?

Language is a powerful and magnificent tool which enables and fosters creativity. It can also become a deadly weapon, a prison or the worst obstacle to creativity, depending on how we use it. Words can feel alive … or dead. Human beings can use language to map their own perceptions of the world around them, of their own feelings, ideas and thoughts. They can also lose the connections between what they say, and what they feel/ know/think about the world around them.

One of the most popular of Descartes' contentions could be proven wrong by any Zen master: existence goes beyond doubts, reflections, thoughts and words. Life pre-exists and persists longer than rational mental activity. From this wider, larger, more comprehensive point of view, we can only attempt to capture in language an approximation of what *reality* seems to be ... trial-and-error; trial-and-success, partial success in an ever growing, ever more complex process of cognition and evolution. Truth – as something absolute, as something unique – lies in the realm of silence.

How can we, then, make use of this fabulous tool, with its complexity and richness, that only we humans share? Learning how it works, learning about its limits and potential may give us some clues about our existence, its meaning, its underlying framework; about our participation in a bigger, wider project, about our position in the evolutionary scale, and the intersection between our individual history and that of the human race. It may also make us understand the reciprocal translation of our senses, the relationship between the parts and the whole, the patterns that point to something persisting and surpassing our restricted nervous systems, of something that pre-existed our limited consciousness (can you remember, if not, your sensations or emotions at 2, 3, or 4 years old?) and that will, supposedly, outlive us: life.

It is life, in a wider sense, which we as humans are called to protect and humbly to attempt to understand.

❖   ❖   ❖

CHAPTER 4

The Motive

Of how an axiom can work in practice but be unsustainable in theory. Of how a hypothesis about the intention of the speaker is absolutely necessary for the interpretation of his speech. Examples from FAO, Bertrand Russell, Stanislavski and the super objective of a play.

Do not interpret what the speaker says but rather what he means is one of the axioms of interpreting, and one of the first things that students of interpretation need to learn. "Forget about the words, think about what the speaker means". And students almost invariably do give a better version once they stop translating words and start translating meanings.

The axiom however brings up a serious problem from a theoretical point of view. How to be really sure of knowing what the speaker means? Considering what parameters? From which point of view?

The problem becomes even more complicated if we take the notion of implication into account. The premise *"do not interpret what the speaker says but what he means"* could even entail that the interpreter's task is to make explicit whatever is implied. Nothing could be farther from the truth. Often the interpreter, like any other listener, knows exactly what the speaker means but will not "say" it if the speaker chooses "not to say it openly".

And even though in a previous example (see page 72) all of those present knew that when "A" said ***"X" es un gran amigo*** he meant exactly the opposite, no interpreter would have dared to say in English "'X' is a bad friend".

> "X" is a good friend.

"X" es un gran amigo.	≠	"X" is a bad friend.

Had he done so he would have found himself later on in an embarrassing situation when having to translate:

"We agree. It is exactly what I have just said".

From all this we can infer a tacit rule, according to which interpreters are obliged to respect the stylistic manoeuvers (such as irony, metaphors,[1] hyperboles), to respect whatever is implied in the original text and to preserve the indirect acts as much as possible.

Another example may prove useful:

During a FAO meeting in Rome in May of 1977, a delegate from an African country asked that a certain measure that affected his country and an industrialized country be reconsidered. He demanded that it be done in the light of the latest recommendations made by UNCTAD in which the developed countries committed themselves to the improvement of their relationships with dependent countries. The representative of the industrialized country in point (The Federal Republic of Germany) asked for the floor to state, in a rather lengthy intervention, that his government could not accept the reconsideration of the measure under discussion. The Chairman of the Group of 77[2] (Brazilian at the time) became the spokesman for the African country and took the floor to say he had been unable to understand what had just been said because he had had problems with the sound or the interpretation; what little he heard over his earphones made no sense for if it did, the developed country's policy would be contradicting itself: industrialized countries had already made a commitment in an international body and were now refusing to live up to it. He was therefore sure he had not heard well and asked the German delegate to be kind enough to repeat his statement. The delegate did so. Attending to procedure the President of

---

1 The translation of "ella es la flor de mi vida" as "she is the cream in my coffee" and not as "she is the flower of my life" shows that in the interpreter's mind the equivalence of the act takes precedence over that of the words. In this case the interpreter is more interested in repeating what the speaker does rather than what he says.

2 The group of 77, also known as G-77, composed only by developing countries, embraces today 133 members.

the meeting then asked the Chairman of the 77 if he had this time understood properly. His answer was given with emphasis and irony:

> "Yes, Mr. President. Thank you very much. *That* was *exactly* what I wanted to hear".

What had the Chairman of the 77 done? To start with, when saying he had not understood the statement and requesting that it be repeated, he caught the ear of all those present and directed their attention to that specific part of the speech. He pretended not to have heard or understood for, had he understood correctly, the lack of consistency would not be due to the *words* but, rather, to the *facts* (the policy sustained by the country in question) something quite unlikely in view of the power relationships at play. By explaining why he believed he had not understood, the Chairman brought to the attention of the delegates the *message* he wished to convey: *there was contradiction and lack of consistency and seriousness in the position upheld by the industrialized country.* To say so openly meant levelling charges with all the consequences such an action might entail. He preferred, therefore, to make this understood, without saying as much, by including it in a conditional proposition: "… If I have understood well … this would mean that …". But he even went further since he attributed the lack of coherence in what he had heard to a failure on his own part to hear or understand properly rather than to the contradictory position of a country assumed to be developed, consistent and predictable. The underlying structure of his argument was "… if I have understood correctly … this would mean that … therefore, I must have understood wrongly".

Using the same mechanisms for reasoning and reflection used by his counterparts, the Chairman of the Group of 77 reverts the accusation so often present in the relations between industrialized and developing countries: *You are contradictory, inconsistent and unpredictable.* Forced to repeat what he had said, the European delegate ratified, against his will, the arguments used by his opposite number. He confirmed that the Chairman of the 77 had heard correctly even the first time and that there was, therefore, according to the reasoning used, contradiction and inconsistency in the policies of his own country. That was precisely the implied accusation in "That was exactly what I wanted to hear!"

"C'était bien cela que je voulais entendre" said the interpreter with the same emphasis and irony in his voice as used by the speaker. The interpreter, through a critical analysis of the speech he heard, discovered the hidden messages and grasped the shades of meaning which he then transmitted without making explicit or trying to explain what the speaker wanted to say.

Where implied meanings are involved, the formula "Do not interpret what the speaker says but what he means" ceases to be valid. Other aspects of the ambiguity of this formula will become apparent in a quotation from *Portraits from Memory* by Bertrand Russell[3]:

> "Human beings are completely exempt from undesirable behaviour patterns only when certain prerequisites, not satisfied except in a small percentage of actual cases have, through some fortuitous concourse of favourable circumstances, whether congenital or environmental, chanced to combine in producing an individual in whom many factors deviate from the norm in a socially advantageous manner.
>
> Let us see how we can translate this sentence into English. I suggest the following: *All men are scoundrels or, at any rate, almost all. Those men who are not must have had unusual luck, both in their birth and in their up-bringing.* But I am afraid any professor who used the second sentence instead of the first would get the sack."

....

3 Portraits from Memory, *London , Allen and Unwin, New York. Simon and Schuster. 1956*

Human beings are completely exempt from undesirable behaviour patterns only when certain prerequisites, not satisfied except in a small percentage of actual cases have, through some fortuitous concourse of favourable circumstances, whether congenital or environmental, chanced to combine in producing an individual in whom many factors deviate from the norm in a socially advantageous manner.

All men are scoundrels or, at any rate, almost all. Those men who are not must have had unusual luck, both in their birth and in their up-bringing.

If interpreters were expected to report only the essential elements of an intervention, they would often remain silent or simply sum up by saying: "The delegate of such and such a country said NO". Indeed, this has sometimes happened, although not without infuriating the delegate of the country in question who had made a long presentation to explain the reasons and subtleties of his refusal. Some syntheses can indeed produce brutal effects.

Let us suppose that a speaker utters a speech comparable to Russell's first version. Let us also assume that there is simultaneous or consecutive translation. Is the interpreter perhaps expected according to the formula we are discussing to give a translation similar to Russell's second version?

Even if an interpreter of genius managed to do so – and his synthesis would be remarkable – some of the effects of the first version would be lost. Indeed, the first part of the Russell text reveals a speaker who is confusing, circumlocutory and pretentious; the second reveals exactly the contrary: a speaker who is direct, clear and concise. These effects, directly linked to style must be taken into account while interpreting, for omitting or changing them can also distort the process of understanding. From the point of view of style, the formula "*Do not interpret what the speaker says but what he means*" also loses validity.

How is it possible for this axiom to be accepted by interpreters and translators and how is it possible that it works especially well with beginners? Because those who are beginning to interpret are generally too concerned with the words they hear and the ones they seek to use; very often they feel they are being judged by a powerful Mr. Bilingual or Multilingual Dictionary who will rule that a certain term was rightly or wrongly translated and therefore they tend to interpret "in the air", "in a vacuum" unconnected to the speaker. It is precisely at this moment that the formula becomes efficient since by telling them: "Forget the terms, think of what the speaker means", it encourages beginners to transfer emphasis – and attention – from the words to whoever is producing them.[4]

The student of interpretation begins then to be less concerned with the equivalent in Spanish or Japanese of words such as "pattern", "background" or "patronizing attitude" to devote more attention to finding out why the person who has the floor is saying what he or she is saying. Instead of processing words "on their surface" the student will try to link and understand them in the light of certain information: "who", "to whom", "where", "when" and "why".

When saying: "... *do not interpret what the speaker says but what he means* ... the existence of two areas or dimen-

---

4 "*Speech acts are achieved not by words but by the speakers who utter them*". *J. Searle*. Les actes de langage. *Paris. Hermann.1972. Page 66.*

sions is implicitly recognized. One thing is to say something, another to mean something. People do not always say what they mean; and interpreters cannot seriously expect to know for sure what somebody else wants to say before they have said it. Interpreters make then hypotheses on the speakers' motives, intentions and objectives.

In retrospect, I find that at the beginning of my career, every time I had a chance to talk to the speaker before the conference, I would ask questions such as "What is the basic point you wish to make? What is your objective? What are you driving at?"[5]

It was sometimes a matter of defending a theoretical point against other prevailing ones; of increasing the sale of a product, or of establishing new contacts with a company or a government. Sometimes the speaker either did not know or did not want to tell me. Often, though, I did obtain the parameters I needed for a correct interpretation – straight from the speaker's mouth – of what he or she was going to say. I seldom do this nowadays since professional practice has especially taught me to elaborate – modify, assimilate, reject or verify – any hypothesis concerning the intentions of the speakers. And this is precisely what the formula "Forget the words ..." summarily keeps in the minds of students of interpretation.

To interpret sentence "n" just uttered by "A", the interpreter simultaneously takes into account that "A" is speaking to his listeners "B" at place "y" at a given moment "t" on a subject "x" and knowing what he knows about "A" and "B" he will draw up a hypothesis, "h", permitting him to understand "n" and interpret that sentence into another language as " n' ".

The formula we have been considering is of undeniable pragmatic value but has serious and undisputed theoretical

---

5 See examples on pages 50 and 68. In the first case the interpreter took a Danish speaker for an Englishman and distorted his speech. In the second, the interpreter refused to admit prostitution could be of interest to bishops.

flaws. Pragmatically, we encourage its use in practice. But we will now propose a new more refined formula for theoretical purposes: *we cannot interpret "what has been said" except in the light of a number of hypotheses we make about the speaker's motives, intentions and objectives. These hypotheses are inferred from the situation in which the utterance occurs, and are based on what speakers say and do and on what we know about them.*

The interpreter as a Bridge

Some will say that not having certain data about the speaker's function, ideas, nationality or background may prevent the formulation of valid hypotheses. In fact, this is quite often the case. The interpreter then generates hypotheses, only to discard them later and replace them with other – hopefully more relevant – ones as the speaker's intentions become clearer.

What to do in those cases? *"What does anyone do when he doesn't understand something? He fastens on to its surface appearance."*[6] The interpreter will turn up the volume to ensure good reception, will place himself as near as possible to the speaker intervention and will intuitively try to put across the feeling of ambiguity he is experiencing.

It sometimes happens that listeners with additional background information fully understand the speaker even though the interpreter is left "groping". In such cases the interpreter will have acted simply as a bridge or as a carrier pigeon. The same happens when we are asked to "… tell Peter the answer is yes", in the understanding that he knows what it is all about. As the messengers we are, we will be left to guess the meaning of this "Yes". For Peter, on the other hand, the message will immediately be clear and comprehensible.

In situations like these, the interpreter will have the awkward and unsettling feeling of proceeding blindly. Far

---

6 *Christopher Isherwood,* A Meeting by the River, *London, Penguin, 1961.*

from being satisfied, he will repeatedly test his hypotheses as the speaker's intervention unfolds, in search of the additional information needed for understanding. Once the pieces have fallen into place, the interpreter will usually be able to follow the thread of meaning without any further difficulty.

Hypotheses concerning the intention of the speaker integrate a vaster network of hypotheses about the participants, their objectives and the more general aims of the meeting and its organizers. We elaborate such hypotheses from data acquired *before* the meeting and information gathered *during* the event itself.

The problem of intentionality in the realm of discourse poses the problem of what is deliberate in speech and what is not. We find ourselves here in a field that psychoanalysis has singled out for special study. It is not my intention to venture into this slippery terrain. It does seem timely, though, to point out that even the elements which we could, from the outset, call *non-deliberate* – such as cultivated or vernacular accents – give us information which we use, often unknowingly, to elaborate hypotheses about the speaker's intent.

Motivation

In another field, that of drama, and approaching the problem from the other end, Stanislavski[7] refers to the objective actors must find for their characters in order to justify their words and gestures, in each act, each scene and each unit of action. If actors do not manage to find those objectives, Stanislavski rightly contends, they will lack in credibility on stage. He also mentions the "super objective" of the play; if

---

7 *Constantin Stanislavski,* La construcción del personaje, *Madrid, Alianza Editorial, 1975, Page 326. (*Building a Character, *Theatre Arts Books, 1989.)*

lost sight of by the director and the actors the audience will not find any sense in the performance.

Much in the way a detective follows the clues left by his prey, we normally try to find the motive behind people's words.

This poses some problems since it is possible to attribute different meanings and different motivations to the same words, utterances or actions. Let us imagine, for example, that we are walking in Paris in early medieval times when we see crowds of craftsmen working on a big building site. We stop to observe from close a small group of men carving stone. They all perform the same act with apparently similar intent. When we ask them what they are doing, though, we may be puzzled by their different replies.

– I'm earning my living – says the first.
– I'm building a wall – replies the second.
– I'm building a cathedral – says the third.

The way these men look upon the work they do can have an incredible impact on the quality of their work – and of their life.

Quino humorously reveals Mafalda's hidden intentions to deliberately modify delegates' interventions so as to super-impose her own more generous motivations.[8]

---

8 Quino, Mafalda & friends, N° 3, *Edición de la Flor, Buenos Aires, 2004.*
© *Joaquín S. Lavado - Quino. Reproduced with the copyright holder consent.*

Etymologically, *motive, move, motivation, motion, emotion* all have the same origin: movement. Doing, acting and speaking are tantamount to *moving* to achieve a goal.

Words, acts and gestures become signs for the interpreter to infer hypotheses about the speaker's intent.

❖   ❖   ❖

CHAPTER 5

Divergent or Contradictory Signals

Of the possible presence of divergent or contradictory signals in speech. Five cases showing what the interpreter does when faced with them. Examples: Chaplin, prostitutes and a good friend. Stanislavski and the sub–text.

S peakers sometimes hesitate while rendering their speech, they pause in doubt, stammer, go back and sound unsure.

At other times, speakers feel they are making a great presentation or delivering a speech without flaws and yet careful listeners perceive inconsistencies, suffocated questioning or signs of uncertainty. We will now take five cases of divergent signals in speech.

Twenty minutes from Nice airport, surrounded by hills and fairly unspoilt countryside, lies Saint Paul de Vence, a wonderful little medieval town mostly inhabited by painters and antique dealers. Within walking distance of the town, close to the Maeght Foundation and in woods overlooking the Mediterranean sea, an American data processing company centre was established in the seventies to host small conferences all the year round. Business was conducted in style; presentations were at the highest level.

I flew south from Paris six or seven times a year for almost twenty years, appreciating the friendly, multicultural atmosphere, the team, the style and the exchange of information at the Unisys Management Centre, previously known as Sperry Univac. It was there in the mid-seventies that I had to visualize and interpret the concept of "electronic mail" for the first time.

The examples that follow were taken from the presentation of a keynote speaker who was introducing a product not yet fully born.[1]

---

1 *A few years later the development had transformed communications all over the world.*

The keynote speaker was presenting the astounding idea in those days of transmitting data electronically within the same company or within the corporate world for normal everyday operations.

Case N° I

Speaker's words	Interpreter's words	
… eh … I should point out that … eh … I have a bias there. I believe that a document is a useful … unit of information transfer and that an electronic office system ought to remember documents even though they may, in fact, physically go away … some day (Nonetheless) there is an assumption in what I'm going to be saying along the way that the document must survive.	*Debería … quisiera señalar que tengo un prejuicio aquí. Yo creo que un documento es algo importante en la transferencia de la información, entonces creo que es necesario que la oficina electrónica recuerde registre esos documentos a pesar de que materialmente no estén más allí. (—) hay un supuesto en lo que voy a decir después en el sentido de que el documento debe sobrevivir.*	I should … I would li-ke to point out that I have a bias here. I believe that a document is something important for information transfer; so I think that it's necessary for the electronic office to remember, to record documents even though they may physically no longer be there one day. (—) there is an assumption in what I'm going to be saying along the way that the document must survive.

If we compare these two fragments we shall find that certain elements (*unit* and *someday*) do not appear in the Spanish version. We shall also find that physically has been correctly translated as ***materialmente***, etc. There is much room for analysis here. However, we are going to pay attention only to the presence of nonetheless and its absence from the Spanish version.

materially.

Let us first describe the "plot" of the situation.

During a seminar organized in St. Paul de Vence (1978) on the latest trends in computer applications, an American speaker introduced the concept of "electronic office". In the future, he stated, computers would not longer be used simply as support instruments; they would become an integral part of the office, its very heart. He was, in fact, announcing the coming of offimatics[2] with all the transformations this would entail for everyday work in offices all over the world.

Just before the above quotation he had said

> "... eh ... the electronic office ought to ... the electronic office system ought to work in the context of ... eh ... documents and ... eh ... generating them, flowing them around in the organization, permitting retrieval ... eh ... it ought to be used in the context of the coordination of people and their work, ... eh ... and it ought to be used in the management of projects and such functions".

He then went on to say that he was biased, and explained why: he believed that a document is a useful unit for the transfer of information and that the electronic office should be able to record the documents ... (But is not that perhaps the main objective of computer science? Why does the speaker call it a bias? ... the interpreter is meanwhile asking herself ...). The speaker continues "... even if some day the documents are not going to be physically there any longer".

Is it not precisely the role of the electronic office to record information without using paper? "However – the speaker

---

2 *"Offimatics", the term used then to refer to the incorporation of computing into the office, did not survive. "Data processing" was replaced by "informatics" or "computing sciences" and today the term "IT" (Information technology) covers an even wider field.*

adds, literally – there is an assumption in what I'm going to be saying along the way that the document must survive".

Let us follow the procedure step by step:

1. The speaker warns that he has a bias;
2. He begins to explain it;
3. His assumption will "therefore", "naturally", "consequently" be underlying his words. But surprisingly, the speaker discards using "therefore" or "obligatorily" and he links the propositions with "nonetheless". Why, if the argumentation requires a consequence? In fact, in spite of having announced it, he does not describe his bias in 2) He will only do so in 3).

What does the interpreter do? Without the slightest pause or doubt in her voice she directly omits "nonetheless". This proves that at normal discourse speed (the rate of delivery was very fast: 170 words per minute)[3] and while doing both things at the same time (reception and delivery of the speech), the interpreter is in addition carrying out a deep analysis of the fragment she is translating. She not only grasps the presence of divergent elements, she also has to make a quick decision on the direction she should follow to reconstruct meaning. To perform such an analysis outside the extreme situation of simultaneous interpretation requires efforts which develop in time: we need to concentrate, find relationships, make comparisons and reach conclusions. Interpreters do all this in a fraction of a second and – for better or worse – make their decisions accordingly.

The subsequent development of the speech will ratify or nullify their decisions. In this case, 28 minutes were needed

---

3 Compare this figure with the rate of 60 to 100 words per minute accepted during the Nuremberg Trials (see page 22) and with the average of 129 of Mitterrand and 148 of Giscard D'Estaing during the 1974 electoral campaign, according to Cotteret in "57.744 mots pour convaincre", Paris, PUF, 1976.

after the statement of the bias to begin understanding something of the knot of interrelated ideas.

> "Now, there are certain things that might be put into an electronic office system that aren't so easily described … eh … for all users … eh … I call them 'client oriented features' and I'm gonna take a minute to talk about that … Oh! … there is one point though that I want to get to because if you don't think about it you miss it. In the electronic mail and message switching issue, if I send a document to … eh … Rigg … what's he going to do with it? Well, if it's a piece of paper, he may … eh … write a note on it and send it back to me, or he may write a note on it and file it, or he may create another memorandum and send it to me or to somebody else … electronic message switching systems have to be able to duplicate that, if they are really gonna work within the office setting. It's tricky. What do you do with a display terminal which has a message on it which I sent to Rigg? He wants to write a note on the side. How is he going to do that with the terminal?"

The speaker had already begun to mention certain "client oriented features" when, as if by chance, he remembers something which he considers imperative to underscore because it is often forgotten: *computers in the office will end up replacing memos, letters and documents*. Because of its superhuman speed the computer has often already replaced paper; in the case of files, archives, and dictionaries and even money. *This is where the true basis of the speaker's bias is revealed* since he clarifies that unless an electronic device was invented to add comments on the margin of the document appearing on the screen, the system would not be truly successful in the office. *According to him, it was not only a question of being able to store or retrieve information but also of being able to add, delete or modify the in-*

formation received. If such device were not invented, the speaker believed it would be better to stay with pen and paper (Oh …! there is one point!). What is the use of offimatics? What's the sense in electronic offices?[4]

All these reasons justify the following hypothesis: what the speaker called a bias, which he described in rather obscure fashion, is no more than a serious questioning of the practical aspects of the system, merits of which he is supposed to be introducing at this seminar. The *"nonetheless"* seems to be the counterpoint, in such a framework, to the silent thoughts of the interpreter.

While listening and translating the speaker's words, the interpreter thought "one of the purposes of computer science is precisely to eliminate paper work". The speaker went on to say – as in answer to the silent questioning of the interpreter – "However, I believe their survival is necessary". Finally, the bias had been explained and the **nonetheless** justified.

The way in which the speaker returns to the subject as if he were beginning to discuss another matter reveals the existence of many linked up fragments of ideas which both reflect and hide questioning, contradictions and internal struggles.

Case N° 2

Speaker's words	Interpreter's words	
Now, I don't want to skip "time sharing". Everybody knows what that is.	*Ahora, no voy a hablar de programas que todo el mundo ya conoce.*	Now, I will not speak of programs which everybody already knows

4 *This conference was held in 1978. In 1983 I had to interpret, at the same place, the presentation of the Sperrylink system which already included the devices mentioned by the speaker. Five years later, the improved electronic office device (our e-mail system) had become a reality in the business world.*

The "plot" of the situation: the character is the same speaker as in case N° 1. He kept the floor to describe some features of the electronic office such as electronic mail, the switching system and other communication devices which at that time (1978) seemed to come from another galaxy and which today are part of daily life even in the developing world. He then mentioned "time sharing".

> – Now, I don't want to skip "time sharing". Everybody knows what that is.

Let us analyse the sentence. In it we find a collision, a clash of ideas. The speaker is saying exactly the opposite of what, in our perception, he wants to say. Both statements as shown cannot be uttered in succession because of the inconsistency in the thread of logic.

He can very well say:

> – Now, I don't want to skip "time sharing"; nobody knows what that is.

This is possible but not likely since we know the concept is well known in the business.

Or else:

> – I want to (I'll) skip "time sharing". Everybody knows what that is.

We can say that this is what the speaker meant. How do we come to this conclusion? Through a number of relationships, especially in this case, between the two statements uttered. The interpreter realizes that two semantically feasible sentences have criss-crossed each other half way through, thus producing the mistaken statement:

> – Now, I don't want to talk about "time sharing". Everybody knows …

and

> – Now, I want to skip "time sharing". Everybody knows …

The interpreter corrects this as:

> – *Ahora no voy a hablar de programas que todo el mundo ya conoce.* (Now I will not speak of programs which everybody already knows).

The fact that the speaker did not eventually mention "time sharing" is definite proof that the option taken by the interpreter was the right one.

It must be observed that immediately after having established a coherent order in the wording, the interpreter becomes vague when saying "programs" instead of specifying "time sharing". Only the interpreter involved could perhaps tell us whether it was a deliberate omission, whether she had not heard properly or whether she had misunderstood something. If it was not a deliberate deviation the following questions seem relevant:

Can a clash of ideas or a break in the thread of thoughts of the speaker produce a *mirroring* effect in the mind of the interpreter, once a "fatigue" threshold is surpassed, even if such a collision or rupture does not happen "at the same place" in the discourse? Do the additional efforts to detect incoherence and clarify it force the interpreter "to take a rest afterwards"? What is the limit in the use of energy (understood as that which permits the production and accomplishment of a job) and of concentration in such cases?

These questions might be a good starting point for future research.

Case n° 3

Speaker's words (*clearing his throat*)	Interpreter's words	
"… cause now I'm gonna talk about hardware … If you were to construct an electronic office system, what should be the hardware required? Well, first of all, if you're going to use the thing for word processing, **it imposes some very serious constraints in the kind of terminal that you can use** … should be eight and a half by eleven inches, now, that is … ah … in the United States. I'm sorry in Europe the paper is longer. So there is an additional … eh … eh … problem.	*Ahora voy a hablar del hardware … Si se va a construir un sistema electrónico ¿que tendríamos como hardware?* *En primer lugar, si se va a utilizar esta máquina para proceso de palabras, entonces se necesita una máquina bastante grande … …* … … … … … … … *digamos de 11* … … *eh* … … … … … … … … … … … … … *que pueda imprimir hojas de 11 pulgadas.*	Now, let's talk about hardware … If you are going to build an electronic office system, what sort of hardware will you have? In the first place, if you are going to use the machine as a word-processor, then you need a somewhat big terminal … … … … … … … … … … … say 11 … … … … … … eh … … … … … … … … … … … … … so that it may print 11 inch sheets.

The "plot" of the situation: The protagonist is the same. We can, from the outset, see that the interpreter did not translate "eight and a half" and that she skipped the reference to the United States and Europe. Her efforts to explain things clearly become evident when she says, for example, "*… que pueda imprimir hojas de 11 pulgadas*".

But let us go deeper into analysis. Ideas have become so intertwined due to what I would call the "irruption" of *I am sorry* that it becomes difficult to disentangle them: if *I'm sorry*

… so that it may print 11 inch sheets.

refs to the U.S.A. as we thought initially and the proposed measurements correspond to Europe, ... where is the paper longer? If, on the other hand, what he said was right and goes on to speak of Europe where paper is longer, why does the speaker apologize?

The only reason I could finally think of after hearing the paragraph and the entire speech a number of times is that the speaker suddenly realized that he was in France, speaking to an audience who was mostly European and apologized for having taken his own country as a reference.

There seems to be a knot of entangled ideas. The interpreter perceives the knot but is unable to unravel it. She does not say a word.

These three cases correspond to a single intervention by a speaker who is visibly used to speaking at international conferences but who, on this occasion, gives the impression of feeling irritated and insecure. From the very beginning his speech had snags in it, words barely whispered, interrupted by throat clearing, doubts concerning the audience's interest in his presentation and even perhaps his presence at the seminar. In the light of Austin's classification it could be said that the illocutionary force of this speech is one of doubt, in spite of the fact that in itself it is an assertion.

In a previous chapter we mentioned which road we felt the interpreter should take in the presence of slips of the tongue. In the speech we are now analysing the interpreter is not even able, for the most part, to set them straight. Rather, she feels bombarded by information fired at her, machine gun style, with a halting delivery. Because of the amount and speed of all this seemingly contradictory information, it is difficult for her to impose any sort of order on it. In the booth my colleagues and I felt somewhat disturbed and insecure when translating this speech. Only when we listened to the recorded tapes – later and several times – did we begin to realize why.

An analysis of differences between speakers' and interpreters' deliveries, as revealed by tape recordings, shows the following:

1. **There is an evident wish to understand and be understood** on the part of interpreters.
2. **There is a search for consistency** which is also evident in their translation.
3. **Interpreters generally prefer to remain silent** – or sin by omission – rather than repeat words whose connection or meaning they are unable to grasp with the elements they have at hand.
4. When overwhelmed by the number, the speed and apparent contradictions of the information they are receiving, **interpreters make spontaneous decisions which seem governed by two principles: a) preserve the essential and b) be logical.** I propose the hypothesis that in such cases, even while obviously striving for consistency, interpreters will reflect doubts, contradictions and inconsistencies, often to their regret, through their tone of voice, breathing or intonation.

When comparing an original passage to its corresponding interpretation and by studying the "locations" where divergences happen (where, for instance, the interpreter omitted *nonetheless, I'm sorry* or where she introduced changes: *I will not speak of programs …*) one feature of speech becomes obvious: *it can, and often does, contain contradictory or divergent signals.*

Every speaker can make use of commonplaces, connectors, adverbs, etc. which, instead of acting as links between ideas function rather as broken links. In such cases ambiguity increases and listeners get confused.

If there is a contradiction between the message to be conveyed and the semantic content of the terms used, ambiguity will prevail; discourse will lose force and the speaker will lack credibility. This phenomenon is common in the oral mode but can also occur in writing.

In everyday life we often cannot perceive these contradictions clearly enough as listeners or speakers. The very nature of interpreting, though, compels the interpreter to perceive them from the start. Benveniste[5] claims that "everything in language must be conceived in dual terms" and this may help us explain the interpreter's irritation with both sound interference (as when the speaker plays with his microphone) and with that other "noise" (or sense interference) even though in the majority of cases they go unnoticed by the audience.

The notion of *divergent signals* fits well with that of *motive* or *intentionality*; the perception of these signals disturbs interpreters by offering them data which are in contradiction with their hypotheses about the speaker's intention.

With such findings in mind we shall now take up an example from a different context.

Case N° 4

Speaker's words	**Interpreter's words**	
Now with respect to fusion. Fusion is just a great idea, but it does have radioactivity associated with it. It has some limitations on fuels because one of the major fuels of fusion at least as we now conceive it is lithium **and lithium is not all that abundant; it is about as abundant as uranium.**	*En lo que concierne a la fusión, es una gran idea, pero no hay que olvidar que la radioactividad es también un problema de fusión. El combustible no es tampoco ilimitado ya que es el litio el que se utiliza en la actualidad para el procedimiento de fusión y **el litio no es tan abundante como el uranio.***	Now concerning fusion. It's a great idea, but we shouldn't forget radioactivity is also a problem of fusion. There are also limitations on fuel since lithium is used at present for fusion **and lithium is not as abundant as uranium.**

5 Benveniste. Problèmes de Linguistique Générale. *Paris. TEL. Gallimard. 1966. Page 40.*

The "plot" of the situation: The example is taken from a Franco-American round table on nuclear energy (April 1975)[6] summed up by D. Seleskovich in an article entitled "Traduire: de l'expérience aux concepts". In the previous examples the interpreter had said somewhat less than the speaker (he had kept silent) or had said something different (he had been less specific or more general) whereas in the case we shall now study not only does he say something the speaker has not said, *he even contradicts him.*

Lithium is not all that abundant. It is about as abundant as uranium.	≠	*El litio no es tan abundante como el uranio.*	Lithium is not as abundant as uranium.

The author of the article where this example appears attributed the mistake to the oral quality (in writing the translator would not have had any problems) and to lack of knowledge of the subject: had the interpreter known the quantitative relationship between uranium and lithium, he would not have made such a mistake. This is certain but not sufficient, since we frequently interpret – orally, by definition – concepts, ideas or mental constructs of which we had no knowledge beforehand. Another explanation is therefore in order. The concept of divergent signals can help us find it. When the speaker says:

> – Lithium is not all that abundant; it is about as abundant as uranium.

he is sending, superficially, contradictory signals. He seems to be saying that something **is and is not** at the same time.

> – Lithium is not abundant, lithium is abundant.

----

6 *Quoted by D. Seleskovich in an article entitled "Traduire: de l'expérience aux concepts" in* Etudes de Linguistique Appliquée. *Paris. Didier, 1976.*

Logic makes us reject these examples. Each premise is valid by itself and perfectly easy to translate; it is their juxtaposition without pause or warning that causes perplexity. The apparent contradiction can only be solved by inverting the term *abundant* in the second sentence which leads to consider "it is about as abundant as uranium" as an irony meaning "it is as *scarce* as uranium".

The problem is yet more complicated for both sentences contain an element of comparison, implicit in the first, explicit in the second:

Lithium is not all that abundant can be taken to mean "*all things considered, lithium is not all that abundant*" but it can also be understood as "*lithium is abundant but not as much as many people think*".

If we keep this last interpretation and compare it with the second sentence as it must be understood, that is, "*it is about as scarce as uranium*" we again find ourselves with a contradictory proposition:

> **Lithium is abundant, lithium is scarce.**

The interpreter's – or any other person's – spontaneous and total rejection of propositions of this kind seems to indicate that we are in the presence of "one of the principles governing speech acts": *we cannot state one thing and then go on to say the opposite without changing the context, the framework or the level.* As Grice says "talking is a special case or variety of purposive, indeed rational, behaviour".

If the speaker were talking slowly or if he had given some warning with the tone of his voice, a smile or a gesture, it is certain the interpreter could have followed him. But pressured by time, trying to discriminate the fundamental from the accessory and processing information at a number of different levels at the same time, the interpreter found himself superficially confronted with:

lithium is not abundant, lithium is abundant, and at a deeper level with: **lithium is abundant, lithium is scarce,** where the terms are inverted. In both cases the propositions thus juxtaposed are lacking in all logic.

The clash of contradicting signals paralysed the interpreter who was unable to avoid an accident on his course.

When the speaker says: "**Lithium is not all that abundant**", the interpreter is saying: "*... y el litio no es tan abundante*".

He cannot complete his sentence correctly (*as we might think*) because at that very moment he hears the speaker saying "**it is about as abundant as uranium**" and the contradictory information catches him on the wrong foot and leaves him speechless. His efforts at in depth explanation prevent him from maintaining superficial ambiguity and he will find a good structural ending to the sentence by adding: "*... como el uranio*".

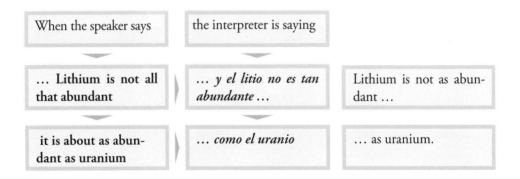

When the speaker says	the interpreter is saying	
... Lithium is not all that abundant	*... y el litio no es tan abundante ...*	Lithium is not as abundant ...
it is about as abundant as uranium	*... como el uranio*	... as uranium.

In this way he sweeps away the ambiguity of the speaker making him establish, ironically, one of the few relationships between lithium and uranium which the speaker had not established.

Case N° 5

The "plot" of the situation: During a conference organized by UNESCO on "intercultural matters" (Paris, June of 1979) one officer enthusiastically defended the need of every nation to protect its identity and the right to preserve its own language. Excited by the ideas he believed he was defending, the South American got carried away by his own loquacity without realizing that by speaking French – when his mother tongue was Spanish – he was cancelling out his statement, at least in part. Although the internal logic of his speech was perfectly good, the juxtaposition of the content with the fact that he was speaking a language other than his own revealed a lack of consistency. *The perception of the whole* (content plus circumstances of enunciation) *can certainly partially modify understanding or globally transform the effects speech can have.*

We are forced to conclude that:

If **A** says "**x**"   we think   **A** believes in "**x**",
but
if **A** says "**x**"   while doing "**z**"; and it turns out that "**z**" is different from "**x**" ($z \neq x$)

we must conclude:

1. that **A** does no believe in "**x**" but wants us to believe he does; or
2. that **A** believes in "**x**" only in certain unspecified circumstances; or
3. that **A** believes in "**x**" but only for others and not for himself, which brings in the question of finding out why **A** uses a different set of criteria for himself; or
4. that **A** is unaware of his own inconsistency or is betting that it will go unnoticed. In both cases attention must be redoubled.

The contradiction must not be sought in the contents of the statement itself but in the confrontation between what is said and the situation in which it is said. When there is contradiction between what people say and what they do, their statements lose force and their credibility is open to question.

This kind of contradictory situation where the speaker is doing exactly what he says should not be done is often the substance of jokes, such as those found in the comic strips by Claire Bretécher, where a dissenting writer explains his reasons for refusing to appear on television while presenting his new book, *Rejection of the Media*, ... on television !

If contradictory signals create ambiguity and mistrust among peers, their effects can be devastating in situations of dependency and/or when the contradictions are not clearly perceived. If a father says to his son: "*Don't swear, damn it!*" the father's friends may find the situation funny and perhaps laugh; the son, on the other hand, will feel the impotence of confusion and dependence. Contradiction and duplicity are at their worst in examples such as: "*Let me help you become independent*" or "*I order you to disobey me*" where parents seem to block all exits, even the emergency ones. Faced with such alternatives, the son can never win whatever he does; if he achieves independence, it will be thanks to his father; if he disobeys him, it will only be because he is following orders.

Gregory Bateson assigned the origin of schizophrenia to "double binds" like these. His studies of schizophrenia used communication analyses and a theory of logical types.[7]

Observe that we have moved in this chapter, in a steady crescendo, to ever higher levels of abstraction at which collisions between signals may occur, whether these come from the same or different levels. In order to detect these collisions, *it is imperative to have perceived, found or created a "whole", encompassing all elements however heterogeneous from different levels.*

By doing this, i.e. *changing the frame of reference or the level of abstraction*, by inserting the conflicting father-son relationship in a wider context, the son may also break free; by accepting the limitations of the restrictive family situation he finds himself in he can transcend it, thus achieving a seemingly impossible victory.

---

7 Gregory Bateson, Steps to an Ecology of Mind, *Paladin Books, 1973, (Vers une ecologie de l'esprit, Vol. 2, Paris, Seuil, 1980).*

Contradictions

Will and motive are not necessarily as clear and univocal as we would like to believe. Mistaken actions, Freudian slips or lapses, contradictions, diverging signals and interference are all proof of this.

Perceiving contradictions in what someone says is sometimes easier than perceiving contradictions between what someone is saying and what he is doing. Western intellectual tradition leads us to detect the contradictions between signs of the same nature which follow one another in time. On the other hand, detecting contradictions between disparate signs presupposes two things:

1. Their simultaneous inclusion in a whole.
2. The capacity to produce a unified response (reacting as a unified whole) beyond any split between linear reasoning and the processing of the information supplied by all our senses.[8]

Contradictory elements can thus appear successively or simultaneously in time. They can create tension or anxiety, especially so if they are not clearly detected.

The opposite holds true as well. As general-semanticist Phil Ardery comments, when things flow together in the same direction, when there is perfect harmony between ideas and words, intent and goals, the message rapidly gets home!

---

8 *Ever since Pavlov we have known about the chain of automatic reponses animals can trigger after repetitive exposure to certain associated signals even in the absence of the first direct stimulus after a certain time. Words and their "semantic reaction" as described by A. Korzybski can trigger some automatic responses in men. Korzybski warned about the pernicious effects of automated responses to words themselves. Just as an example, think of how you reacted when someone called you something you did not like. Just a word ... which of course will vary from one person to the next (communist, reactionary, stupid, gay, etc.)*

Concern, or suspense, generated by ambiguity disappears when it becomes possible to identify the conflicting divergent elements. Conversely, it is possible, by inverting the procedure, to awaken a feeling of anxiety or to create an effect of momentary paralysis through the use of contradictory instructions.

Manipulation

Let us imagine a high mountain road prepared for a car race where contradictory signs have been placed before a perilous bend separated by only a few feet: one sign showing a *right* turn and the other a *left* turn. Let's suppose one of the car drivers has been informed about this: he knows the track well enough and without any hesitation or pause takes the right turn. What would a driver do if he is not in the know? What would you do if confronted with contradictory indications? Stop and think. Yes, the sensible reaction would be to slam on the brakes. Guess who wins the race ...

Magicians and prestidigitators train themselves to control and divert other people's attention. This ability plus the dexterity of their hands allow them to distort perception and create illusions. Pickpockets manage to develop the same talents for different ends.

During negotiations or parliamentary debates, two equally passionate and contradictory interventions concerning a very minor point can distract the attention of delegates when they have to decide on a fundamental issue. Concerted operations to deflect attention away from the main issue could be more frequent than we would like to believe. Non-concerted interventions can sometimes have the same effect, to the detriment of the common good.

Attention is dispersed and dispelled by boredom and fatigue. Bankers, negotiators and diplomats know that it is towards the end of a meeting, when their opposite numbers and counterparts have been made drowsy by endless statements and confusing reports, that they have the greatest chance of getting their most precious and controversial proposals accepted. Blah blah serves to put both distrust and … the participants … to sleep.

During a rare moment of relaxation at a very important political conference, I found myself sitting at the same table as a number of well-known statesmen from various countries. Knowing that I should not ask questions that were too personal or political[9] but wanting to make the best of such an exceptional situation, I asked them what qualities, in their opinion, defined a good politician. Some faces lit up, focus was made and conversation enlightened.

"*A political man is a strong man*", was the prompt but measured reply of who was destined to become the head of government of one of the smallest but most powerful countries in the

---

9 *As pointed out by P. Watzlawick, an important part of communication is to know what you are NOT supposed to say, think, see or hear, (In "La réalité de la réalité", Paris, Seuil, 1978).*

world. A look of bewilderment in my eyes encouraged him to go on: "*Yes, he who is physically stronger than the others, just as in ancient times, he who can resist, endure and continue while the others have fallen asleep.*"

Some military tactics are well known to the layman as well: in order to win, you must confuse and tire your enemy. Divergent signals and endless speeches can thus become useful weapons on a different sort of battlefield.

Among our tactics these are the best: mislead, confuse, disrupt and exhaust your enemy...

Top operative decisions are often made fast, and taken by a few people. The rest is "intellectual, sometimes passionate and even fascinating debate".

CHAPTER 6

The Two Axes

Of the work of the interpreter, and its organization along two axes.

Of how these two axes are – or should be – used in any type of discourse or exchange.

Ferdinand de Saussure – frequently considered the father of 20th century linguistics – contends that language must be considered a social phenomenom, a structured system that can be viewed *synchronically* (as it exists at any particular time) and *diachronically* (as it changes in the course of time). These two concepts – synchronicity and diachronicity – and a few others he introduced, proved fundamental for the development of several theories within the social sciences.

I will now borrow these concepts in order to apply them to the interpreters' world. We will see these axes at work at two different levels: first in discourse at a macro level and then at a micro level with phonemes. They can also be found at some other intermediate levels between phonemes and discourse: with prefixes and suffixes, lexemes or words, phrases, combinations of them, etc.

We will bring back some of the examples given in the previous chapters to illustrate the functioning of these axes. Whereas their functioning is similar at the macro and micro levels, we will contend that we can consciously use them only at the former level. At the micro level, it is only *a posteriori* that we can reconstruct their spontaneous involuntary work.

Speaker's words	**Interpreter's words**	
Amendment number ... eh ... deals with the first paragraph ... ... one ...	*... eh ... eh ... la enmienda diez se refiere al primer párrafo ...* *... al primer inciso.*	... eh ... eh ... amendment ten deals with the first paragraph ... ... the first inset

See page 48.

Case N° 1

Let us begin by returning to an example we saw at the beginning of Chapter two. It will be remembered that the transfer from "one" to *"al primer inciso"* could only be explained by the presence of the interpreter in the act of enunciation which allowed him to draw on extra-discursive elements both for understanding and transmitting meaning. He could have said *one* but instead he opted for another solution.

first inset

These extradiscursive elements which justify the transformation of "one" into "al primer inciso" show the functioning of the **synchronic axis** thanks to which the interpreter integrates visual elements of relevant use into his oral perception.

Case N° 2

Speaker's words	**Interpreter's Words**	
1 Thank you Mr. Chairman …	*Gracias señor Presidente …*	Thank you Mr. Chairman …
2 There are … three … eh … activities	*Hay tres actividades que aparecen en el proyecto de recomendación … …*	There are three activities which are in the draft recommendation …
3 which are…eh…in the draft recommenda-	*… … … … … … …*	
4 tion which are not in the amendment.	*… … … … … … …*	
5 … eh … (inaudible)	*… … eh …*	… eh …
6 data collection in the social sciences, the	*acopio de datos en las ciencias sociales, las*	data collection in the social sciences, the activities
7 … eh … activities related to patents and	*actividades sobre patentes y licencias y la*	related to patents and licences and translation and
8 licenses and translation n production	*traducción y la publicación … … … … …*	publication … … … …
9 of S and T books and periodicals. I s want to	*…*	…
10 confirm that this is a deliberate omission	*¿Esto es una omisión voluntaria? Porque esto no*	Is this a deliberate omission? Because this is not
11 and not … eh … just hadn't been over-	*aparece en la enmienda propuesta … o es simple-*	mentioned in the proposed amendment … or is
12 looked in this rearrangement.	*mente … se debe a cuestiones de ordenamiento.*	it simply … or is it a question or rearrangement?

Case N° 2

First, the situation: we are dealing with the "Meeting for the International Standardization of Statistics" at UNESCO, in Paris in June 1978. The delegates are discussing another amendment and a member of the Canadian delegation comparing the draft of the original article with a new version, detects the omission of three elements and wants to know why.

We must keep in mind that the speech rate is quite fast and the speaker has a peculiar accent which makes interpretation difficult.

The recording allowed us to go back over and over again and also have two persons whose mother tongue was English listen to the speech. When listening for the sixth time one of them thought he heard "*the general*" in the space in line 5 of the transcript and which until then we had considered inaudible. The conjunction "*and*" was almost totally assimilated by the final sound of "n" in "*translation*" (line 8) and the adverb "*just*" (line 9) was contracted to an "s".

We can also see that, starting with the hesitation in line 10 of the last part of the speech, there is a break in the grammatical sequence: the sentence has no subject and the listener is left to juggle with the ideas and re-accommodate them. The speaker's fast, halting rhythm, sprinkled with hesitations, "eh … eh …" contrasts with the more deliberate version of the interpreter who nonetheless pauses when omitting "which are not in the amendment" in the fifth line. In spite of the gap, her delivery does not lose coherence and the interpreter goes on to mention the three activities just mentioned. There is another "blank" in line 11; the interpreter does not translate "S and T books and periodicals" (S and T refer to science and technology) but does render *y la traducción y la publicación*

and the translation *and* the publication

There are a number of divergences between the two texts, but what we want to analyse here is the introduction of *porque esto no aparece en la enmienda propuesta* in the interpreter's version, which is equivalent to "**which are not in the amendment**" (line 4 in the speaker's version). It is surprising to hear the interpreter introduce further on what she omitted in

for this does not appear in the proposed amendment.

Line 4. And I say "surprising", because I was the interpreter in this case and I know for sure that I did not hear the words when they were spoken. I was only able to infer them later from the context. This points to the existence of another axis, which we shall call the *"diachronic axis"**.

We can therefore note the functioning of two axes in speech: *the synchronic axis and the diachronic axis.*

Through the *synchronic axis*, we create a relationship between elements which can be of diverse nature: a fragment of speech and other objects or actions. A relationship is thus created at a specific point in time between two different perceptions: what someone hears or sees, feels, or senses, etc. It is like the vision one might have of oneself from above, looking at oneself listening, watching, sensing at a given point in time.

Through the *diachronic axis* which unfolds in time we create a relationship between elements that could be of the same nature but while some are still present, others no longer are. We establish a link between what we perceive now and what we sensed before, between our present perception and the memory of previous perceptions.

There seems to be a double to-and-fro movement: one following a horizontal wave along the synchronic axis and another one following a vertical wave along the diachronic axis. As the speech unfolds, the interpreter checks his past predictions, makes new ones and still hears the speaker's new input; as he gives his own rendering, he also continues to take in the speaker's intervention as well as other elements from the environment. He also remembers what he said, goes back and self corrects in a double movement of feed-back and feed-forward.

Case N° 3

We shall now apply this concept of the two axes to a case in which the interpreter made a mistake: the two axes worked at the micro level – on the surface, we might say – but the interpreter did not manage to consciously apply the two axes at the macro level so as to avoid producing the mistake.

During a conference on computer science held in Rio de Janeiro in 1993, a French delegate said "*lorsque l'ordinateur fonctionne à plein temps...*" which was rendered in Portuguese as "*quando o computador funciona na primavera...*"

Speaker's words	**Interpreter's words**	
Lorsque l'ordinateur fonctionne à plein temps ... When the computer is working (full time)...	*Quando o computador funciona na primavera...*	When the computers work (in springtime ..)

Let us see what may have happened.

The Portuguese interpreter did not catch the word "*plein*" /plɛ̃/ since he missed one of its sounds: /l/. Then, something resembling a *simultaneity axis* may have functioned there without his being aware. Thus, phonemes /b/ /s/ /d/ /f/ /g/ /z/ /t/ /p/ /v/ etc., which cannot be found in this combination of sounds in French were automatically discarded. As a result of that implicit processing, the only ones left were:

		↓	
a p	j	ɛ̃ t a
a p	w	ɛ̃ t a
a p	R	ɛ̃ t a
		↑	

The only phoneme that can make sense in this combination, in addition to /l/ is, of course, /ʀ/. Unconsciously, the interpreter changed /a/ for /o/ and obtained a sound chain intelligible in French:

$$/\text{opʀɛ̃tɑ̃}/ = \textit{au printemps}^1$$

This replacement of sounds happened beyond (or beneath, certainly before) the interpreter's consciousness. It is only *a posteriori* that we can infer that something of the sort occurred. The interpreter – or any speaker for that matter – is faced with a certain "sequence" of sounds and cannot, on the spur of the moment, go back. But the interpreter in question could have done something else: consciously apply the axes at another level.

If he had used the *diachronic axis* at a macro level, relating **primavera** to the foregoing, he would certainly have realized that seasons, whether he liked it or not, have little to do with the functioning of computers. Regrettably the interpreter did not relate what he had understood (in the springtime) to the subject matter of the talk and made a mistake.

If we were to take into account only sound linearity when interpreting, mistakes of this kind would be frequent, especially in the Western world where interpreting is generally done into the mother tongue.[2] It is the use of these two axes at macro levels and using ever larger units in discourse which permits us to detect this kind of mistake and correct it.

----

1 *It is not very important to know if he had rightly heard /a/ or if this was precisely the sound that was lost, replaced by /o/ in the paradigmatic axis, which compelled him further on to change /pl/ into /pʀ/ or if indeed he had not heard either one and all he received was /p–t/. This is only an effort to try and explain, step by step, what can happen in such cases: it goes without saying that neither the interpreter nor any other speaker would consciously do something like this.*

2 *According to A.I.I.C rules (International Association of Conference Interpreters) interpretation should always be done from languages B and C (acquired) into A (the mother tongue).*

Furthermore, as soon as we contrast the concept of *plein temps* to that of *mi temps* in the field of information technology, we realize that the use of one or the other is of vital importance from the point of view of profitability. The dichotomy *à plein temps/ à mi temps* is not only relevant in this matter, it is even fundamental. The interpreter should have known this. His mistake shows he was working only on the surface, at least at that moment. [full time / part time / full time/part time]

Now, most speakers are not aware of the functioning of these axes in speech. Interpreters' examples have revealed their existence and showed that interpreters knowingly make use of them. It is precisely the correct management of these two axes that enables interpreters to correctly interpret simultaneously. But an interpretation mistake was used to prove that these axes also function at micro levels with a significant difference though: neither speakers nor interpreters are aware of them, let alone use them. We will then call these axes which we cannot consciously manipulate: the *paradigmatic axis* and the *syntagmatic axis*.

But the problem does not end here. Let us go back to the second example in this chapter. When the interpreter hears "which are not in the amendment" and translates it, the speaker is saying "and not eh … just hadn't been overlooked" which the interpreter hears since he will introduce it in his delivery. The linear development of the interpreter's version *overlaps* the functioning of the diachronic axis (memory); he does not say, "they are not in the amendment" but rather proposes the adequate linkage: – *porque no están en la enmienda propuesta*. If we go back to the first example we shall also see that the operation of the *synchronic axis* is superimposed on the linear operation of the *diachronic axis* of the words whose temporal succession the interpreter hears and repeats. When the interpreter says *… al primer inciso* the speaker is saying: "and it suggests that we should drop the word …", which the interpreter hears, as evidenced by the fact that he says it. [Because they are not in the proposed amendment / the first inset]

The simultaneous functioning of these two axes in speech brings with it the dislocation and the disrupture of the one and only single point of view: elements at work showing the existence of the two axes are not of the same kind nor do they belong to the same levels and the "time" dimension is considered simultaneously from at least two different viewpoints. As I stated above, in a somewhat clumsy effort to put into words something I find particularly difficult to describe, on the synchronic axis (or simultaneity axis) one gets the vision one might have of oneself from above – as in a kind of snapshot – looking at oneself listening, watching, sensing at a given point in time. On the diachronic axis, one feels the unfolding of "memory" and time, the succession of elements coming one after the other … It is in the actual "here-and-now" that we face the intersection of both axes. Their intersection at the macro level appears as a synthesis of many other intersections. When things flow at the micro levels, we are not, and we cannot possibly be, aware of the functioning of those axes, we are simply aware of their results; we can, though, become conscious of their malfunctioning when errors occur – but only *a posteriori*.

Conscious and Unconscious Acts of Perception and Memory

Summing Up

Perception of a given element allows us to identify it and isolate it from the rest of the elements, associate it with a word or a name and to memorize it as a given unit. *Perceiving* implies seeing, listening, sensing, feeling, tasting, smelling, intuiting, and recognizing. We know, though, that we perceive and store in our memories much more than what we are aware of. We also know, since Ribot,[3] that perception and

---

3 *Théodule Ribot (1839-1916) was a French psychologist who studied mental processes and memory disorders. I will eventually refer to his works and to the concept of "affective memory" he created.*

movement are closely linked. There are certain movements that are too fast for our consciousness to grasp separately: so, we group them. Experiments have proven that perception takes place through the detection of a slight movement or its consequences.

In order to work "simultaneously" the interpreter exacerbates some typical mechanisms of speech and in so doing he becomes an expert in the manipulation of two axes that silently operate in discourse: the *synchronic axis* which relates simultaneous perceptions of different nature and the *diachronic (or successive) axis* which relates present to absent elements. "Time" is simultaneously considered from two different viewpoints: *diachronically* thanks to our memory and *synchronically* thanks to our senses.

Certain examples taken from conference interpretation and others from psychological experiments (as we will see in chapter 16) disclose the functioning of these two axes below the threshold of our conscience. We said we would call them differently in order to differentiate the voluntary and automatic levels. Those axes whose function it is to present to our conscience already structured units were called the *paradigmatic* and the *syntagmatic axes*. The elements they handle move at such a fast speed that consciousness can only seize them in units or groups. The notion of "time" becomes even more complex because a third viewpoint should be added to the other two already mentioned: the infinitely more rapid one of our "unconscious".

The automatic functioning of these two axes would explain why we cannot listen to a series of phonemes following one another when we listen to somebody speak. We normally cannot "disintegrate" words into sounds in normal speech as much as we cannot disintegrate objects into atoms and molecules when we open our eyes and look around. Perception seems to operate holistically: a "whole" can be conceived as a unified entity – different from the sum of its parts, but from which several pieces can be detached so as to create new and different entities. Some of the principles of the Gestalt theory can be easily applied to discourse perception. We can set a parallel between these two types of perceptive phenomena:

- Boundaries between objects – as between words – can create some perceptual problems.
- In the same manner we infer the invisible faces of a cube, we also consummate the incompleteness of what we hear.
- Every visual, auditory, tactile element announces more than it contains.

Parallels made between several examples suggest that the perceptual processes at work for *understanding human speech* are similar to those for understanding what we see. *Seeing and speaking are similar ways of structuring* the environment through different means. "The art of seeing" and "the art of talking" would thus be more than just good friends.

It is perhaps easier to use a visual example to perceive that feeling of uneasiness and uncertainty – as if in quicksands – when confronted by some ambiguous images our paradigmatic and syntagmatic axes have not yet circumscribed. The following pictures enable us to stay for a while in that intermediate "no man's land" where multiple virtual probabilities are still possible.

What sort of woman can you see on your left? An attractive young lady looking to her right or an old big-nosed woman looking down?

Both are possible. This illusion was first published in Puck in 1915 and it was entitled "*My Wife and my Mother-in-law*".

These visual perceptive exercises were a favourite brain tickler at Harvard Business School for years.

Can you see the Dalmatian?

Can you see the cow?

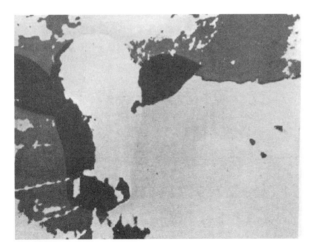

Can you experiment with how you end up structuring the image of an animal, almost voluntarily in this case?

Perception lies at the roots of knowledge but knowledge often helps not only to "adjust" perception but even to perceive. Perception, knowledge and memory are closely interrelated. Their inter-relatedness is more difficult to reveal at the non-conscious or automatic levels. But we should be able to explain one day how we can perceive, store and process information without really being aware of what we are doing.

❖ ❖ ❖

CHAPTER 7

Simultaneity
of Operations

Of the multiplicity of elements and processes being handled simultaneously as revealed by an analysis of the example "now I understand the amendment …"

The following example will show how the interpreter handles the two axes at the same time
while he elaborates a hypothesis about the objectives of the speaker and perceives and communicates the
implied contents. Our purpose is to underscore the *simultaneity* of these operations, which overlap in time those of
translation and delivery of the speech. The task of description is complex in itself, since the spoken word is, by definition, fleeting and the processes of perception, reasoning
and thought difficult to apprehend.

The situation is as follows:

During the meeting of the International Standardization
of Statistics (UNESCO, Paris, June 1978) the Chairman of
the meeting announced a new amendment to be considered
by the delegates. It was a proposal submitted by the United
States calling for a change in the placing of article 2.g.4.
referring to the "translation and publication of books and
periodicals". The delegate from the Soviet Union asked his
American colleague for an explanation: "What did he mean
when he referred to the publication of books?" The Secretary of the meeting explained that there had been a change
in the amendment which now mentioned "translation and
publication" whereas the original document referred to
"translation and **production**". In his view it was merely a
problem of terminology, but this did not detract from the
fact that the two texts differed.

The American delegate took the floor to state:

Speaker's words	Interpreter's words	
Thank you, Mr. President. I would like to thank the delegate from the Soviet Union for pointing this out and apologize to the Secretariat and to the other members. This was my mistake … I meant to duplicate the words exactly … but … eh … in my haste I fear I picked up the wrong word. My intention was to … eh … move the … eh paragraph on translation and production … eh … of S and T books and periodicals exactly as it is written **to the section dealing with Science Information.**	*Muchas gracias, Sr. Presidente. Me gustaría agradecerle al delegado de la Unión Soviética por haber hecho esta observación y pedir disculpas a la Secretaría y demás. Este fue un error de mi parte … En mi apuro creo que inserté la palabra errónea. Mi intención era trasladar el párrafo sobre traducción y producción de libros de la misma manera, exactamente como aparece escrito, a la sección que se refiere a las ciencias.*	Thank you, Mr. President. I would like to thank the delegate from the Soviet Union for pointing this out and apologize to the Secretariat and others. This was my mistake … … In my haste I think I used the wrong word. My intention was to move the paragraph on translation and production of books, exactly as it is written, **to the section dealing with Sciences …**

At this point, the Chairman of the meeting takes the floor again:

As I understand the amendment then that is on the floor it is **essentially** to use the identical text which was under 2.g.4 but to move it to an **earlier** part of the text in there …	*Entonces entiendo que la enmienda que estamos discutiendo es simplemente usar el texto idéntico – el mismo texto – que aparece en 2.g.4. "Traducción y edición de libros y Publicaciones", pero pasarlo a otra parte del texto.*	So then I understand that the amendment we are discussing **simply** consists in using the identical text – **the same text** – which was under 2.g.4. "Translation and production of books and periodicals" but to move it to **another** part of the text.

A lag should have appeared in the transcript to reflect the brief lag in time between both speeches and remind the readers that when the interpreter says something he must at the same time listen to something else.

Let us analyse the example. We see, first of all, that the interpreter begins to speak only after the speaker has uttered five words, only after hearing the adverb *then* and it is precisely with the Spanish word **entonces** that he begins his delivery. This adverb of little content is used here as a link to understand what came before and will come after. We could paraphrase it by *this being so*, *in that case* or *after what we have just heard*, for what the chairman of the meeting is saying is that after having listened to the previous comments, like those mentioned by the author of the amendment, his understanding of it has changed and he would like to share his new interpretation with us. The implicit content of *then* underscores the contrast between the old and the new understanding of the amendment.

then

We are thus able to see that there are discrepancies between the speaker's words and the interpreter's delivery. They are underlined in the examples. There are elements in the interpreter's delivery, which are not found in the speaker's words. There is also a semantic element in *earlier* – the concept of previousness – which disappears when translated as **en otra parte**.

in another part

A prosodic analysis and analysis of intonation curves – using Lilia Armstrong and Ida Ward's IPA System – shows:[1]

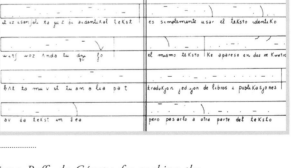

1 With acknowledgements to Adriana Boffi de Cánepa for making the transcript available to us.

The analysis of the intonation curves shows that the interpreter not only underscores *identical text* as does the speaker (manifested in the transcript by the highfall accent on *identical*) but also repeats the idea in other words and with an

the same text even more marked intonation curve in **el mismo texto**. The interpreter knows that an extended discussion has taken place because of an inadvertent mistake made by the author of the amendment. He also knows, since he has been present at the conference since its opening, seven days before, that the chairman wants to be clear and concise in order to save time. And the interpreter *knows* it not only because the chairman said so a number of times but also because he acted accordingly: setting schedules which he was the first to adhere to and chairing the meeting in an active and vital manner. The interpreter thus knows that the chairman wants to make it clear to all the delegates who are going to vote on the amendment that he is not proposing any change in the text. The repetition of the same idea and the tone of voice seem to be indicating: "*Beware! No change is contemplated here as we believed at first.*" We once again find here the implicit dimension of speech and the hypotheses about the speaker's intent.

As from Jones, Kingdom and O'Connor onwards (and studies conducted firstly in English) we know that the tone of voice, the intonation, is a carrier of meaning. Stanislavski[2] even said:

> "The accent is like a pointed finger. It stresses what is essential in a phrase. For it is in the word thus underlined that we shall find the soul, the intimate essence, the highest point in the sub-text".

---

2 *Constantin Stanislavski*, La construcción del personaje, *Madrid, Alianza, 1975. Page 177.* (Building a Character, *Theatre Arts Books, Reprint edition, June 1989).*

If in the framework of the situation described above, the interpreter had accentuated the number of the inset, *2.g.4.* for example, or emphasized that it was a matter of transferring the text to an earlier part of the document, he would have lost focus and misled his listeners. Had he emphasized *inset 2.g.4*, he would have created a mistaken cross-reference, for every term that is emphasized requires, at the very least, a second term of comparison. In the situation described there is no such opposition. To signal non-existing oppositions in the speech is tantamount to putting out false clues for establishing relationships and recreating meaning. "A misplaced accent malforms a word or mutilates a sentence ...[3]"

It took the speaker 17 seconds and 36 words to say what he wanted to say. It took the interpreter 16 seconds and 35 words to hear, understand, translate and make his delivery, communicating the implied contents, and drawing up at the same time a hypothesis on the intentions of the speaker. His many simultaneous tasks did not end there. During that same brief period the interpreter was also able to "read" the title of the amendment: "*Translation and publishing of books and periodicals*" and include it in his delivery without losing the thread of the statement. He strayed from what the speaker said in order to complete the information. This addition shows the functioning of the *synchronic axis* overlapping the functioning of the *diachronic axis* within a time span of 16 seconds. This addition reveals the simultaneous functioning of the two axes.

Did the interpreter not hear well? Or did he not understand? Or was it his purpose to stress even more the idea of

-----

3 *In this fashion, a report on the proceedings of a meeting can alter the description of what happened without any omissions or inaccuracies; the change in emphasis, the insistence on a specific idea rather than another can bring about deep alterations of meaning. It is sometimes amusing to compare different versions of the same conference in the media. The comparison of headlines of local and national newspapers on the days following the Mar del Plata Summit (November 2005) provides good examples of this.*

the same text as opposed to *another part*? It does not matter. When listening again to the recording we realize that 18 seconds before the American delegate had indicated the place where the new text should go: *the section dealing with science information*. Be that as it may, whether he heard correctly or decided not to include this concept, the interpreter *knew* that this information was not necessarily relevant since it had recently been made explicit somewhere else. The diachronic axis is in action; the memory of the earlier parts of the speech comes to the rescue of the interpreter and lets him: 1) interpret a new fragment and 2) decide what elements to keep and which to eliminate.

It is precisely in these "spots" of the speech where the interpreter underlines, adds, eliminates or transforms, where we can see most clearly that he is taking responsibility for his version and becomes the true enunciator in this twofold act of enunciation. This is where the contract between speaker and interpreter is sealed, a contract we have called "of complicity", wherein the interpreter commits himself to adopt the point of view of whoever has the floor.

This case has allowed us to underline the importance of stress and intonation, detect the number of elements which are handled in the same period of time and the juxtaposition of simultaneous activities.

It also allows us to see how the interpreter respects the *four cooperative principles** as spelled out by Grice[4] (and even how he modifies them depending on the speaker).

According to H. P. Grice, human conversation implies a cooperative effort: there normally is a purpose or set of purposes – or at least a mutually accepted direction – when we engage in conversation. Within a certain logic then, at each stage, some possible conversational moves should consequently be excluded as conversationally unsuitable. Grice's *general*

---

4 *H.P. Grice, "Logic and Conversation" in* Syntax and Semantics, Pragmatics, *edited by Peter Cole, London, Academic Press, 1975.*

principle of conversation implies you should make your conversational contribution such as is required, at the stage at which it occurs. Four principles derive from that:

1. Make your contribution as informative as is required for the current purpose of the exchange. Do not say more than necessary.

2. Try to make your contribution one that is true:
   a. Do not say what you believe to be false.
   b. Do not say that for which you lack adequate evidence.

3. Be relevant

4. Be perspicacious:
   a. avoid obscurity
   b. avoid ambiguity
   c. be brief
   d. be orderly

Let us see what the interpreter does:

1. **Quantity.** The interpreter finds and adds the title of 2.g.4. *"Translation and Publishing…"*

2. **Quality.** Now that he knows that an error has slipped into the previous explanations and desirous to be truthful, he chooses to complete the information.

3. **Relevance.** He omits the concept of previousness in his translation of *earlier* for *otra* (another) since he knows it is not necessarily relevant.

4. **Clarity.** Committed to be clear he feels free to stray from the speaker's words. (Listeners and readers will decide if he was successful or not).

Talking for Grice is a special case or variety of purposive, indeed rational behaviour. We find this classification useful even if we know that not always do our daily exchanges meet this requirement. Not only emotions, feelings and confusion often complicate the logic of the exchange or the rationale. We are also aware of cases of intelligent conversation not really fitting into this frame, like the koans by Zen masters for example.

And then the wish to be clear is often not enough, nor is the addition of a personal note a guarantee of clarity of meaning, as we recall from the illustration taken from R. Ekvall[5] who witnessed the misunderstanding created by the interpreter during negotiations about North Korea under the chairmanship of Belgian statesman Paul Henri Spaak in 1954 (see page 52).

The Concept of the Whole

Working "in simultaneous" implies working with organized "wholes" (or structured units) and respecting the relations between the various elements which make them up.

The three following figures contain the same number and kind of elements. Changing one single relationship changes the perception of the whole.

....

5 R. Ekvall, In Faithful Echo, *New York, Twayne, 1960. Cited by P. Watzlawick in* La réalité de la réalité, *Paris, Seuil, 1978.*

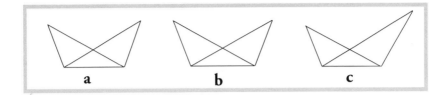

When a group of subjects are asked to copy figure "a", there are basically two reactions: some improve the symmetry (b) and the others exaggerate the asymmetry (c).[6]

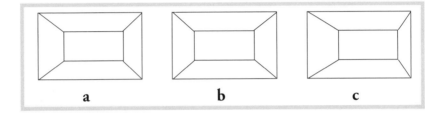

"An ill placed accent can malform a word or mutilate a sentence" in Stanislavski's[7] words.

In this way, the minutes of a meeting can misrepresent what happened, even when nothing of what was said is omitted and nothing false is added; the displacement of emphasis, the prevalence of one idea over another, a minor change in whatever was implied can all produce deep semantic alterations. It is thus sometimes amusing to compare the versions of the same press conference as reported by newspapers of different tendencies.

❖   ❖   ❖

---

6 *R. Arnheim,* Art and Visual Perception, *Buenos Aires, Eudeba, 1962. Page 47.*

7 *In* La construcción del personaje, *Madrid, Alianza Editorial, 1962. Page 177. (*Building a Character, *Theatre Arts Books, reprint edition 1989).*

What the Interpreter Does

"The true meaning of a term is to be found by observing what a man does with it, not by what he says about it."

P. W. Bridgman

Part II

THE FUNCTIONING OF THE INTERPRETER

In this section, we will get into the nitty-gritty of interpreting itself, describing the strategies used, both verbal and non-verbal. Before going into this we shall recap what we have done so far. Instead of announcing what I was going to do in the introduction, I did it first and then stopped to observe what I had done.

The itinerary I am inviting readers to take is not linear; it takes a spiral path: I will touch upon a subject and then I will eventually go back to it from other perspectives. Looking at the same events or processes from other viewpoints brings new light to our vision.

As I start describing my initial almost intuitive research approach, I realize that I am describing what some have called the "scientific orientation in everyday life".

CHAPTER 8

Recapitulation about our Working Method

Of how this research started and of how it eventually evolved. Of its initial aim and its initial working method. Of its later expanded scope.

L et us recap on what we have seen so far.
What I have been trying to do so far is to find similarities and differences between different objects.
In chapter 1, one linguistic example allowed me – through
the use of several stereotypes – to build plausible scripts and
thus show how the interplay of invariant elements may give
birth to a *number of variations*.

In chapters 2 to 7 and thanks to simultaneous recordings, I
was able to make a few comparisons between a fraction of the
speaker's speech and a fraction of the interpreter's speech.

Simultaneous recordings can make interpreters aware of
their performance and help them find the causes of their difficulties, giving them a perspective of their own work. Eventually they become an invaluable tool for approaching their
work in a systematic and more objective manner. Two-track
recordings also allow researchers to occupy briefly the place
of the professional interpreter and provide insights into the
mental processes inherent in interpreting.

The examples quoted in the previous chapters are taken from
a recording of a conference lasting three hours and twenty-five
minutes. The simultaneous recording of speakers and interpreters on a two-track tape has allowed me to examine simultaneously fragments from this conference in which the *two versions*
supposedly convey the same meaning. By interrupting the flow
of speech along its diachronic axis and by splitting speech as it
unfolds into a number of smaller parts, we can compare smaller
units of the two versions, as if it were on a simultaneous horizontal axis. This comparison facilitates the detection of various
dimensions and characteristics of discourse.

What were the criteria for selecting the examples? At first
I acted intuitively, selecting the cases which I found "interest-

ing". After analysing some of them I realized that I had always stopped at those moments when the interpreter seemed to say *less* or *more* than the speaker or when he seemed to be saying *something different*. I therefore decided to apply this criterion systematically. *The study of the "gap" – or difference between the two versions – became my working method.* From these discrepancies I chose the ones which seemed clearest or most representative to me for further analysis. This method requires the assumption that bilinguals[1] know when there is equivalence between two texts in different languages and when there is not, and can therefore detect deviations of meaning and gaps.

To say it in other words, within the framework of an *abnormal* communication exchange (i.e. when an interpreter is needed), the study of abnormal cases (when the interpreter seems to say less or more or something different from the speaker) reveals some of the mental processes involved. These processes are the *same* as those involved in *normal* exchanges, where their transparency and universality makes them almost impossible to detect. Pressed by time and cornered in space, interpreters exacerbate them making them thus more easily perceivable: thanks then to this magnifying glass, we can unveil the scaffolding of the operations involved.

Comparisons showed, first of all, the importance of the co-presence of the speaker and his interpreter at the time of delivery. The comparison of the first example – composed of *two* parts – with a second example – also made up of two parts – suggested the existence of two levels: the textual surface (what is said) and the meaning (what is conveyed). It was therefore possible to see that the equivalence between the "textual surfaces" does not necessarily ensure an equivalent message. In other words, there are dimensions in speech which are

---

1 By "bilingual" we mean persons who have a deep and thorough knowledge of two languages at the phonological, prosodic, structural semantic and pragmatic levels and who can understand and express themselves easily in both of them.

not contained in the utterance. Other fragments revealed the existence of implied messages, of a permanent *process of hypothesizing* about the speaker's intentions, as well as the presence of *divergent signals* and the simultaneous functioning of *two axes* in discourse.

The importance of this approach lies in the way that simultaneous interpreting relies on everyday processes for making sense of on-going interactions between people. The analysis and comparison of two discursive pieces delivered in the same place and at the same time by two different persons, one of whom is trying to mirror what the other is saying, allows us to pinpoint not only *what the interpreter does* but also *what we all do* while talking and listening and trying to understand each other.

When writers on semiotics and discourse analysis refer to meaning, they usually do so only after having reached the final full stop of a paragraph, a chapter, a speech or a book. Interpreters working "in simultaneous", however, do not wait for the end of a speech to start interpreting; they do not even wait for the end of a sentence to start its translation. It is the simultaneity of this operation that bewilders the scholar. It was and still is, indeed, a perplexing factor and my belief was that its study could provide fundamental clues concerning the psychological and cognitive ingredients at work when humans engage in dialogue. *These processes concern us all since they have to do not with the characteristics of one given language but with the human capacity of language at large, i.e. the human capacity of creating, sharing, conveying and interpreting meaning.*[2]

When linguists speak of meaning they do so often on the basis of the meaning of words, structures and their combinations. They seek the unvarying components in the system that enables us to communicate. But interpreters – as some of our

---

2 *My intuition proved right: the disparate conclusions of my original doctoral thesis eventually propelled me out of the interpreting world into the wider and vaster universe of human communication.*

examples have demonstrated – know that intonation, accent, gestures, silences and actions are as important for the recreation of meaning as the words themselves and that it is on the basis of this constellation of variables that it is possible to capture and restore the meaning of an act of communication.

What we have just done, then, is to set an objective for study different from what most theoreticians have set for themselves so far – even if conversation analysis and paralinguistics are by now well-established research areas that not only examine the sounds, structures or signs which allow us to communicate but the fleeting and complex act of communicating by two persons in each other's presence.

This act, unique in its realization by definition, evanescent and almost impossible to seize through traditional lenses of research became candidly exposed through our method permitting "snapshots" or synchronic cuts of two simultaneously recorded speeches.

Confronted with the finding that communication is "embodied" and the complexity of the variables simultaneously at work most linguists, prudently, avoid this area of study. Conference interpreters, though, have to face the complexity of these problems pragmatically day after day. And since simultaneous interpretation has existed in practice since the Nuremberg trials, that is, for over sixty years, there should be a theoretical framework accounting for the simultaneity phenomenon involved.

The single "object", i.e. "the one that cannot be distinguished from its surroundings or compared with others, is unapproachable for the human intellect", as Magariños de Morentín[3] likes to say. Its characteristics and composition can only become apparent if contrasted with another object or against a background. Since a single object is unapproachable,

---

3 J. A. Magariños de Morentín, Curso de Semiología Estructural, *Buenos Aires, ILAE, 1976.*

only the confrontation of two objects can become the source of information.

In our approach, it was the confrontation of two objects that revealed various discursive dimensions. Interpretation gave us the possibility of comparing two versions and thereby gave us information on the components of spoken discourse in general. This comparison and this information enabled us, in turn, to infer certain cognitive mechanisms.

From a completely different viewpoint, with the aim of obtaining the best possible performance from his actors, Stanislavski used a similar contrastive method – that of making actors compare texts to emotions or emotions to actions. He made them tap into their emotional memory to draw on their perceptive and associative capacities so as to unleash their creative power, thus identifying many characteristics of discourse by bringing into play not only words, or texts, but words and actions and feelings and emotions and intangible forces and energies.

The starting point of this research (back in 1977) was my curiosity to find out how interpreters managed to convey what speakers *implied* – not only what they *said*.

It becomes apparent to me now that what I was trying to seize, understand and describe then were the intangible processes that enable a simultaneous interpreter to meaningfully *anticipate* in real time somebody else's flow of thought and *make sense* of his words, acts and motivation. The difference between normal speakers and interpreters is that the latter have to maximize their capacity to make associations, inferences and hypotheses at very high speed within a very restricted time frame. They need to focus and to multiply their power of attention.

What we call "simultaneity" in conference interpreting refers then to that very brief space where attention is geared to its peak so as to enable interpreters to scan outside and inside in search of those invisible elements that may help them build the most appropriate hypotheses and become aware of the inferences implied by the speaker or revealed by the situation.

My object of research was then necessarily different from everybody else's in the linguistic or semiological field. Undertaking such an object for study, with the constellation of innumerable variables that come into play, was a task especially complex and extremely ambitious. It was justified by the existence of the profession as such and by my own personal experience as an interpreter.

❖ ❖ ❖

CHAPTER 9

Preliminary Conclusions

Of the need to draw some conclusions on what we have seen so far. Of how the interpreter reacts to contradictory signals. Of our need to "unlearn" certain things or to rectify our hypotheses.

L et us go back to some of the examples chosen, compare them and draw some conclusions from them.

Speaker's words	Interpreter's words
Nonetheless …	(—)

See page 104.

The interpreter correctly heard the expression "nonetheless". She could immediately have translated it by ***sin embargo.*** However, the processing of the data she was receiving sent her a warning; since she could not find a logical connection between "nonetheless" and the preceding or following sentences she chose to remain silent. Her choice proved valid since it was congruent with what the speaker said later. She could also have transmitted the ambiguity by using a "one fits all" expression in Spanish, such as "*de todas maneras*" (anyway) or "*sea como fuere*" (be that as it may).

nonetheless

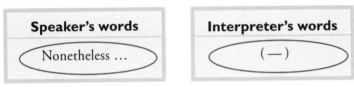

Speaker's words	Interpreter's words	
Now, I don't want to skip time sharing. Everybody knows what that is.	*Ahora, no voy a hablar de programas que todo el mundo ya conoce.*	Now, I will not speak of programs which everybody already knows

See page 108.

The interpreter heard the speaker correctly; she sensed the presence of diverging signals and detected, quite accurately, the place where the two contradictory statements occurred, all of which allowed her to correct the speaker. The re-established coherence gave her confidence to continue but this additional effort caused a loss of precision when she went on programs to say *programas* instead of **time sharing**.

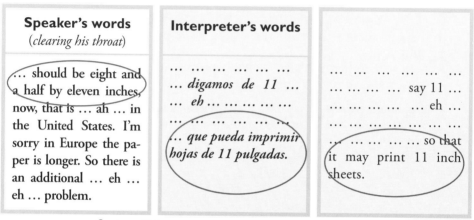

Speaker's words *(clearing his throat)*	Interpreter's words	
… should be eight and a half by eleven inches, now, that is … ah … in the United States. I'm sorry in Europe the paper is longer. So there is an additional … eh … eh … problem.	… … … … … … … *digamos de 11 …* … *eh* … … … … … … … … … … … … … *que pueda imprimir hojas de 11 pulgadas.*	… … … … … … … … … … … … say 11 … … … … … … eh … … … … … … … … … … … … … … … so that it may print 11 inch sheets.

See page 111.

Once again, the interpreter realized she was getting contradictory information. She could not, however, detect how this was happening and therefore did not repeat it. She processed in depth, as shown when she said "*que pueda imprimir hojas de 11 pulgadas*". The listeners who heard the speaker directly did not, of course, understand much more than those listening to the Spanish version; the audience heard more words but was probably unable to digest them since they were not very clear.

Lithium is not all that abundant. It is about as abundant as uranium	≠	*El litio no es tan abundante como el uranio.*	Lithium is not as abundant as uranium.

See page 114.

In the absence of a distinct signal or warning to announce irony and thus ratify the meaning of the second phrase (the speaker could, for instance, have added "in fact" before saying "it is about as abundant as uranium"), the interpreter – confused by the ambiguity – got lost in the middle of the sentence. Trying to find a way out, he ended up losing a few words in the process ("lithium is not ~~all that abundant; it is about~~ as abundant as uranium") thereby causing a true accident during his delivery.

We can already draw some conclusions about these examples:

1. The four cases we have analysed show "real time" processing of information in depth; if interpreters had been working "on the surface", they could in all four cases have said exactly what the speaker had said.

2. Confronted with divergent or contradictory signals, interpreters often make use of the "strategy of silence". By doing so, they give themselves more time to process the conflicting information and/or to allow for the reception of new signals pointing to the path to follow.

3. When interpreters receive contradictory signals and are unable to locate the place, level or way in which the ideas got mixed up they end up remaining silent or making a mistake. When erring, it is frequently due to the fact that they have already said too much to remain silent. When they remain silent, however, their silence proves two things:

   • their reluctance to say something lacking in logic and
   • the numbness created by contradictory instructions.

4. When interpreters receive divergent signals and manage to detect accurately the place, level or way in which the ideas got tangled up, they spontaneously make the correction of the error in their own speech, translate the lapse spontaneously or subsequently explain what happened.

5. The presence of contradictory information or divergent signals produces ambiguity. Interpreters sense this much more

clearly than the rest of the listeners since they are on the alert: their profession requires them to listen to the speaker carefully, to try to follow the logic of what the speaker is saying and to permanently make decisions about what they think the speaker meant.

Let us now consider the two cases in which the interpreter got the impression of not having heard – or understood – what the speaker said.

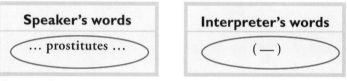

Speaker's words	**Interpreter's words**
... prostitutes ...	(—)

See page 68.

Speaker's words	**Interpreter's Words**	
There are ... three ... eh ... activities in which are ... eh ... in the draft recommendation which are not in the amendment ... eh ... (inaudible)	*Hay tres actividades que aparecen en el proyecto de recomendación ... ...* *... ... ...* *... ... ...* *... eh ...* *acopio de datos en las ciencias sociales, las actividades sobre patentes y licencias y la traducción y la publicación ... ...* *¿Esto es una omisión voluntaria? Porque esto no aparece en la enmienda propuesta ...*	There are three activities which are in the draft recommendation ... ... eh ... data collection in the social sciences, the activities related to patents and licences and translation and publication ... ... Is this a deliberate omission? Because this is not mentioned in the proposed amendment ...

See page 128.

The comparison of these two examples can give us some clues to the mechanisms of comprehension.

In the first case, the interpreter believed she had not heard the speaker; she could not even hear the word "prostitutes" which she only got as "noise". The analysis had allowed us to formulate the hypothesis that it was *precisely* because she had heard the word correctly that she rejected it. From this standpoint, and according to the interpreter's personal mental framework, what took place – at top speed and unconsciously – was a collision between two opposing elements: the disreputable subject of "prostitution" did not "fit" the highly dignified framework of a Conference of Bishops. We would therefore be in the presence of yet another case of divergent signals, but with a fundamental difference: the interpreter here did not choose to remain silent and omit the word "prostitutes"; she was compelled to do so for she was not aware of even having heard the word.

Instead of becoming a bridge across which new elements could be incorporated into the existing context, the hypothesis framework prefabricated by the interpreter became too rigid and acted as a barrier to understanding. Without the help of her colleague, the interpreter would have been guilty of mistranslation attributable to an internal blockage caused by her own web of hypotheses (an instance of "cognitive rigidity", we might say).

In the second case, the interpreter was unable to understand what the speaker said: she did not get the words "which are not in the amendment" and all she got was obscure and diffuse blurred sounds. But, in contrast with what happened in the previous example ("prostitutes"), the dynamic incorporation of contextual elements made it possible for her this time to recover retroactively the words which seem to have remained in blurred suspense in her mind. The interpreter had just heard the speaker ask a question; the speaker wanted to know if it was a voluntary omission; he spoke of a draft recommendation, they were debating the amendments to that text. There must have been a comparison between them. The underlying reasoning seems to be: if there is "B", there must have been "A" since a comparison has been established between "B" and

"A". Due to this inference process taking place at the same time that she was listening to and translating the speaker`s words, the interpreter managed to recover the blurred sounds, remember them, understand them, translate them and incorporate them suitably into her own version: *porque esto no aparece en la enmienda propuesta.* A few things to do in only 15 seconds providing an instance of "cognitive flexibility".

because this is not in the proposed amendment.

We can draw some more conclusions from the latest examples:

1. The fact that the interpreter was subsequently able to include "which are not in the amendment" shows that it is possible to store information and keep it in "abeyance" even when poorly or partially processed.

2. If the web of hypotheses we draw up as we go through the process of understanding is not flexible and dynamic enough to re-adjust new elements, it can paradoxically end up functioning as a barrier to understanding. The flexibility of this network allows us to cancel, change, modify, increase and incorporate new data; it permits us, finally, to know something more or something different from what we knew at the outset.

3. If the web of hypotheses gets too rigid or proves not to adapt to what happens "out there in the real world", we should readily eliminate it altogether or eliminate some of its components; in other words, *we should unlearn something we have learnt.* And try again experimenting with some new hypotheses and new webs.

❖   ❖   ❖

CHAPTER 10

Strategies

No interpreter, translator or bilingual person in his or her right mind would translate ***entre nomás y tome una silla*** by "**between no more and drink a chair**". However, each of the French or English words corresponds to a possible translation of each Spanish word. Finding a logical connection between each word and the ones preceding and following it is the fundamental law of translation.

come in please and sit down

With no change whatsoever in sounds, the mere changing of accents will transform the meaning and offer a number of variations of /entrenomas/:

| Entré nomás | = | I came in. |
| en ˎtre no ˳mas\| | | Je suis rentré sans plus. |

| Entre Nomás | = | Come in, Nomas. |
| ˎentre no ˳mas\| | | Rentrez, Nomas. |

| En tre´* nomás | = | Only in three of them. |
| en ˎtreh no ˳mas\| | | Dans trois seulement. |

(Argentina and Uruguay vernacular (no /s/ sound at the end of some words).

| Entre nomás | = | Come in! or Come in, please! |
| ˎentre no ˳mas\| | | Allez rentrez! o Rentrez s.v.p. |

The fact that *"entre no más"* is followed by *"tome una silla"* eliminates the three first possibilities and makes the fourth option mandatory. It also conjures up the image of the speaker in his office in some Latin American country (but not in Spain because of the use of *"nomás"*) at the moment when he is, for instance, welcoming a customer.

Even if:

Entre	=	between; among
		parmi, entre
no	=	no
		non
más	=	more, most, etc.
		plus, etc.

Entre nomás y tome una silla.	≠	Between no more and drink a chair.
		Parmi non plus et buvez une chaise.

But rather

Entre nomás y tome una silla.	=	Come in please and sit down.
		Rentrez s.v.p et asseyez vous.

A thorough knowledge of English and Spanish and of certain mechanisms of translation have led Basil Thompson to develop this kind of linguistic humour and share it with his numerous readers in the *"Buenos Aires Herald"*. The aforementioned quote is one of his examples.

After an initial surprise due to the non-sense of the sentence there comes, for bilinguals, a zigzagging movement from English into Spanish and back to English; it is the itinerary covering the distance between the false English version and the correct one, indispensable for understanding the joke, that makes its functioning transparent and produces hilarity.

This example allows us to make explicit *the fundamental law of translation* and an important *strategy* of the interpreter: relate the matter to be translated to what precedes and to what follows it; relate the part to the whole; relate what is heard or read to what is already known, and what is heard to what is seen or felt.

Let us take a look at the other strategies used by interpreters.

The examples given, carrying divergent signals (*nonetheless*) show that one frequently used strategy is *silence*: if you do not understand something, you had better remain silent and wait.

When translating *"time sharing"* as **programas** (see page 108), the interpreter brings to light another strategy: when speed, difficulties in content or terminology create problems or when incoherence and fatigue are great because of the information overload, she will go from specifics to generalities. In such cases, if possible, she can seek protection in the use of a *deictic** rather than repeat long terms difficult to articulate.

programs

Thus, in a Colloquium on Adipositis (held in Montecarlo in March of 1982), when the speaker, mentioning thyroid hormones said: *"la différence entre les effets de la tiroxine (t4) et de la triiodotironine (t3) est que la triiodotironine (t3) ... "*, the interpreter simplified by saying:

The difference between the effects of thyroxine (t4) and triiodothyronine (t3) is that triiodothyronine (t3) ...

Speaker's words	Interpreter's words	
La différence entre les effets de la tiroxine (t4) et de la triiodotironine (t3) est que la triiodotironine (t3) produit ...	*La diferencia entre los efectos de la tiroxina (t4) y de la triodotironina (t3) es que (ésta) produce ...*	The difference between the effects of thyroxin (t4) and triiodothyronine (t3) is that (this one) produces ...

"This", "this last one" or even "t3" were enough in this case for an unambiguous reference to triiodothyronine.

Another strategy for gaining time is the transformation of an indirect act into a direct one, as in the example (see page 128) where the interpreter transforms an indirect request into a plain and simple question thus saving time enabling him to include "for this does not appear in the proposed amendment".

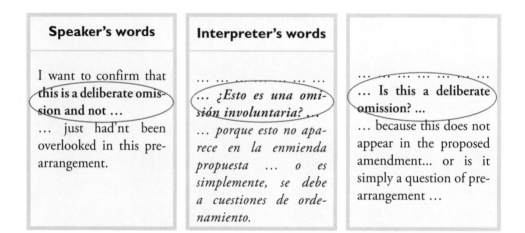

Speaker's words	Interpreter's words	
I want to confirm that ~~this is a deliberate omission and not ...~~ ... just had'nt been overlooked in this pre-arrangement.	... ... ~~... ¿Esto es una omisión involuntaria? ...~~ ... porque esto no aparece en la enmienda propuesta ... o es simplemente, se debe a cuestiones de ordenamiento.	... ... ~~... Is this a deliberate omission? ...~~ ... because this does not appear in the proposed amendment... or is it simply a question of pre-arrangement ...

Let us now consider those cases where there undoubtedly was an interpretation error. The example on page 131 shows how the Portuguese interpreter, when not understanding *à plein temps* ended up saying *lorsque l'ordinateur fonctionne au printemps*. He used the relationship strategy only at a superficial level. Had he gone into a deeper level, he would have rejected "*au printemps*". One could argue that if he had not heard "*à plein temps*" and if he had rejected *au printemps*, what else could he have said? Knowing that probably he could clear up the information subsequently, thanks to the possible repetition of the concept; thanks to his own capacity for retroactive inference, or to the assistance of his colleague in the booth, he could – and should – have used the *generalization strategy* and say, for instance: "when computers function in these conditions" or "when computers are in operation."

full time

when computers work in springtime.

in springtime

In the example on page 114 the interpreter makes a mistake because he has already said too much and cannot remain silent ("lithium is not as abundant as …") and not being able to detect the ambiguity (Is lithium more or less abundant than uranium?), he must somehow complete the comparison – and the sentence – in one way or another. Since he has already said "lithium is not as abundant …", the interpreter covers up the "hitch". He could correct himself later on if necessary.

Any speaker can make mistakes or talk nonsense. He can hesitate, mutter, restart, interrupt himself or leave some sentences unfinished. So can the interpreter. But there are some types of mistakes that a speaker normally does not make and which the interpreter must consequently avoid. We would have serious doubts about our speaker's clarity of mind if he repeatedly interrupted his sentences before the completion of the expression of an idea or of a certain unit of meaning, for instance:

> **"Having reached this point of … I believe that …",**
>
> **"… The entrance is next to …",**
>
> **"… What matters most is the …"**

In these cases, the final blanks would leave interlocutors amazed.

Formal pulchritude in the use of the language must be added to the *strategy of silence*. When the interpreter does not understand something he prefers to remain silent and sin by omission; in this way he can skip a whole phrase, a subordinate phrase, some qualifiers or some elements inside a listing. When he has said too much and cannot remain silent he will prefer, in any case, to give the sentence a good ending, at least from the syntactic point of view. He will leave no sentence half finished. In other words, it is not a question of just skipping something. It is a question of knowing exactly what can be omitted[1]. And in any event the interpreter keeps in his hands the thread of the *diachronic axis* which will let him complete the information *a posteriori*.

There is another characteristic of interpreters that greatly helps them at work.

I consider it so important that I have, in fact, taken it so far for granted: their versatility, flexibility or capacity to adapt to the most unexpected turns, both structurally and semantically. Suppose the interpreter, anticipating the speaker, has already said something – she has used for example a feminine article in Spanish only to perceive an instant later that she should have used the masculine one. While beginners would most probably go back and self-correct themselves, professionals take the challenge to go on, looking for synonyms or turn around expressions (for ex.: "*la … razón; el … motivo*"). If a word stays in the tip of their tongue, or if simply they had never heard it before, interpreters will often find a way out – sometimes through colourful images or metaphors. "Hand shoes" was for example Mansilla's spontaneous explanation of the meaning of "gloves" to some Ranqueles indians who had never been acquainted with the object or the concept before. Adaptation and creativity should also be added to their strategies' list.

Our last example will be another joke taken from an actual conference. During a seminar on Business Management held in Wiesbaden in 1983 a German speaker ended his presentation with a joke. What does the interpreter do? With the greatest of ease, instead of translating the joke, he drops the first person singular – typical of simultaneous work – and says with seductive complicity to his listeners: "The German speaker is telling a joke … Please laugh now to make him happy. I'll tell it to you later." The participants, surprised

---

1 See chapter 15, "Tying Up Loose Ends", page 245.

by this change in enunciation began to laugh. A complicity was thus created between the audience and the interpreter (everybody knows how difficult it can be to translate certain jokes or puns) and if everybody in the room laughed at the same time, each half did so for different reasons; the German auditors laughed at the speaker's joke, the English-speaking participants because the former simply did not know that the latter were laughing at something else.

This joke is exactly at the opposite end of the one at the beginning of this chapter. In the example "between no more and drink a chair" the imaginary bilingual gets stuck at every individually translated word without being able to even construct a meaningful sentence in English. In the last case, however, the interpreter – taking all liberties – interrupts the speech, changes the enunciation, does not repeat what the speaker is saying but does however manage to get the same result: his public breaks out laughing. This is proof of how, by recreating and not reproducing an *illocutionary* act,* it is possible to obtain an equivalent *perlocutionary* act.*

A fleeting "view of the whole" – situation, context, tone – the quick evaluation of the speaker's objectives and the conviction that the joke, if told in another language, would fall flat, led the interpreter to stray totally from the speaker's words. His strategy was to relate not only one word with those coming before and after but the joke as a whole with the context, situation, objective and means within his reach even before the speaker had finished telling it. His objective, amply attained, was to produce an equivalent effect in the audience by different means.

Strategies in Conversation

A quick look at our daily conversations or the analysis of television or radio interviews will show that the strategies used by the interpreter are the same we use in our daily talk.

It sometimes happens that we understand something different from what has been said – something bizarre or funny, ridiculous or irrelevant. On the whole, we remain silent and wait. The continuation of the dialogue sheds light on the matter and we come to grasp both the original meaning and the sound-based reasons for the incident. But we seldom confess to this. When we realize what has happened and can own up to it without losing face it is already too late. To do so would interrupt the flow of conversation. Often, also, we hide our ignorance or embarrassment behind a curtain of silence.

To this day Grice's principles of conversation are the best description I know of what happens when we indulge in conversation, where not only roles, functions and power can be at stake but also strategies and tactics to consolidate, change or overturn them.

What can we do, for example, when we are asked in public a question we do not want to give an answer to?

Faced with questions we would rather not answer, we can divert other people's attention by referring to analogous or similar subjects to those proposed. We can also cover up the clues with contradictory information so as to send our listener directly back to Square One.

Faced with questions for which we have no answer, we also tend to react through association or connection: "*I don't know much about that but I can, however, tell you something regarding this other subject ...*" We often go from specifics to generalities: "I can't remember the year exactly but it must have been towards the end of the war".

Other possibilities are also at hand: we could, in either case, directly reply: "*I don't want to tell you*" or "*I do not know*" which could be considered a spontaneous manifestation of utter sincerity or a well pondered choice after a quick assessment of the available options. Any of these replies closes the exchange: after such manifestations it is necessary indeed to start anew.

But it is equally possible to relocate the issue in another context through a comment or a question on the type of exchange: "*Are you asking me that out of courtesy?*" or "*Why do you insist on cornering me like this?*" We shift from one level to another to communicate on how to communicate.

When our interlocutors bring in ideas that are troublesome for us or double meanings through the use of subordinate clauses or when we are involved in a situation just by being mentioned in passing, it is better to clear matters up to avoid feeling trapped. This is not always easy. The flow of communication must be stopped and the ball sent back using, if possible, also a subordinate clause. I recall, for instance, an exchange at lunch time between a rising socialist French minister and a French businessman where the topic was politics and commerce: the minister gave a long explanation in the middle of which he verbalized the assumption that the businessman had never visited one of the unpretentious neighbourhoods in the East of Paris. Surprisingly, the businessman happened to live in that area, a fact which facilitated his chance to get back to the fleeting comment and at the same time help break the minister's stereotype.

Defense strategies in conversation are therefore basically the same as those used when interpreting: relate or associate; delay response or remain silent; go from specifics to generalities or go up the abstraction ladder; react to hidden meanings, or at least uncover them. As for an offensive strategy, it will mainly depend on the objective pursued when asking the questions.

❖   ❖   ❖

CHAPTER 11

Expectations and Social Anticipation

Of how interpreters – and humans – learn to predict at different macro and micro levels.

L ong before their working day begins, interpreters are already implementing strategies. They arrive early to examine the conference hall; they check the view from their booths or select the best location to work in consecutive. They read the list of participants carefully, observing the place assigned to the various delegates; the seating plan is often a good guide to the forces at work[1].

Although interpreters do not resort to physical relaxation exercises as actors do when trying to find what Stanislavski called the "zero point", they do consciously interrupt their internal monologues and put any private concerns and personal problems behind when they enter the booth. Once inside the booth, they become immersed in the conference: agenda, list of participants, reference documents and even, quite frequently, texts of speeches submerge them in the subject-matter and connect them with whoever takes the floor.

When engaged for the Bush-Putin Summit in Bratislava in February 2005, interpreters were able to *predict* many of the items on the agenda: the fight against terrorism; the post-war situation in Iraq; the "threats" of Iran and North Korea; the state of "democracy" in the world; the Middle East.

Similarly, interpreters at the Franco–African Summit in Paris in 1981 were able to predict that delegates would speak

---

1 *The Vietnam peace negotiations scheduled to begin in Paris in November 1968 were delayed for three months because the participants were unable to agree on the shape of the discussion table. "This was not", as Henry Kissinger pointed out, "a trivial issue (...) By this proposal (of a four sided table) Hanoi sought to use the beginnings of the negotiations to establish the National Liberation Front as an alternative government."* (The White House Years. London, Weidenfeld and Nicolson, 1979. Page 52).

about relations between rich and poor nations, about the exchange of raw materials, technology transfer and aid for development as well as anticipating that the political situation in Chad would most probably be discussed.

Interpreters at the meeting of the Paris Club in October 1987, where certain Latin American countries were renegotiating their foreign debts, expected mention to be made of the social and economic crisis, interest rates, stand-by credits, debt rescheduling, preferential rates and International Monetary Fund programmes, just as interpreters at a high level meeting of European executives in 1988 were prepared for frequent references to the Single European Market which was to come into force by 1993.

And interpreters at the UN Millennium Conference in New York during Clinton's last year of office knew that the presence of Fidel Castro and the Iranians would be commented on by the 188 delegations.

But what does an interpreter do when he or she has no prior information whatsoever about the participants, the subject or the meeting?

We shall use this extreme case to outline another two strategies the interpreter commonly resorts to: 1) negative reversal and 2) inference.

It is possible for the interpreter not to know the subject of the meeting while still being able to infer which subjects the meeting will not deal with. Let us take an example: the only thing the interpreter knows is that he must show up at a certain address on a certain day and at a certain time for a meeting of the French Coal Association and contact Mr. X (whose assistant hired him on somebody's recommendation). The interpreter has, in fact, very little information. A beginner would feel very much in the dark. However, this information is enough for a professional to start predicting and preparing a framework of hypotheses. If the meeting is to be held at "Charbonnages de France", there is little chance of the participants discussing matters concerning architecture, cinema, fine arts, astronomy or agriculture. Such terminologies and sets of problems can therefore be discarded. If only Europeans attend, the latest problems of the European Union will certainly arise as will problems of production, imports and exports. There are coalmines everywhere in Europe except in Switzerland. We associate coal with peat, lignite, anthracite and coke. It is a traditional source of energy and it can be compared with oil, fuel oil, hydraulic, solar, aeolic and nuclear energy. They will certainly speak of energy problems, of oil substitution, production costs, markets, labour employment.

– Who is that man in such a hurry?
– The Secretary General.
– Where will the President sit?
– He's not coming. The Director General will preside.
– Who is the President?
– He has just been appointed by the new government.
– He belonged to the Communist party and there are some people worried about it who may want to ask questions on the subject.
– How often do they meet?
– Four times a year, but always in a different country.

These questions – asked by interpreters as in passing – can prove fundamental: the information thus obtained can allow them to dispel the ambiguity of a sentence or detect an irony which would have otherwise eluded them.

To interpret a sentence it is necessary to relate it to a specific framework resulting from the situation of enunciation. The more we know about it, the easier it will be to interpret.

Nevertheless, care is necessary. Expectations and anticipations can facilitate and speed up understanding and the task in hand – just as stereotypes do. But one should always be on the alert and ready for the unexpected in an increasingly complex world.

Anticipation and Foresight

In Edinburgh, two famous phoneticians are members of the same University jury. Seeing from afar one of the students who would be sitting for his exam, one of them said:

– He is British R.P. (Received pronunciation)
– How do you know?
– By the way he walks.

He was right.

This is a true story and it was told by Kenneth Pike during the 7th Congress of Applied Linguistics (Brussels, 1984). It shows how we relate different types of sensory information to make our predictions and how our senses translate themselves reciprocally. We know from looking at a piece of cloth what it will feel like because of prior experience and we experience no difficulty in imagining what our trip will be like depending on what bicycle we choose.[2]

We can also imagine the face of the other person at the other end of the telephone from clues we receive from her voice.

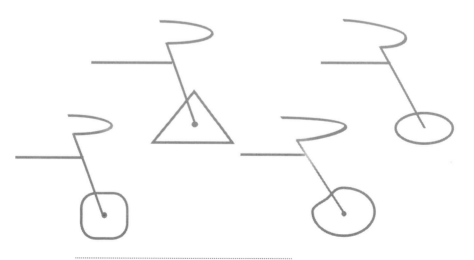

---

2 *Example taken from E. De Bono,* The Mechanism of Mind, *Great Britain, Pelican, 1971.*

186 | THE HIDDEN SIDE OF BABEL

We use our previous experiences to anticipate events at all levels. In conversation we make phonological, grammatical, syntactic, semantic and even pragmatic forecasts, as it has already been noted.

Some psychologists are currently debating the question of knowing whether it is the phoneme or the syllable which allows access to the lexicon. We have shown that even before hearing the first sentence, the first word, syllable or phoneme, the interpreter has already activated one or more areas of his lexicon. He has opened, so to speak, his own personal thesaurus to a certain page and is anticipating at other levels. It would be interesting to learn how the confirmation of a forecast at one level fires forecasts at other levels and how the layers of this complex system interweave with one another.

In an experiment reported by Arnheim,[3] a square projected on a screen became increasingly brighter. If the subjects expected a square, they recognized the image much sooner than if they had been led to believe that the figure was going to be a circle. The reaction of interpreters to unexpected sentences shows the same inclination, as shown by Chernov's experiences (see page 71). In another experiment, related this time by Vernon,[4] subjects who at the outset made false guesses concerning a sequence of images that gradually became less ambiguous and more precise tended to hold on to their initial false guesses much longer than a control group who began to observe the series when it was already half way through.

When one is led to expect something and it does happen, the time for the reaction needed to identify it will be shorter than when the expectation is upset and the information has to be reorganized.

---

3 *In* Arte y Percepción Visual, *Buenos Aires, Eudeba, 1962, Page 43.*

4 *M.D. Vernon,* Psicología de la Percepción, *Buenos Aires, Ediciones Hormé, 1979, (Page 170).*

It not only appears that we are permanently looking forward but also that our expectations affect our reaction times.

The consequences of this can be far-reaching. If at the moment we are trying to give a name to a perception/feeling/emotion/idea, somebody else provides one, we may feel our freedom restricted since our own personal exploration was forced to end. First impressions, first suggestions tend to suppress others, to prevent them from "appearing", from "coming to the surface".

Foreseeing, anticipating, predicting is therefore basic to work "in simultaneous". And also to directing a nation, a company, or even one's own life, provided we also become more and more aware of the enormous number of unexpected events that may occur in an ever more complex world.

We project our past onto our future, thus interweaving them with our present.

Like actors before going on stage, we should know certain basic facts about every interaction: who, to whom, when, where, what, for what purpose. On the basis of these data, we will possibly be able to correctly infer others.

When	Where	Who Main actors	On what Issues on the agenda
The 70's	USA	Carter	Human rights Hostages in Iran War Iraq-Iran The arms race
	France	Giscard d'Estaing	The Middle East Problems in Africa La *"crispation"* The Soviet invasion of Afghanistan

When	Where	Who	On what
	Argentina	Perón, Isabel, the military	Terrorism, inflation Repression Riots, strikes, disturbances
The 80's	USA	Reagan	Starwars Central America Economic success
	France	Mitterrand	Socialism - *Gauche caviar* Liberal economic reforms Big architectural works Berlin wall comes down
	Argentina	Alfonsín	Back to democracy Inflation soars up Military revolts Human rights
The 90's	USA	Clinton	Prosperity Medicare Stability The Lewinsky affair
	France	Chirac	Enlargement of EU Unified European Market Internal disruptions Growth of the National Front
	Argentina	Menem	Privatizations Peso pegged to US$ Stability-Economic boom Increase in poverty Corruption

The following diagram, simplified for reasons of space, gives an overview of the permanently changing factors at play. It contains data which were fundamental for interpreters working at the IV Summit of the Americas (Mar del Plata, november 2005). Colleague Victoria Massa-Bulit prepared it and generously circulated it among us.

Panamerican System – 2005

Country / Capital city	President/ Governor General/ Prime Minister	Minister of Foreign Affairs	
Antigua and Barbuda / St. John's	Sir James Carlisle, GG Baldwin Spencer, PM		Antiguan / Barbudan
Argentina / Buenos Aires	Néstor Kirchner	Rafael Bielsa	Argentine
Bahamas / Nassau	Ivy Dumont GG Perry Christie PM		Bahamian
Barbados / Bridgetown	Sir Clifford Straughn Husbands GG Owen Seymour Arthur, PM		Barbadian
Belize / Belmopan	Colville Young, GG Said Musa PM		Belizean
Bolivia / La Paz	Eduardo Rodríguez Veltze	Armando Loaiza Mariaca	Bolivian
Brazil / Brasilia	Luis Inacio Lula da Silva	Celso Luiz Amorim	Brazilean
Canada / Ottawa	Adrienne Clarkson GG Paul Martin PM	Pierre Pettigrew	Canadian
Chile / Santiago	Ricardo Lagos Escobar	Ignacio Walker	Chilean
Colombia / Bogota	Alvaro Uribe Vélez	Carolina Barco Isakson	Colombian
Costa Rica / St Jose de C R	Abel Pacheco de la Espriella	Roberto Tovar Faja	Costa Rican
Cuba (*) / Havanna	Fidel Castro		Cuban
Domenican Republic / St Domingo	Leonel Fernándes Reyna	Carlos Morales Troncoso	Dominican
Dominica / Roseau	Nicholas O Liverpool, Presidente Roosevelt Skerrit, PM	Charles Savarin	Dominican
Ecuador / Quito	Alfredo Palacio	Antonio Parra Gil	Ecuadorian

Country / Capital city	President/ Governor General/ Prime Minister	Minister of Foreign Affairs	
El Salvador / San Salvador	Elías Antonio Saca González	Francisco Lainez	Salvadorean
Grenada / St. George's	Sir Daniel Charles Williams GG	Elvin Nimrod	Grenadian
Guatemala / Guatemala	Oscar Berger	Jorge Briz Abularach	Guatemalan
Guyana / Georgetown	Bahrrat Jagdeo Samuel Hinds PM	S. Rudy Insanally	Guyanense
Haiti / Port au Prince	Boniface Alexandre Gérard Latortue PM	Hérard Abraham	Haitian
Honduras / Tegucigalpa	Ricardo Maduro Joest	Leónidas Rosa Bautista	Honduran
Jamaica / Kingston	Sir Howard Cook GG P.J. Patterson, PM	Keith Knight	Jamaican
Mexico / Mexico	Vicente Fox	Luis Derbez Bautista	Mexican
Nicaragua / Managua	Enrique Bolaños Geyer	Norman Caldera Cardenal	Nicaraguan
Panama / Panama	Martín Torrijos	Samuel Lewis Navarro	Panamanian
Paraguay / Asuncion	Nicanor Duarte Frutos	Leila Rachid de Cowles	Paraguayan
Peru / Lima	Alejandro Toledo Manrique	Oscar Martua de Romaña	Peruvian
St Lucia and Castries	Calliopa Pearlette Louisy, GG Kenneth D. Anthony, PM	Petrus Compton	Saintlucian
St Vicent and the Grenadines / Kingstown	Dr. Frederick Ballantyne Ralph E. Gonsalves, PM	Michael Browne	Saintvicentian
St Kitts and Nevis / Basseterre	Sir Cuthbert Sebastian, GG Denzil Douglas, PM	Timothy Harris	
Surinam / Paramaribo	Runaldo Ronald Venetiaan	María Levens	Surinamese
Trinidad and Tobago / Port of Spain	George Richards Patrick Manning, PM	Knowlson Gift	Trinidadian
Uruguay / Montevideo	Tabaré Vázquez	Reinaldo Gargano	Uruguayan
USA / Washington DC	George W. Bush	Condoleeza Rice Secretary of State	American/ NorthAmerican
Venezuela / Caracas	Hugo Chávez Frías	Alí Rodríguez Araque	Venezuelan

For the sake of argument, let us now take one subject and freely associate with it as many words/concepts/ideas that first come to mind. We shall see how fluently and easily we start developing "semantic fields".

Geographical Information systems – GIS

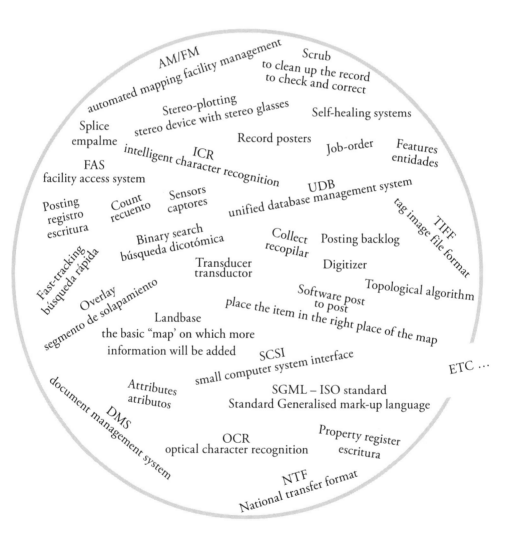

Antarctic Treaty

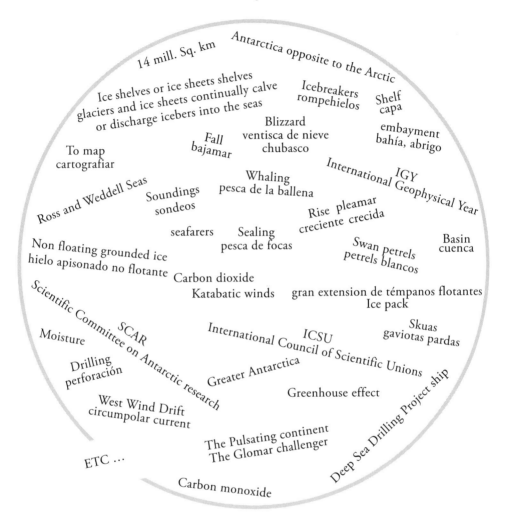

So, depending on the subject, we shall bring certain words to the surface so as to have them on hand when needed. We will thus start outlining a *semantic field*. The lists could go on indefinitely since we can hardly ever exhaust a subject. Doing this preparatory work, we become more and more aware of the links and *connections* between ideas, and concepts, orientations and words, of the abstracting mechanisms at play, of the different ways in which languages organize the "outside world", of the way our mind works ... We become readier to understand and recognize elements at different levels. We bring these words to the surface knowing that our efforts will only be tentative, that speakers will always be able to say more or differently; knowing that, in practice, some of those terms may never come up even though many others will, thus confirming the "non-allness" principle: the lists of associative elements of a semantic field go on indefinitely. But lists are not enough. Priorities, levels and categories must be set, concepts classified, levels of abstraction determined. It is this structuring which facilitates *understanding*.

The answers to the basic set of questions (*who, when, where,* etc.), and the development of some semantic fields provide the interpreter with a minimum foundation from which to start making predictions. Of course, attention should be paid so as not to stick to simple stereotypes.

When I wrote these observations about "predictions" in 1989, I did not know that for some brain researchers predictions would play such a fundamental role.

"*Prediction* – not behavior – is the proof of intelligence" says, for example, Jeff Hawkins while trying to explain how the brain works in his *memory-prediction framework.*[5]

He says,

> "Prediction, is the application of invariant memory sequences to new situations. Therefore all cortical predictions are predictions by analogy. We predict the future by analogy to the past ... You look for expected patterns and you are on the alert for new ones ... This kind of behavior is a creative act. Prediction by analogy – creativity – is so pervasive we normally don't notice it."

---

5 *Jeff Hawkins,* On Intelligence, *New York: Times Books, Henry Holt and Company, 2004.*

He goes on,

"To make predictions of novel events, your neocortex needs a way to memorize and store knowledge about sequences of events. To make predictions of novel events, the cortex must form invariant representations. Your brain needs to create and store a model of the world as it is, independent from how you see it under changing circumstances.

To make predictions of future events, your neocortex has to store sequences of patterns ... to make predictions ... you need to have memorized sequences of events. To make predictions of novel events you should resort to invariant representations."

My examples from the interpreting world have helped me – perhaps clumsily, I admit – to show these processes at work at the phonological, grammatical, structural, logical and pragmatic levels. My hypothesis is that these processes operate *permanently* and *simultaneously* at different micro and macro levels.

❖ ❖ ❖

CHAPTER **12**

Protocol
and Ritual

Of shape and
substance.
Of background,
figure and form.
Of the ritual
framework
of conference
interaction.

At the beginning of the 20th century Vienna was a centre of cultural splendour at the forefront of some trends in art and sciences. While Freud was formulating his psychoanalytical theory, his native city also saw the flourishing of other ideas which were to give birth to group psychotherapy and psychodrama. J. Moreno´s book "Theatre and Spontaneity" divulges the psychiatric concept of "role" and the therapeutic possibilities of "acting out".

The accent on the *individual* and his "personal history" was transferred to the *group of persons* interacting in the here and now. The rich complementariness of individual and social approaches, of forces *in praesentia et in absentia* would be taken up again by Saussure in his famous dichotomies which paved the way not only for modern linguistics but also for most social sciences in the 20th century. At the beginning of the 21st century, accent has shifted once again to focus not only on the individual's history and his network of relationships, but on his genealogical tree and hidden influences through long chains of ancestors.[1]

In the sociological field, E. Goffman,[2] in the United States, took up the theatrical metaphor used by Kenneth Burke and tried to give formal shape to formal codes for interaction in daily life by using the concept of "role".[3] Ac-

---

1 Anne Ancelin Schüztenberger, The Ancestor's Syndrome, *London, Penguin, 1999. (Aïe mes aïeux!, Paris, La Méridienne – Desclée de Brouwer, 1993.)*

2 E. Goffman, Strategic Interaction, *Oxford, Basil Blackwell, 1970, and* The Presentation of Self in Everyday Life, *London, Penguin, 1978.*

3 A "role" is an orderly model of behaviours in relation to a specific position of the individual in an interactive context. Diccionario de Psicología, *Frederic Dorsch, Barcelona, Editorial Herder, 1985.*

cording to this theory, all of us in society permanently take on roles which vary with the activities we develop or with the social group with which we interact. Thus, within the family we shall assume roles of sons, fathers, brothers or all of them jointly (or their feminine equivalents). In the street, we can be pedestrians, car drivers or passengers. We can be tennis players, club employees or spectators at a tennis match; doctors, patients, nurses or assistants at a hospital; buyers or sellers, office workers, managers, secretaries or executives[4] in the business world, etc.

Two or more players together may produce a unit of interaction. This can be seen as a small theatre piece where, in addition to a cast and a stage, certain implicit rules of social behaviour prevail, inherent in the distribution of roles and actions. Most of us know these rules for, in fact, when interaction works it is because we apply them; this does not mean however, that we consciously know how to identify them, recognize them or explain them. Every interaction, no matter how commonplace it may turn out to be, is inscribed in a ritual. Since nothing is more difficult to see than that which is obvious[5], Goffman chose cases where daily rituals were disrupted in order to make them more apparent and reveal their grammar.

The more elaborate or sophisticated a ceremony or an action, the more specific and codified the ritual will be; and the more visible, too. The older a tradition is and the more respected its details are from generation to generation, the

---

4 *In* Descripción de Puestos en Hoteles, Restaurantes y Bares / México, Cía, *Editora Continental, 1982, Sixto Báez describes the functions of each one of the 26 jobs (from managers to order takers including waiters, barmen, pastrymakers, hostesses, etc.) within the section "Food and Beverages" and then continues with the rest of the sections defining in this way not only roles and functions but also the social networks of hierarchies and expectations in the labour hive).*

5 *See Lacan,* The seminar of "The Stolen Letter" *based on Edgar A. Poe's short story.*

greater the interest in its codes and in the recovery of their meaning.

In this way the traditional pomp and ostentation of religious and royal celebrations responded to meticulous organization and planning. Currently, the functions of protocol and ceremony are important to any self–respecting government. Rules may vary from one country to another; what we wish to emphasize is that they exist and that knowing them makes work easier, even if we decide not to respect them.

A conference is not exempted from all this.[6] There are rules and codes, which must be respected, going from the seating of participants to the way in which the meeting is organized, with its pauses and intermissions. There will be a President of the Session at the centre of the podium, a Secretary seated to his right, a *"rapporteur"*, delegates, advisors, observers and in some cases participants and members of the public.

Let us recall an example already mentioned where seating was important: the Vietnam peace negotiations. These were scheduled to begin in Paris in November 1968 but were delayed for three months because the participants could not agree on the *shape* of the discussion table. As Henry Kissinger pointed out in *The White House Years*:

> "This was not a trivial issue (...) By this proposal (of a four-sided table) Hanoi sought to use the beginnings of the negotiations to establish the National Liberation Front as an alternative government."

The language of the Conference must also be adapted to a certain ritual and a certain register. There are pre-established ways to ask for the floor or to grant it, begin an intervention or develop a subject; and the example here shows a profes-

---

6 *See an article by Eduardo Kahane. "La interpretación de Conferencias o el teatro como metáfora" in* Cuadernos Hispanoamericanos, *No 431, May, 1986.*

sional interpreter thoroughly complying with the ritual which the delegate apparently ignores but whose substance is in the end respected.

When we speak of rituals we speak of figures, background and forms. Form is significant in itself. Whoever organizes the forms, frames the action and consequently holds some of the threads of the interaction so framed – which may thus allow for pulling some of the strings. In this sense, knowledge of the forms helps interpreters to assess the substance and helps everyone to better understand what is at stake in the interaction. To know who finances the interaction may also be significant. Medical or Data Processing Congresses, meetings of experts in any field, political conferences are always organized and paid for by somebody. Knowing who is financing the event is sometimes fundamental for understanding the different forces at work.

Every society, however primitive it may seem, is governed by certain codified rules of conduct. It may seem surprising to Western observers how well defined and clear-cut the laws are governing social relations in some indigenous societies.

It may be interesting to observe that certain of the so called nomad "primitive societies" seem to have preserved their *social harmony* throughout the centuries better than some of the so called sedentary "developed societies". The latter have fostered and developed an astounding range of measurable elements of progress (scientific, educational, commercial, etc.) but often seem to suffer from a loss of harmony in the relationships among their members, on the one hand, and with the environment on the other.

Nomad societies, at least in my interpretation of the data found by some researchers,[7] seem to have guaranteed through certain rituals and codified ceremonies (like initiation ceremonies, for example) the preservation of certain constant human values even if they lack other types of modern developments. The preservation of an intangible web of harmonious relationships has perhaps enabled these hunters-collectors to compensate for the fact of being constantly on the move in search of food. The harmony some of these tribes seem to have preserved – at least for some time – could be compared to the harmony members of an orchestra or a ballet achieve on stage during their performance. (This in no way should be interpreted as a naïve attempt to go back to the "noble savage" theory, but rather as a conscious generalization which only attempts at integrating the seemingly contradictory values of different types of societies).

The complexity of some linguistic codes among some indigenous societies may come as a surprise to some. According to writer Lucio V. Mansilla,[8] Araucanians had three modes of speech: family speech, conversational speech and parliament speech. It is surprising to find that even the role of the interpreter was well defined among them, as related by Mansilla when describing his expedition.[9]

> "A lot of patience is needed, brother, to deal with the Ranqueles. I do not know if you have any idea of what a parley is in Christian lands; and I say Christian for things are different in Indian land. A parley is a diplomatic confer-

---

7 *Like Carlos Valiente Noailles and his studies of the Bushmen.*

8 *Lucio V. Mansilla (1833-1913) was an Argentine colonel and writer who knew both the refinement of Parisian life and the tough and rich experiences of interaction with some indian tribes in Argentina. He was sent to Cordoba to persuade the Ranqueles indians to leave the lands in that province. He summed up those experiences in an interesting book full of wit and humanism.*

9 *Lucio V. Mansilla,* Una excursión a los indios Ranqueles *(An Expedition to the Ranqueles Indians), Buenos Aires, Kapelusz, 1972.*

ence. The committee is announced by a "*lenguaraz*" (tongues man). If it is made up of twenty individuals all twenty will introduce themselves. They start by shaking hands with each other in order of hierarchy, and they place themselves, with considerable poise, on the chairs and sofas which have been offered. The "*lenguaraz*" or interpreter-secretary sits to the right of the man in the centre who is acting as chief. The chief speaks and the "*lenguaraz*" translates; but it should be remembered that, even in the cases where the plenipotentiary understands Spanish and speaks it fluently, the rule does not change."

The same happens nowadays at the highest levels when men of state, conscious of the political weight of their own language refuse to use other languages, at least officially. (As an example reported by the media, on March 23, 2006, French President Jacques Chirac left a meeting in Brussels when a French entrepreneur insisted on using English instead of French).

It proves somewhat curious to find today how some typical rules of behaviour of the most advanced societies do not differ much from some of the old uses and customs of some indigenous tribes in Latin America.

It would be useful to study how we infer the implicit rules which govern our behaviour in society from our acts.

From this point of view, accepting a role implies accepting certain rules. In democracy we are all equal before the law. Nevertheless, our relative social importance will depend, at any given moment, on the role we play.

It is worth noting that societies tend today to define better the different roles individuals can assume, and often encourage them to shift from one role to another as a way to acquire experience and training from different perspectives. A great flexibility of roles benefits society as a whole and gives individuals more opportunities to explore and develop their skills. It is not infrequent these days as part of the training of managers to make them take up different subordinate positions (as doorman or butler in the case of a hotel manager for example). Similarly, we sometimes hear of future lawyers, advertising agents or surgeons paying for their studies working as car washers, dishwashers or hotel night clerks. The more flexible a person, the more he or she can achieve – and this is true of societies, as well.

Discipline and flexibility seem to provide a good synthesis of figure and background, the good equation for balance between fixed rules and spontaneity, between protocol, ritual, "good manners" and creative freshness. Or to put it in a bigger macro framework – and in British sociologist Desmond Morris' words – "the success of any society largely depends on the balance it achieves between innovation and tradition".

The Ritual of Words

Just as we organize our actions into sequences, so we organize our words into formulas or linguistic rituals which may vary according to culture. Some cultures seem more aware of those sequences than others, which may explain their greater facility for telling – or inventing – stories and tales.

The repetition of certain words may constitute by itself a ritual in certain circumstances. We will go back to the example provided by Lucio V. Mansilla in *An Expedition to the Ranqueles Indians*[10] to see how the repetition of words functioned there as a ritual. It was not the meaning of the words but rather the repetition itself or the transformation of the sequence during the repetitions that created the melody, the rhythm, the structure and ultimately the situation itself.

"The galloping horses came to a sudden halt; there were no more than twenty steps between the group of Indians on the one side and Colonel Mansilla and his men on the other,

---

10 *Lucio V. Mansilla,* Una expedición a los indios ranqueles *(An Expedition to the Ranqueles Indians), Buenos Aires, Kapelusz, 1972.*

in this unexpected and dust covered face-to-face encounter in the middle of the desert".[11]

Two spokesmen, equally distant from their respective groups, one looking North and the other South, spoke in succession. Each spoke in Araucanian for approximately fifteen minutes. Mansilla asked Mora, his interpreter, to tell him what was going on. "Nothing – was the answer – they are simply greeting each other". "For Heaven's sake" – was Mansilla's reply – he spoke that much only to wish me good morning!"

Mora then explained that conversations during a "parlamento" were carefully codified and subject to very strict rules; the speakers could not interrupt each other and should respect the "question-answer" formula.

The statement or question: "Ask him what his trip was like yesterday" or "What condition are his horses in?" is called a "*razón*" (literally "reason"). The better the speaker, the larger the number of "reasons"; it is a question of conveying an idea in the largest possible number of sentences, changing the word order or the mode (active or passive). "In such fashion", adds Colonel Mansilla, "the speakers of the pampa excel in rhetoric as much as Molière's grammar teacher who, at the request of the Bourgeois Gentilhomme, wrote to a certain lady:

"*Madame, vos bels yeux me font mourir d'amour*" but, since his student was not happy with this, he changed it to "*Vos bels yeux, Madame, me font mourir d'amour*" and then "*D'amour me font, Madame, vos bels yeux mourir*" to finally

11 Idem

please the Bourgeois with "*me font mourir d'amour, vos bels yeux, Madame*".[12]

This kind of exchange was used in official visits among indians and its charm resided in the uniformity of intonation and the drawing out of the last syllable of the last word.

> Madam, your beautiful eyes kill me ... or Madam, your beautiful eyes make me die of love ...
>
> Your beautiful eyes, Madam, make me die of love ...
>
> Out of love, Madam, your beautiful eyes make me die...
>
> Out of love, your beautiful eyes, Madam, will make me die ...

"You cannot know – wrote Mansilla in his diary, imbued with the biases of his time – the degree to which these barbarians were funny and ceremonial."

A witness unaccustomed to a certain protocol in the General Assemblies of the United Nations might experience today the same feelings when listening to the delegate of a member country congratulate the chairman for his election when taking the floor for the first time: even if over a hundred delegates did so before, he may choose to repeat the formula. We wonder whether we are truly so far from the Araucanian ritual.

If most delegates respect the ritual, some these days do not, without this neces-

> Thank you, Mr Chairman, before starting my intervention on some of the important issues on our agenda, I would like to take this opportunity to congratulate you on your election to preside over the work of this Honourable Assembly and to tell you up to what point our delegation appreciates and welcomes your appointment and will gladly follow your orientation and your guidance during our debate ...

---

12 *In French in the original text. (Molière,* Le Bourgeois Gentilhomme, *Act II, Scene IV).*

sarily implying a lack of respect. Others exert their power through their thorough knowledge of silent codes.

Communication is framed by culture and custom. Every act of communication is inscribed in a ritual: the more day to day and familiar, the less easily the ritual element is perceived.

We normally have a choice: we can either respect rituals or ignore them. But we should at least be aware they exist.

Manipulation through Words and Ritual

According to the Oxford Advanced Learners' Dictionary, *ritual* is the series of actions used in a religious or some other ceremony; or the procedure regularly followed in precisely the same way each time. Ritual implies "systematic repetition", or repetition of patterns. Once familiar with the pattern, it proves easier for the interpreter – or for any human being – to concentrate on the changing elements within the pattern.

Protocol is defined as the system of rules governing formal occasions, e.g. meetings between governments, diplomats, etc.; official etiquette, where once again the concept of repetition is implied.

In a world of infinitely varying forms and ever-shifting perceptions, the stability of certain forms or patterns fosters and speeds up *understanding*. Our brain rapidly scans the whole in search of meaningful differences.

To manipulate, according to the same source, implies to control or handle something with skill; control or influence somebody cleverly or by unfair means.

Some people delight in formalities for their own sake and sometimes use them as devious means to their own ends. It is possible, for instance, to repeat certain formulas in an exaggerated manner so as "hypnotize" the audience, as it were, and shift the focus of the discussion. Repetition can produce reinforcement – a fundamental step in any learning process – but also drowsiness. Two different effects of the same phenomenon.

During an AGM (annual general meeting) I once was witness to a strange exchange: the newly elected president of the association took the floor to give his formal support to the proposal made by Mr. "X", its former president. While starting by openly stating his support, the newly appointed president went on pompously recalling all the titles and previous offices held by Mr. "X" and while apparently in admiration of his former achievements, he ended up reverting the contents of his proposal. While emphatically recalling Mr. X's achievements, the new president proved that he was deliberately torpedoing the former president's proposal by distracting the audience with unnecessary details. There was no *lapsus linguae* here, just sheer effrontery. The distorted proposal was passed. Mr. "X", aware of the dubious success and dishonesty of the manoeuvre, stood up and left the room. The most revealing thing for me in the communicational field was to realize that no one else seemed to have followed the exchange and understood what had happened; no one else, at least, reacted. Myself included.[13]

---

13 *There are times when leaving a place or a position appear as the only possible way of responding to a certain situation. Sometimes figure and ground, protocol and ritual, manners and codes leave a too small margin for action. During President Valery Giscard d'Estaing's state visit to Moscow in 1980, the Soviets invaded Afghanistan. The French president – a Soviet guest on the occasion – felt he could not openly criticize their action while being their guest. He thus decided to shorten his visit and return home.*
Once back in Paris, at a press conference, he explained his attitude as follows: "Comme je ne pouvais ni parler ni me taire, je suis parti". "As I couldn't either speak or keep silent, I left!"

The Wear and Tear of Rituals

On one occasion I was entrusted with the task of keeping the minutes of a meeting. I had the very strange feeling that I could complete my work long before the end of the discussion. Everything, or almost everything, seemed to be a foregone conclusion.

According to Watzlawick,[14] only one fifth of each communication is a true exchange of information; the rest is devoted to defining, confirming, rejecting or re-defining interpersonal relationships. The exchange may be even less informative when rituals take over and roles and situations are frozen. Communication is blocked.

The continued and repeated use of certain codes can end up eroding the exchange. As with certain family or personal situations, it becomes necessary then to reframe them or change the perspective so as to vitalize the forces at work.

Structures, background, figures and forms can get eroded or devoid of sense. Repetition can produce fatigue, boredom, absentmindedness.

Interpreters become used to distinguishing between different types of speakers. They recognize those who are almost rigid *rule and ritual followers* and distinguish them from those who are more likely *rule and ritual breakers*.

Would it be possible and ethical for an interpreter to exert some indirect subdued influence to favour a good negotiation? was the interesting question humanist and former NASA astrophysicist Stuart Jordan once asked me. The answer is yes. Through subtle changes in vocabulary or tone, an interpreter *could* facilitate a successful negotiation between one "rigid" speaker who wants material presented in a well defined format, and another who is more "loose" and who may even try to use "shock" tactics to get his way, recognizing a certain vul-

---

14 *See Paul Watzlawick,* How Real is Real? Communication, Disinformation, Confusion, *New York, Random House, 1976.*

nerability in his more rigid and possibly anxious counterpart across the table.

An interpreter *might* choose to contribute in the negotiating process by presenting the "rigid" speaker's position in a more informal way better attuned to the "loose" listener's style (probably enhancing his respect for his counterpart in the process) and the "loose" speaker's remarks more in conformity with accepted procedures (which might make his counterpart more comfortable). In some cases, interpreters do so without clearly realizing what they are doing, unaware of the subtle nuances involved. In other cases, they can choose to do so voluntarily and subtly facilitate the exchange. They could do the opposite, as well.

❖　　❖　　❖

CHAPTER **13**

Raising
the Curtain

Of the usefulness
of a scenario,
script, storyline
or plot.
Of how to
understand a
dialogue in "Checo",
a non-existing
language.
Emphasizing
the concept of
"whole".

After having referred to it a number of times, the moment has come to go directly into the theatrical world and reach some conclusions beyond the restricted field of interpretation itself.

Back in the seventies I enrolled in an actor's course in Buenos Aires, with well-known Austrian-born actress Hedy Crilla and Argentine director Julio Ordano. One of the many exercises we were asked to engage in was the "Checo" exercise. Like most of the other activities, this was directly inspired by the method applied by Stanislavski and his brilliant American successor, Lee Strasberg.

"Checo" was a language we had to invent which should resemble as little as possible any other known language. In fact, it was not even a language but simply a series of utterances of unintelligible sounds.[1]

Our drama instructor gave a clear description of the storyline (who, to whom, where, when and why) and a number of students began to improvise on stage. The rule of the game was that, at a given moment, another student would come on stage and carry out an action, known only to the actor and the director. This action, which would unleash a conflict, would take all the other actors by surprise. As from that moment, the "miracle" of communication in "Checo"

---

1 *This is what is technically known as "glossolalia", the history of which goes back to the Bible. Charisma of tongues or glossolalia (First Epistle to the Corinthians, 12,10) is to praise the Lord by uttering unintelligible sounds under the influence of the Holy Spirit and in a more or less ecstatic state. It is what Paul calls "to speak in tongues". This charisma goes back to the most primitive Church where it was the first discernible effect of the coming of the Spirit.*

often occurred. When it did, the future actors developed a cohesive sequence of actions and dialogue. Everything said on the stage was in "Checo" and even the audience managed to understand.

How is it possible to understand a message conveyed by a set of sounds, which have no separate meaning?

What can we learn from the following dialogue?

From the very outset we are tempted to answer "nothing".

> A – *Brumpt javist. Kapuntant air?*
>
> B – *Svausja marinue ile dumpt.*

But although the words seem unintelligible, our comprehension does not equal "zero": the transcription of this dialogue gives us a number of facts:

1. That there are two actors: "A" and "B";
2. That they are communicating verbally;
3. That "A" is asking a question, and
4. That "B" reacts to it.

In this linguistic "whole" – in this linguistic exchange – we have included not only the words but also the way they have been grouped and the speakers uttering them.

The "Checo" exercise was oral. In such circumstances even if the content of the "words" cannot be processed, it will always be possible to process intonation. Intonation is a carrier of meaning and it reveals not only individual feelings and moods but also relationships between the speakers. Important prosodic studies (initially, in English) have described the intonation patterns which accompany different emotions. It is true that beginners may find it difficult to recognize an intonation pattern in isolation and assign it to a certain mood (even if they constantly do so in everyday speech); but what they can do as a useful starting point is use a "reverse technique" and say, for instance, what emotions a particular intonation does not convey: indignation, anger, impatience, etc.

Stanislavski[2] uses the following anecdote to stress the importance of intonation. When hearing one of his friends speak enthusiastically about the wonderful performance of an actor during a poetry recital, he wanted to know which verses had moved him most. His friend answered he had no idea since he had not understood a single word, the poems having been recited in German. How can anyone be moved by words in an unknown language? "Because the spectator" – says Stanislavski– "is reached not only by the thoughts, impressions and images related to words but also by the colour and tone of the words, by their intonation, and by silences which complete what the words have left unexpressed. Intonations and pauses can, by themselves, cause a great impression on the listener".

In a situation of oral communication, the following indications might also have been gathered from our previous dialogue in "Checo" if it had been spoken and not written down:

5. That "A" is asking a question in a gentle tone, and
6. That "B" replies in an indifferent tone.

But "Checo" was not only an oral exercise; it was supposed to be acted: "A" and "B" were supposed, respectively, to be a man and a woman carrying out certain actions as part of their role. (*Visual perception is therefore added to auditory perception*). A café was represented on stage and "A" was obviously meant to be a waiter because he could be seen going, tray in hand, from the tables to the counter. "B" arrived a little later, sat at one of the tables and put down a stack of

---

2 *Stanislavski,* La construcción del personaje, *Madrid, Alianza Editorial, 1975, Page 170.*

books. "A" approached and in a correct but indifferent tone said:

> *– Brumkt javist. Kapuntant air?*

To which the woman (B) replied, almost absent-mindedly:

> *– Svaushja marinue il dumpt.*

There was no difficulty in understanding what was going on. We have all witnessed situations like these a thousand times:

– Good morning. What will you have?
– A cup of coffee, please.

As is also the case with "Who do you ... (noise   ) ... speak to?" where we can easily supply the missing words, *the perception of the whole often facilitates the perception of one of its parts. This means that when, by association, analogy or contrast, we manage to identify some of the elements of a situation, we can often work out or guess the meaning of the rest. The unknown is thus revealed by inference.*

It could be argued that no one listening to "Checo" can be dead sure that "B" had ordered coffee. It is true that she might just as well have ordered milk, tea or soda, or a bottle of wine. However, knowing the kind of beverage ordered does not have the slightest importance here, since it is not indispensable to understanding what comes next. Not being relevant, this information can remain in limbo. What is indeed indispensable is to know the context given by the storyline; that "B" has just come into the café and ordered something. (Needless to say, when the spectators see the cup of coffee, other possibilities are discarded automatically).

Inference

Linguistic barriers prevent us from understanding only *part* of what is going on.

Our powers of inference are evidenced by omission, and they are working *at full speed*.

Automatic Processes

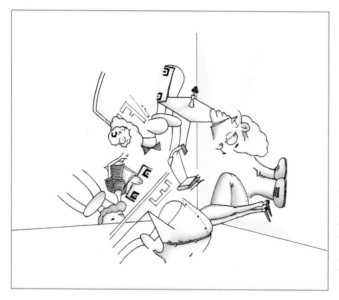

Our nervous systems provide us with "automatic structurings and organizations of the "world" we see and perceive around us.

In the same way, some complex processing of signals allows us to "automatically" infer a web of social relationships and power in our daily interactions.

If, after tasting the coffee, the young woman turns to the waiter and reprehends him:

> *– Kramptuchgaka topu zercofa, ham, pukt!*

we might conclude that the coffee was cold; that instead of black coffee she was given white coffee, which she hates; or that the waiter had confused the salt with the sugar. We could imagine different possibilites. But what we know for certain is:

1. "B" was angry.
2. She found the service wanting.
3. She blamed "A".

There are concrete data intertwined with hypotheses.

Now, if the waiter arrived with the coffee and, turning to the girl, said to her indignantly:

> *– Maritecomputi, kakaredo vouzian!*

we would certainly be nonplussed for there would be no action, gesture, look, or word to justify "A"´s tone and reaction. (The tone of voice is especially important. We cannot speak to just anybody as we please without provoking a reaction; tone of voice is a significant indication of the relationship between speakers)

This shows that *comprehension is not exclusively rooted in words, that it is not only linked to logic and reasoning as expressed through words but is also related – perhaps even predominantly so – to the logic and energy of actions …*

To convey her indignation to a patron at a neighbouring table, the young woman would certainly have used a different tone from the one she used with the waiter, whom she made at least partly responsible for the ill tasting coffee. In the same way, the unexpected reaction of the waiter is all the more surprising, considering waiters are supposed to be courteous to their patrons. The understanding of a situation also depends on a tacit awareness of an entire network of social laws.

Those influencing these actions were, explicitly:

1. You do not use an angry tone of voice without any apparent reason, and
2. It is expected of those waiting on other people to show courtesy and good manners.

All of which brings us back to the theory of wholes, in this case whole sets of characters and roles, plots, scenes and sequences. Our starting point was one of these instances of understanding, or perhaps we should say misunderstanding, due to breakdowns in the ritual. The "miracle" of communication in "Checo" led us to integrate speakers, their role, functions and relationships, their acts and the social laws governing them, their attitudes and their intonation patterns into the linguistic whole.

Once we have identified the social roles of the speakers and their relationships to one another, our knowledge of social rules will provide the silent framework of logical possibilities allowing us to generate hypotheses about the speakers' intentions. As we said (page 95) hypotheses about the speakers' intentions fit into what we may now call "scenario" (script, libretto, storyline or plot) after our incursions on stage. This larger framework would operate permanently to facilitate and hasten comprehension. There are not so many plots, as Borges once said. Basically, there is a restricted number of stereotyped scenarios with endless different nuances. Of the elements that make up a script, it is the linguistic one that is missing in the "Checo" exercise. It is often some of the other variables that are missing in everyday life. Here again it is also more difficult to detect how the "scenario" works since in "the fray" there is a bundle of hypotheses with confirmed data; the explicit information gets intertwined with information that can be implied, assumed or inferred. Only when a mistake occurs, do we perceive the functioning of these overlapping mental processes.

During a state banquet held at the presidential palace in Helsinki I had the honour, as an interpreter, to sit at a small presidential table between former Chancellor of the Federal Republic of Germany, Willy Brandt, and a former President of Venezuela. During a very pleasant after dinner conversation full of personal anecdotes, and after having stressed the exceptional virtues of the Finnish president, Brandt turned to me and asked me to tell the Venezuelan some of the salient facts about the Finnish President's life. My initial astonishment at such an unusual request was immediately overcome by the idea that, being in Helsinki, the former Chancellor must have thought I was Finnish and so would know the outstanding details of the president's life he wanted to recall. Building a hypothesis that was in accordance with his experience of similar situations, the former Chancellor had assigned the character I represented a Finnish nationality. (The fact that I was blonde and we were speaking English not Finnish also helped.) I would never have found this out if this request had not been made explicit. With an almost imperceptible gesture, I encouraged the former Chancellor to go ahead with the story himself and I limited myself to a very careful translation. A slight movement of my eyes was enough to make him understand that there was an error in his hypothesis. It was not wise to interrupt the conversation to let him know that I was Argentine; my gesture proved clearly enough – at least, I think – that I was not Finnish and that in all certainty I did not know the Finnish President's life as well as he did.

The silent dialogue between the Chancellor and myself made transparent the manner in which we "process" various kinds of information simultaneously, how we link information conveyed by a gesture, a look or a silence with other information explicitly mentioned before: we thus weave a "plot" of self-correcting hypotheses which eliminate one another, get modified, verified or cancelled as the conversation, the speech or interaction develops.

If implicatures showed that it is possible to say one thing and mean another, the "Checo" exercise showed that what is not understood linguistically can be deduced through a series of calculations based on the information available on the situation, the speakers, their relationship and the hypotheses drawn up concerning their intentions. The sound-carrying intonation reveals the mood and attitude of speakers and becomes a valuable instrument in order to detect relationships among them and the power allowed to them by their roles.

To understand a dialogue in "Checo", one must be physically present. Visual access is indispensable since the perception of sensorial indications must be optimized and account must be taken of the actions performed by the characters and their logical sequence. Quite evidently, "Checo" does not lend itself very well for philosophical disquisition and ranting.

Nor are there implied meanings in a conversation in "Checo" for what we call "implicatures" or "sub-texts" in normal conversation is all that is left in Checo and thus, paradoxically, becomes the explicit basis for understanding.

To visualize how the semantic effects of acts – and words – depend on the relationship between actors, let us for a second imagine Einstein arriving at a conference to which he has not been invited and where nobody knows him. During the debate, upon hearing the discussion of subjects which are dear to him and which he knows well, he insistently asks for the floor. When he finally manages to seize a microphone and explain his thesis, he is only met with indifference made worse by the impatience and scorn of the chairman presiding over the meeting. His theory might well be the same that earned him the Nobel Prize; the relationship between the forces present and the power so instated would have sufficed, in this case, to make a genius appear to be a madman.

In the same way we can visualize the hidden sides of a cube, by inference, we can also elaborate the elements missing in a stereotypical scenario based on previous experience, social norms and the logic of the action.

The concept of "scenario, plot, storyline or script" has allowed us to explain how and why we can infer the unknown, even when it is the linguistic variable itself.

Cracks in Scenarios

We can only smile at the idea of an interpreter seeking verbal confirmation for something as loud and clear as a declaration of war.

D´après a cartoon by French humorist Fez.

In most scenarios involving "declarations of war" there is no room for ambiguity: tension can almost be breathed, read in the eyes of others, guessed at in the tone or the exaggerated or repressed gestures of concern of the participants.

Striking a note of sympathy for the interpreter and a veiled criticism of certain forms of communication, the illustration sketches the opposite situation and in so doing makes us laugh.

It is true that it so happens that in some drafting committees it is possible to perceive certain delegates' deliberate intent on maintaining ambiguity in some statements: the more ambiguous the resolution or the recommendation, the easier it will be for everybody to find it acceptable. In the long run, though, there will be a greater risk of getting lost in a dense fog of words. The cost can be higher to pay than if things are clearly stated.

Ambiguity as a semantic effect may prove useful to immobilize your opponent by clouding his perceptions, as certain types of nerve gas do, paralyzing or postponing an adverse reaction. These effects are not, however, everlasting and so the day comes when things have to be called by their name. It is possible that, undermined by excessive use, words and certain mechanisms will no longer suffice to convey a clear message and if communication becomes imperative at such a stage, it will then function at its best through silence, gestures or acts.

❖   ❖   ❖

CHAPTER 14

The Standpoint of the Interpreter

Of his role.
Of the tacit "pact
of complicity"
between speaker
and interpreter.
Of its boundaries.
Ethics, submission,
freedom and
responsibility.
An interpreter's, a
psychoanalyst's and
an actor's approach
to speech.

Throughout the book parallels are drawn between interpreting, everyday language and the theatrical environment. There are, however, substantial differences between the work of an actor and that of an interpreter.

The actor learns his lines and discovers his character beforehand; on the basis of a complete, memorized script he will try to reconstruct an architecture of feelings and sensations. The actor delves within himself to find the "raw material" with which to mould his character in an environment delineated by the script as a whole and by his own role in it. He responds, from his own creation, to the creation of the other characters or counterparts in the different scenes of the play. On the basis of the playwright's script and following the director's instructions, actors work on their characters and they rehearse.

The interpreter often interprets – and this is perhaps the gist of his work – spontaneous off-the-cuff speeches. If speaking in public is daunting for many people, having to speak in public without even knowing what the speech will be about can be even more so. We have shown, nevertheless, that one of the tasks of the interpreter is precisely to formulate hypotheses concerning the participants, their objectives and the purpose of the meeting; from this point of view neither the substance nor the shape are – strictly speaking – chosen freely by the speaker or totally unknown to the interpreter. "The act of taking the floor is not free or gratuitous" as Ducrot[1] said, referring to the codes which implicitly rule social behaviour and which the interpreter (like any other speaker) knows and uses,

---

1 In Dire et ne pas dire, *Paris, Hermann, 1972. Page 8.*

"[The speaker] is not free in the sense that certain conditions must be satisfied in order to have the right to speak, and to speak in this or that fashion. It is not gratuitous in the sense that every word must be seen as motivated, as if in answer to certain needs or aiming at certain ends".

In this sense, only a psychoanalyst interprets spontaneous speech, where free associations – of thoughts and words – find or can find expression. "Free association" is, after all, the only prescription in therapy. The analyst needs not only a perfect command of his patient's language, but also a vast and deep knowledge encompassing myths, customs, general information and cultural references. These greatly facilitate the job of the interpreter and the actor as well.

One of the main differences between these professions is basically rooted in the fact that *an actor plays at making believe that he becomes somebody else* (when we see Sir Laurence Olivier as Hamlet or Gades as Don José in "*Carmen*", the actor is fulfilling his role), whereas *the interpreter only plays at making believe that he believes in what the speaker says*. He spontaneously places himself by his side and tries to look at things from his point of view: it is what we have called the "*pact of complicity*"[2] between speaker and interpreter.

Interpreters sometimes get passionately involved – or pretend they do – in mirroring the speakers. This is what happened to me once with a group of American journalists who had come to Buenos Aires to interview the presidential candidates just before the elections of March, 1973. Our first appointment was at the home of Ricardo Balbín, a politician well known for his

---

2 It is precisely the opposite, a "non complicity pact", which seals the agreement between the psychoanalysed and the psychoanalyst. It is precisely by not necessarily adopting the point of view of his patient and by not restricting himself to what the patient says, that the psychoanalyst will try to uncover the patient's unconscious thoughts, his hidden fears and beliefs. The psychoanalyst will mostly work on what his patient does not say, re-framing his patient's speech and interpreting his patient's words in accordance.

vehement opinions. I interpreted his speech *in consecutive* (he spoke for a moment, then stopped to let me translate). It was then the turn of the other candidates. Towards the end of the day some journalists came up to me to share their surprise: during their first interview they had quite candidly thought that I was a member of the party of the candidate being interviewed and only realized that this was not the case when getting the same impression during their second interview!

The vehemence and passion with which a speaker takes the floor depend not only on the issue and the situation, but also on the different personalities and cultures involved. I remember the disappointment expressed by certain Latin American delegates when listening to the English version of one their colleagues' Spanish speech on one occasion: they felt the words were there but the heart was not.

American actor Jack Lemmon once said during a television interview at the Actors' Studio that there are two basic approaches to acting: either the actor lets his character seize him completely or he stays in command of his character. Jack Lemmon preferred the second approach. Thus, he could be telling jokes and having fun with colleagues, be summoned to the set for a dramatic scene and play it marvellously without transition, pause or preparation. Once it was over, he would become his old carefree self again. Had he been submerged in or consumed by the tragedy of his character, he would have had to do something to snap out of the mood before going back to telling jokes.

Something similar may happen while interpreting. Where interpreters identify too closely with the speaker, they need to get rid of any remaining energy from the speaker before leaving the booth. If their style is more detached, however, and they remain in command of the situation, greater serenity is possible and interpreters will find it easier to return to normal after work.

At first sight, the role of the interpreter seems easy to define. Interpreters allow people of different languages, cultures and civilizations to communicate. *Their task is to find equivalence in difference and to connect separate worlds.* This creative work is always subject, however, to strong constraints: the only aim of any liberties taken by the interpreter is to be faithful to the speaker. Liberty? Yes. But above all, submission. We are here confronted with a first paradox.

The more the interpreter enters the speaker's *world* and understands the speaker's *mission*, purpose and intent, the more easily the interpreter will accept *submission* to the speaker and – paradoxically – the more liberties the interpreter will take. Understanding and acceptance favour submission if purposes are clearly understood.

Seated at the negotiating table, to the right of a Head of State, with the lucidity needed to understand and explain the options available, the interpreter learns to negotiate, but the interpreter can never take the president's place, not even for an instant. The interpreter's share of the limelight next to the powerful and the famous is short-lived and he or she will fade into the background as soon as the performance is over.

Although they carry a rich baggage of experience and knowledge of international relations,[3] interpreters are seldom asked for an opinion. Their role takes them, paradoxically, from the spotlight to backstage in the twinkling of an eye.

The better the interpreter's work is, the less his listeners notice his job and its complexity. Or, as an officer of the United Nations liked to say,

"Interpretation was excellent today since we did not realize it was going on".

Having said this, and keeping in mind the sociological classification made by E. Goffman in *The Presentation of Self in*

---

3 *The appointment of Quai D'Orsay French interpreter, Brigitte Sauzay, as advisor on French matters to the German Chancellor shows perhaps the beginnings of a new trend.*

Everyday Life,[4] we would be tempted to place interpreters, as servants, in the category of *non–persons*.

> "It is expected of these persons that they be present in the central spot while the host is being hospitable to the guests of the establishment. Even though, in a certain sense, the servant is part of the host's team, he is defined in other cases both by the main characters and the other participants as somebody who is not present, like children, the very old and the sick".

What is paradoxical in this situation is that if servants, children, older persons and the sick are considered "non persons", it is because they are denied the right to speak or because there is great reluctance to give serious consideration to what they say; whereas the function which defines the work of the interpreter is precisely speech, one of the most specific human activities. It must be admitted, however, that even though it is true that interpreters have the *right* to speak (we could even say, the "*duty*") what they say is taken seriously only during the meeting, interview, negotiation or conference – in other words, when speaking on behalf of somebody else. This indispensable mediator in the communication process can only act as a proxy.

Interpreters' role is exceptional in that they travel the world moving from one environment to another, from a technical congress to a political meeting or a scientific colloquium. Even more exceptional is the way in which they handle the "I" and the "you" in the same act of enunciation. It would be difficult to find a parallel, however hard one tried. A number of speakers may follow one another in quick succession; the same interpreter will use the *same* word "I"

---

4 E. Goffman, The Presentation of Self in Everyday Life, *Great Britain, Pelican Books, 1978. Page et seq.*

to refer in each case to someone *different* who is never the interpreter.

This rapid shift from role to role may also facilitate a letting-go, a certain distancing from people and events, which helps the interpreter to display great composure. This reminds me of a German colleague, Professor Heinz Göhring who used to talk about the interpreter's serenity, calmness and growing capacity over the years to view things with equanimity. This would correspond to the second option in drama (as described by Jack Lemmon), that is, when the interpreter (or the actor) does not wholly identify himself with the speaker (or character).

The interpreter can also interrupt the thread of the enunciation, make an aside, take distance from the speaker and make his own presence more visible in other ways by saying into an open microphone, for example, "the President adds" or "he is now thanking us, the interpreters, for the work we have done".

Even when working "in consecutive" – that is, not in the booth but next to the speaker and taking the floor after him from time to time – professional interpreters will stick to the first person and use "I" as if they were the speaker himself.

In my thirty years as a professional interpreter only once was I not able to speak in the first person. To have done so would have been to deny my own existence. I was engaged to interpret the interview between a journalist of a well-known American newspaper and a high ranking officer of the Argentine government. The newspaperman, who was in fact one of the main editors of *The New York Times* on a good-will visit to the newly elected Peronist government in the early 70's, had explained to me the reasons and purpose of his visit. During our tremendously long wait in an anteroom, we amused ourselves by looking at some newspapers lying on a small table. On the front page of one of them something caught my eye: an article directly linked to the subject of the journalist's visit. When the journalist heard this, he grew extremely interested in all the details and asked me to give him a careful sight translation. When we were finally conducted into the minister's office, the pressman waited till practically the end of his interview to take up the subject of the story in the paper, and he did so almost as if in passing.

I was very young in those days and I was amazed to see the officer show surprise and *deny* not only the content but even *the fact* than an article of that nature had appeared in the newspaper at all! He could not of course know that only an hour earlier I myself had translated the item published on the front page of *La Nación*, one of the most prestigious newspapers in Buenos Aires. When my work was over, I realized that when the officer *told his lie*, not only did I abruptly *abandon the first person singular* but I also took all the necessary precautions to safeguard my integrity, stating repeatedly: "The Minister of the Interior says that ..." I also realized that in proceeding so, my message was twofold: the newspaperman could follow the discussion through my interpretation but he was also getting strong *alarm signals*: the slight change introduced in my speech *underscored the Minister's lie*.

The problems of truth and deceit are not especially easy to deal with as we become aware of the diversity of perceptions, perspectives, and interests in discourse. But there were no relative points of view to consider here. The minister did not criticize a position, reject an idea or question an opinion; he simply denied the existence of something we had seen with our own eyes. This was quite a unique case since I had previously had to translate the same article whose existence would later be denied. To a certain extent, I was being caught up in a somewhat schizophrenic situation where I had revealed something I was supposed to deny with similar conviction. The issue here has not to do with interpretation, opinions or ideologies of any kind. It has to do with *sanity* and with our *responsibility* as speakers. In such a case, it seems to me, we find the ethical boundaries of the "pact of complicity" between speaker and interpreter.

Personal Responsibility and Ethics

Interpreters are, of course, bound to secrecy. According to the AIIC[5] code of professional ethics: "members of the Association shall be bound by the strictest secrecy, which must be observed towards all persons and with regard to all information disclosed in the course of the practice of the profession at any gathering not open to the public". This rule of confidentiality lies at the very basis of the profession and professional interpreters make of it a question of honour[6] as I do myself.

I feel, though, that the exceptional characteristics of the previous case justify – thirty years later – this breach of silence. The open attempt at deceit plus the need to preserve my own integrity put limits on my responsibility as an interpreter. It is my responsibility as a human being that is in question here beyond my responsibility as an interpreter. At crucial moments in our lives, inherited rules and codes of ethics that govern most of our actions and interactions to ensure a civilized existence must sometimes give way at particular cross-roads of our private lives so that we may, in a spirit of absolute freedom, assume our own personal responsibility in a given situation.

What the Minister of the Interior was denying was not an inference or an assumption, it was a *fact*. He took his collaborators as witnesses asking for their approval and confirmation. They nodded in consent. The Minister's implied belief seems

---

5 *In an independent and global activity like interpreting, in which most professionals work free-lance, belonging to an invisible network of relations with shared standards and rules has been fundamental for interpreters and their clients. It proved fundamental even when the rules to be applied the world over were normally defined by a small group of people in the so-called "first world". Since societies and markets and conditions differ, some of these universal rules are today being questioned.*

6 *Nevertheless, in certain sensitive areas, like defence or intelligence, this is not enough and ministries or agencies accept only permanent interpreters of their own country and demand certain special clearance tests.*

to have been that his verbal denial sufficed to disintegrate physical evidence.

Since "I" deny "it", "it" does not exist.

This seems to reveal another hidden belief:

Since "I" am in power (as minister)" I" have more power than others, consequently my word (ensuring my will/wish/whim) has greater authority and will prevail …

Under several layers of analyses, a hidden "double bind" seems to emerge. How does this officer exert power? The government he belongs to, his political party and his political interventions emphasize the need for *democracy for all*, defending people's rights, and helping the less favoured in society. How can he reconcile those ideas with the manner in which he speaks, which seems to hamper people's *first* right: the right to their own perceptions? How could he pretend to believe in *equal rights for all* when the language he used showed that he used language to exert power at his discretion?[7]

This is quite an exceptional case; one in which both the limits of the situation and the rules are clear.

The fact that the interpreter must listen and speak at the same time makes him a much more attentive and sensitive receiver than others.

Normally, whether the interpreter agrees or not with the speaker's position, it is clear that he must be faithful to it and respect the speaker's point of view. It sometimes happens, though, "in simultaneous" that the interpreter switches his microphone off to make some marginal comments to his colleague in the booth, as if he needed to express his own thoughts out loud to somebody. It can indeed be quite unpleasant to have to do some speeches in the first person. Here is where taking distance may be helpful to avoid identification. When working in totalitarian regimes, Western interpreters often

---

7 *This example shows a clear case of what general-semanticists call "the allness disease". See Irving Lee,* Handling barriers in communication, *New York, Harper and Row, 1956.*

take geographical distance and interrupt their stay for a few days just to "breathe some fresh air" for a while.

There are situations when the interpreter feels fascinated by the originality of certain outlooks, the meticulous descriptions of certain processes, or by the flexibility and negotiating ability of certain speakers. There are cases where the interpreter feels moved by the magic blend of ideas, emotions and sensations some speakers are able to produce or by the truthfulness of certain attitudes. There may be other situations, though, in which gaps in an argument, muddled reasoning or faulty rhetoric make the interpreter *feel* the speaker's insincerity or insanity. Let us imagine for a moment having to interpret Hitler or Stalin.

There are yet more paradoxes. If the version of a professional interpreter becomes the lens through which the public gets to see the speaker clearly, the version of an amateur may cloud the view or make it opaque or blurry. But professionals may find themselves at times confronted with a paradox. If the interpreter is faithful to the speaker and translates what is said the way it is said, the translation can magnify and worsen the inconsistencies of the speaker. This may, in turn, put the interpreter at risk: because of their respective status, it is the interpreter (and not the speaker) who will be suspected first of talking nonsense. The assessment of the situation in each case and the trust placed in the interpreter by his employers will help him decide what to do. (Let us remark, in passing, that the discerning listener will detect a slight tone of irritation in the voice of the interpreter when he feels forced to correct the speaker too often).

During a conference in which the participants ended up proving that rather than working *for* a cause, they were working *against* one, I questioned my role. However modest my participation, I became aware of my own responsibility in the flow of the exchange. I then realized that if the objective of interpretation is to allow communication, this objective entails, at least to me, a still more ambitious one: make people communicate so that they *understand* one another. This does not mean that they must necessarily end up agreeing; but certainly each should be able to grasp where the others stand.

No interpreter is obliged to accept a contract. It is interesting to observe that one can *feel* different interpreting the *same* Head of State in the context of a United Nations conference and in the context of a meeting organized by the country itself – especially if the Head of State does not preside over an open democratic society. It may feel different, for example, to interpret President Khadafi at a United Nations Conference or at a meeting in Tripoli organized by the Libyan government. Knowing *who* organizes the conference, and who ends up paying the bill may be important factors to take into account before accepting a contract.

The interpreter can also help break the ice and establish a good relationship; he can give confidence to the shy visitor coming from far and ease communication between people from different environments, cultures or civilizations by explaining some tacit codes of behaviour. As Fernando Savater reminds us in the book he addressed to his son,[8] unwritten "hospitality" laws have formed a part of ethics in all parts of the world and at every period in history: to show hospitality to those in need (as hosts do when they welcome visitors) is a sign of humanity.

One advantage of being an interpreter is the possibility of continuing to learn throughout one's professional life. Another is the satisfaction of feeling useful when a real transfer of knowledge takes place, for example, between surgeons, professors or researchers and their disciples and public.

Grasping the importance of information and learning to be respectful and tactful is also part of the interpreter's job.

From this perspective, skilful interpreters may contribute to conflict resolution or favour cross-cultural developments and fertilizations through their rendering of what is said. Some interpreters have contributed to humanistic professions of re-

8 *Fernando Savater,* Ética para Amador, *Barcelona, Editorial Aula, 2004.*

cent development such as intercultural coaching for example. Beyond differences of cultures, positions and viewpoints they seek to establish step by step a common ground for *understanding*.

If, as Grice says, "speaking is an essentially rational activity", if the standpoint of the interpreter is the rational-emotional mesh underlying speech and its effects, the choice of this profession seems to be *an act of faith* in *the rational and emotional capacity of man*, two abilities that, crossing the barriers of language and culture, should throw wide open the doors to human understanding – and creative evolution.

❖   ❖   ❖

Borrowing from other Disciplines To
Explain its Functioning

"The real voyage of discovery consists not in seeking new landscapes, but in having new eyes."

Marcel Proust

Part III

HOW SIMULTANEOUS INTERPRETING WORKS

In the previous section, we made some comparisons and drew some preliminary conclusions and strategies.

In Part III, I will go on establishing comparisons but on a larger scale. I will take some of the examples from the interpreters' world and will compare them to some experiments led by psychologists and psycholinguists; I will take others and compare them to some experiences in the theatre world; and then I will dare plunge into that "difficult to grasp" sphere of interferences and *lapsus linguae*. In a world where variations seem endless, I will look for invariants.

CHAPTER 15

Tying up
Loose Ends

*Of how interpreters
do, in a condensed
fashion, what
speakers do when
they speak.
Four conclusions
on perceptual
integration.
Four conclusions
on the conscious
and subconscious
nature of perception.
Could speaking and
seeing be intimately
related?*

The approach adopted by psychologists and psycholinguists to language and speech production processes is quite different from that used by interpreters. The itinerary along these pages does, however, allow me to come to similar conclusions, although following different paths.

Indeed, introspection and observation led me to detect one of the simplest strategies used by interpreters: generalization (see page 173). In the same way, the results of an experiment conducted by Guy Denhière,[1] who studied the way children 6 to 12 years old recalled a simple story, pointed to a similar strategy leading to a loss of specificity. The children often simplified sentences such as "the giant uprooted the oaks ... and balanced them on his shoulders" during recall, using *lexemes* * which are more general than those of the story. Thus, "the giant uprooted the oaks ... and balanced them on his shoulders" became "the giant took the trees ... and put them on his back". The rigorously controlled results of this experiment coincide with those obtained by introspection and direct observation. We can infer from this that we find ourselves in *the presence of one of the general principles in conversation* or any type of exchange: when confronted with obstacles, we climb a step up towards generalization.[2] This, in turn, confirms Arnheim's principle[3] according to which perceiving (seeing, hearing) is to go into an abstraction, for it consists

---

1 *Guy Denhière.* Le rappel d'un récit par des enfants de 6 à 12 ans, *January 1978. Document 97, Université de Paris VIII. Laboratoire de Psychologie.*

2 *It goes without saying that only exceptionally in cases of need will the interpreter use this strategy. Otherwise, he would wind up saying things such as: "The device of the instrument is inside the machine", but he would not long survive as a professional.*

3 *In* El pensamiento visual, *Editorial Universitaria de Buenos Aires, 1971. Page 65.*

more of obtaining structural features than registering details in an undifferentiated manner.

Denhière also found that when the children were asked to retell the story they had heard, they tended to fill in the gaps. And the propositions they added corresponded exactly to those required to interpret the basic text and extract a coherent macro-structure. The frequence of propositions such as "the giant swallowed the boat" and "the giant carried the firewood" which did not appear in the story clearly showed that the children tended to build the necessary links between the actions and the main events in the story line.

The example "that was *exactly* what I wanted to hear" (see page 92) shows that the interpreter had understood the dialogues and the facts, and that he had successfully chained them together, but unlike the children in the experiment, the interpreter *knew that he should not make explicit what was implicit* if he wanted to remain faithful to the words of the speaker. We can deduce another *general principle of conversation* valid for any type of exchange: *we automatically forge the links needed to join different elements.*

"The lion from its paws."

J.L. Borges.

"The consummation of the incomplete is one of the fundamental acquisitions of intelligent behaviour."[4]

Just as we can infer the hidden sides of a cube, we can also infer the "invisible" or hidden elements in a speech. But the interpreter needs to make sure that he passes on only those elements which the speaker decided to make explicit, maintaining hidden those which the speaker chose to hide.

The phenomenon of differentiated retention of "nuclear" and "secondary" (or modifier) elements is amply established

4 *See Merleau-Ponty,* Fenomenología de la percepción, *México, Fondo de Cultura Económica, 1957.*

in psycholinguistics.[5] It has been shown that the probability of retention (and reproduction) is higher for nouns and verbs than for adjectives and adverbs.[6] Seguí and his collaborators suggested that such results are linked to perceptive integration processes implemented by the subjects.

These processes entail a selection of words in the light of their potential function, determined by the grammatical category on the one hand and by context on the other.

Similarly, an analysis of a professional interpreter's delivery when he is forced to follow abrupt accelerations in the rate of speech of a speaker will show that the first things he gets rid of, when delivery becomes too fast, is adjectives, adverbs, subordinates or any other secondary element.

This shows that there is a selection of the information which takes place at the very moment of reception and that said selection obeys laws of logic which do not necessarily fall within purely linguistic limits. (See example: "Let us say 11... eh ... that can print 11 inch pages". Page 111.)

What remains to be determined is how, in real time during oral reception, an interpreter knows how to decide the *relative importance* of an element or a sentence without an awareness of the overall direction of the speech he is translating. The answer given by Denhière concerning the readers of a text seems perfectly appropriate:

"Because such elements must certainly be codified in a privileged way and because there may be indicators on the surface pointing to the presence of important information."[7]

---

5 See J.Seguí, J. Domergues, U.Fraunfelder, J. Mehler, L' intégration perceptive des phrases, Bulletin de Psychologie.

6 See Forster et Ryder (1971), Holmes et Foster (1972), and Mehler, Seguí, Pittet et Barrière (1978).

7 See Joel Pinte et Guy Denhière, Influence de la thématisation et du statut syntaxique des propositions sur les temps de lecture et de la mémorisation de récits, 1980.

We can draw from all this a number of conclusions:

> **1.** There are processes of perceptual integration that are set in motion by any type of exchange;
> **2.** The object is perceived as an organized whole and not as a kind of accrual of varied elements;
> **3.** How the elements are integrated is in itself an expression of how they have been given hierarchy, and
> **4.** Our perceptual apparatus detects indicators emphasizing certain aspects of information, whether linguistic or of another kind.

At the end of chapter 12 we agreed with Grice when he says that speaking is an eminently rational activity. Nevertheless, we know very well that communication is far from being wholly rational or even controlled. It is precisely why a study of the difference between automatic and controlled processes is one of the subjects of most interest for research by psychologists and psycholinguists at the present time. Some experiments have shown there are processes that are triggered much too fast for the subject to control them, direct them, avoid them or even perceive them.

In this way, if you flash the word **"table"** on a screen for an extremely short period of time (30 milliseconds) most people will not recognize it but they will take less, soon after, to identify the word **"chair"** than the word **"flower"**. *This proves the existence of a contextual semantic connection, which is automatic and operates* per se *independently of our will.* The work of psychologists and psycholinguists normally stops at this finding.

But this experiment also poses the problem of perceptive functioning, not only in what pertains to linguistic perception but also in what pertains to perception at large, for the subjects *have seen something without realizing that they have.* The only thing they thought they had seen was a blur, transient and unclear; subsequent behaviour demonstrated, however, the contrary.

Merleau-Ponty mentions a similar experiment[8] in which the word "heat" is shown to a subject for so short a time that he cannot decipher it but admits to a "hot" feeling immediately afterwards. In both cases the spontaneous reaction of the individuals indicates that they had unknowingly identified the word and that such identification had unleashed a movement within themselves. *The existence of that movement proves the existence of a subconscious act of perception.* The study of automatic phenomena brings up then the problem of perception.

This experiment takes us back to the "*phi*" phenomenon: two lights, which go on and off in sequence will be perceived as just one moving light. In other words, given a space, a distance between the observer and two observed objets, "A" and "B", given a certain distance between them and a certain time between two actions (the turning on and off of the two lights) of a specific duration, the space-time-action relationship transforms the final perceptive result in the observer who will not perceive the isolated flashes but rather a movement integrating them.

Movement implies displacement in space. For there to be movement there must be an object, a background and an observer. We can then perceive movement in any of the three following cases:

• When the background is moving in relation to the object.

• When the object is moving in relation to the backdrop.

• When the observer is moving in relation to both.

---

8 *In* Fenomenología de la Percepción, *México, Fondo de Cultura Económica, 1957. Page 259. Quoted by Aldous Huxely in* The Art of Seeing, *London, Chatto and Winds, 1977. Pages 30 and 31.*

Ribot[9] said:

"Movements are the fundamental condition of cognition for they are the instrument of the law of consciousness, of relativity and change".

We can therefore say – and this will be our first conclusion – that *without movement there is no perception*.

In addition to the existence of an automatic contextual semantic link, this experiment shows that:

1. Mental activity/cognition is far from being totally conscious.
2. Consciousness is instated in a space-time continuum, shortcuts to which are known to the subconscious which often jumps ahead at the speed of lightning.
3. The subconscious works at speeds much greater than what can be handled consciously.
4. Consciousness integrates into an organized "whole" the elements which it cannot otherwise detect separately.

By tying up some of my observations with some experiments in psychology and psycholinguistics I arrived at two general principles of conversation and at some conclusions which go beyond the exclusive field of linguistics and cover perceptual processes in general. My approach has posed, implicitly, an association between the perceptual infrastructure of different senses. *The mechanisms brought into play to understand what we see and what we hear seem analogous.* Were

---

9 *Th.Ribot*, La vie inconsciente et les mouvements, *Paris, Alcan, 1914.*

this so, it would be by far, the most important conclusion of all.

The integration of elements into hierarchical and structured groups just "happens" as a whole. *To see*, according to Arnheim, is to dominate the simultaneous multiplicities.[10] So is *hearing* what somebody says and understanding it. If *seeing* is a way of structuring the environment, *speaking* is also a way of organizing the world around.

Words And Looks

The empty space does not stop us from seeing a square. In the same way, in

"**Who do you** ... (noise   ) ... **speak to?**"

the missing words do not stop us from getting the full sense of the sentence.

We cannot make much of what "A" and "B" are saying but we can infer that two people are trying to communicate verbally:

> A: *Kapuntksdot midr.*
> B: *Traputonka.*

Exercises "in Checo" had shown that when, through association or analogy, we can identify various elements of a given "whole" with previously known elements, it becomes

---

10 El pensamiento visual, *Editorial Universitaria de Buenos Aires, 1971.*

possible to find out the unknown elements through deduction or inference.

There is not much to see, but Charlie Chaplin comes to mind.

A "whole" or "meaningful unit" can be structured at different levels and can have varying degrees of complexity. Nevertheless, the principle of completion of the incomplete is applicable everywhere, both to what is seen and to what is heard.

In the case of a cube, only three sides are visible but we infer the presence of the other three because we *know* that a cube has six sides.

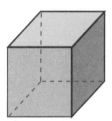

In the same way, we know that the armchair continues beyond the table and that the cabinet begins behind it because of a simultaneous spacial adjustment (as a result of a number of non-voluntary calculations and perceptual adjustments regarding *space* and *position*). To predict the course of an automobile travelling at high speed, we should also include some *temporal* adjustments.

We might add that *understanding* is the integration of simultaneous multiplicities. The processes of perception used for understanding seem similar to those at work in seeing. Seeing is a way of structuring the environment as much as speaking is a way of structuring "reality". Would this mean that some mechanisms at work while *seeing* and while *speaking* may have a common root?

A tacit law seems to compel the interpreter to reproduce only those facets of speech which the speaker decides to share explicitly with his listeners even if the interpreter also needs to reconstruct the hidden facets in order to understand. An interpreter's competence involves drawing a very fine distinction between the different kinds of implied and contextual information, between the lines boldly drawn of a cube, and the invisible one indicated by dots, or projected in the shadings.

Perceptual processes at work for understanding speech seem similar to those at work for seeing.

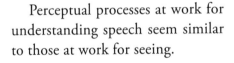

The ways our nervous sytems process information seem to be similar, whether the signals are visual or auditory.

Chain Reaction

For a long time now, psychologists have been trying to detect how lexical access functions during sentence comprehension. They have designed experiments during which they place subjects in front of television screens where words or strings of letters appear while the subjects listen to a given sentence through earphones. It is the access to one word in the sentence psychologists aim at evaluating through the response times elapsed when subjects are asked to recognize other related or unrelated words on the screen. They have thus proved the existence of *semantic priming* or automatic contextual reactivation processes of associated words, for example, which can be defined as the phenomenon by which presentation of a word reduces response time for a semantically-related word.[1]

The results of an experiment conducted by J. Seguí in the laboratory for experimental psychology at France's National Centre for Scientific Research (CNRS) seem especially interesting. An experiment was carried out in which a number of subjects were asked to look at a television screen at the same time as they heard some sentences through their earphones. Their task consisted in identifying as quickly as possible words appearing on the screen. In French one of the examples chosen was *"la fillette est entrée dans la boulangerie pour acheter una glace pour sa maman"* where attention was focused on the ambiguity of the word *"glace"* with its two possible meanings in French: **ice-cream** and **mirror**. When, before the end of the sentence, the words *sorbet* or *miroir* flashed on the

The little girl entered the bakery to buy an ice-cream for her mother.

---

1 See also Swinney, David. *Lexical Access during Sentence Comprehension. Consideration of Context Effects, in* Journal of Verbal Learning and Verbal Behaviour. *Academic Press, 1979.*

We could use the following sentence as a comparative example in English:

"The young lady went into the optician's to buy some glasses for her mother."

Attention should be focused on the word *glasses* with its two possible meanings: *eyeglasses* or *tumblers*.

screen coinciding with the audition of the word "*glace*" over the earphones, the results showed that the time needed for identification was shorter than for any of the other words appearing on the screen. When the subjects heard the word after having heard the entire sentence, only the term "*sorbet*" was more easily recognized.

This proves the existence of an *automatic process* of *semantic facilitation* – or semantic priming – and demonstrates that the process of contextual facilitation, also automatic, happens only after the first stages of the processing of the target word. However, what is most amazing in this experiment is that it proves that when hearing the word "*glace*" – and in just a few milliseconds – not only the meaning demanded by the context appears as the only one we are aware of but that others also do (in this case "*miroir*"). This automatic reactivation of the semantic network is of very short duration, since a few milliseconds later – after hearing the end of the sentence "*pour sa maman*" – the subjects will only retain the sole meaning fitting the context.

A perfectly legitimate inference from all the above is that the mere hearing of a word permanently activates its semantic network, *without our being aware of it,* and drops it immediately after at the bottom of our subconscious with the exception of the single and sole meaning required by the context. If this is true at the level of words, it is plausible to think of analogical operations at the level of *phonemes**, *morphemes** and groups of *lexemes**.

There would be, at least, two different kinds of networks activated then with each word: the contextual semantic network – or priming (like **tree** → plant, flower, birds, etc.) – and the semantic network of the word itself embracing different referents or meanings (**bank** → financial institution; → slope by the river).

We could even go as far as to say, taking up again the old image created by Freud,[2] that upon hearing a word, some elements start moving in the huge anteroom of the unconscious

---

2 *In* Introduction à la Psychanalyse, *Paris, Payot, 1982. Page 276.*

to place themselves in the first ranks (pre-consciousness) on the threshold of the great hall of consciousness.

This is of special interest when considering that in chapter 6 (page 131) in an effort to explain the mistake made by the interpreter, we had formulated the hypothesis which says that when he did not hear the sound /l/ in the word *"plein"* in *"lorsque l'ordinateur fonctionne à plein temps"*, the interpreter had implicitly reactivated the web of French phonemes that could occupy that sound position. Phonemes such as /b/, /v/, /s/, /d/. /f/, /g/, /z/ and /p/, etc., that cannot occupy that place in French were immediately discarded. The only ones left were:

when computers work full time.

a p	↓ j	ɛ̃ t ɑ
a p	w	ɛ̃ t ɑ
a p	R	ɛ̃ t ɑ
	↑	

Since /r/ was the only one to offer the possibility of a meaningful combination, he ended up changing /a/ for /o/ and interpreting *"lorsque l'ordinateur fonctionne au printemps"*. We had taken for granted that it was merely a tentative explanation of what could happen in such cases for, since no one would consciously make such a choice, we were left with the impossibility of verifying our hypotheses. But the results of the experiment we have just described give them additional strength by pointing in the same direction.

when computers work in springtime.

In that same chapter we had demonstrated that the understanding of speech is made easier by the *parallel functioning of the diachronic axis* which recalls data announced a few seconds (or years) back and the *synchronic axis* which facilitates the functioning of all our senses at the same time. This functioning is often spontaneous but it can be detected and controlled at will (this being precisely one of the abilities of interpreters). We can also perceive here an extremely subtle double movement in the orientation of our attention: along the diachronic axis, it is drawn "inside"; along the synchronic axis, we pay attention "outside".

But the result of the experiments described by Seguí strengthens our hypothesis about the functioning of two other axes operating below the threshold of our will and at a number of levels.

The automatic operation of the two axes probably offered, at lightning speed, a plausible solution (*"au printemps"*) to the interpreter who had not heard *"à plein temps"*. The inclusion or non-inclusion of *"au printemps"* in the computing context should already have been part of the conscious handling of the two axes. This is what failed. We find here again the difference sought by psychologists and psycholinguists between automatic and controlled processes. (Even if the interpreter had found *automatically* a potentially correct option, he should have *consciously* rejected it).

springtime
full time

We have thus found a new set of axes whose functioning is automatic and which always function without our control. In order to distinguish them from the first pair we will call them: *paradigmatic** and *syntagmatic**. They overlap the controlled or controllable functioning of the other two axes, the simultaneous and successive ones.

Each element in a group announces more than it contains. In the same way, as Gestalt theory states, a particular aspect of an object relates back to others adjacent or underlying. Each phoneme, each morpheme, each word or group of words would also remit to others, also adjacent or underlying. These referrals are multiple in character but they must be governed or articulated by certain laws. According to Ribot:[3]

> "The typical mechanism of mental life is the "continual coming and going of internal events, in a sort of parade of sensations, feelings, ideas and images which are mutually at-

---

3 Th. Ribot, Psychologie de l'attention, *Paris, Felix Alcan, 1916. Page 5.*

tracted or repelled according to certain laws. It is not a chain or a series but rather an irradiation in many directions and at various layers, a movable aggregate which is constantly made, undone and remade".

Let us now take a word at random – "disc", for instance – and examine the network of semantic associations it evokes and their levels of organization.

Perhaps what first comes to mind today is a flat circular plate coated with a magnetic material on which information (audio, images or text) can be stored in a form that can be used by a computer. We think of CD's, CD ROM's, hard discs, floppy discs, etc. Only then, perhaps, do we think of the layer of cartilage between the vertebrae in the spine; of a round and apparently flat surface, like the moon seen from afar, of the flat plate in brakes, etc. This is a chain of associations by similarity. If we deepen the analysis we shall see that to the extent it is a round and flat object which allows the recording of voices and sounds, *disc* is opposed to other recording media like tapes and cassettes. And a *compact music disc*, a flat and circular object for voice recording is opposed to all other flat and circular objects serving other purposes, such as brake discs, intervertebral discs, intramuscular discs, identity discs, tax discs, etc. This is a chain of *visual associations* through *similarity* of one element or aspect and *differentiation* of others.

On hearing the word "disc" we can also think of /pɪsk/, /tɪsk/, /sɪsk/, /fɪsk/, /mɪsk/, /bɪsk/, /wɪsk/ and all the other English phonemes that can take the place of /d/ in the acoustic context: /phoneme 0 + ɪsk /. We could also think of /dæsk/ /desk/ /dɒsk/ /dʌsk/. And all the other phonemes which could replace /ɪ/, /s/, /k/ and /ɒ/ in their respective positions. These are sound *associations by opposition* of one element and *by similarity* with others, whether or not the alternatives have any meaning.

It is necessary to stress that every now and then breakdowns happen in these associative chains. Even though it is true that

/dısk/ is opposed to /mısk/ and /rısk/ in the same way, the fact that /rısk/ is a meaningful unit in English makes a big difference. We thus see that out of the seventy odd possible combinations according to English phonological laws, only four have meaning as linguistic units of their own: risk, desk, dusk, and duke.

A breakdown takes place when meaning comes into play for even though it is true that /dısk/ is opposed to /rısk/, /desk/, /dʌsk/, /djuːk/ from an oral point of view, it is also true that *disc is not directly opposed to desk, dusk, and duke,* etc. as members of the same paradigm, as elements which can be related to each other under the same governing law. In other words, in Hjemslev's terminology this means that the level of expression does not correspond to the level of content.

But when hearing the word *disc* we can also think of disco, disc-jockey, disc-player, disc-harrow, discus, Discobolus, discontinue, discord, discordant. These are *sound associations by contiguity*, which may or may not keep the meaning of the initial nucleus.

> "It is also possible for one idea to evoke another, not because of common similarity from the point of view of their visual or oral representation but because there seems to be a single emotional event bringing them together and enveloping them[4]" (like the effects of Proust's madeleine).

All this permits the conclusion that *there are association networks produced by opposition, similarity or contiguity which proliferate at different levels and which can be transformed or displaced by the arrival of new elements.*

If, when hearing a simple word, the succession of only four phonemes unleashes such a propagation of associative chains, what then produces the selection of elements to be

---

4 Ibidem

preserved? How do we manage to understand one another at all? Because words do not function as isolated elements, we may tentatively reply, there is always somebody who utters them at a specific point in space-time and with a certain intent.

Let us put *disc* back into the initial sentence whence we borrowed it. "I went shopping with Luis in San Francisco because he wanted to buy some souvenirs and also some compact discs of classical music since the choice is not so large in Argentina and the quality of the recordings not too good."

If we take into account the results of the aforementioned experiment (*glace* = "*sorbet*" or "*miroir*") it is legitimate to think that the simple hearing of the word *disc* reactivates not only the meaning appropriate to that context but also others which do not wholly become conscious and which will sink in only a few milliseconds later into the depths of the unconscious. We can also assume that when hearing the word "classical", tax discs and spinal discs sink into the subconscious and make room for other options concerning compact discs such as "*jazz, bossa nova, folklore or rock and roll*".

Let us now suppose we did not hear "compact discs of classical music" well. This gap in sound reception makes us bring up to our consciousness the paradigmatic possibilities the context brings into play. "I went shopping with Luis in San Francisco for he wanted to buy some souvenirs and also some ... [ ] ... books, flowers, eyeglasses, perfumes, sweaters ..." and as many other possibilities as can be inserted in the contextual breach.

But the speaker goes on to say ... "since the choice is not so large in Argentina ..." which makes us discard "flowers" since we understand that Luis wants to buy them in San Francisco and take them to Argentina in which case, unless they are made of plastic, the likelihood of their wilting eliminates them from our paradigm.

Once the syntagmatic axis is totally unfolded to include the sentence "... and the quality of the recordings not too good", we are compelled to abruptly cancel out all other terms in the paradigm ("books, flowers, vases, eyeglasses, perfumes and sweaters") for none of them fit "the quality of the recordings is not good"

The possibilities of paradigmatic selection are reduced in inverse proportion to the incorporation of new elements in the syntagmatic axis, and this explains why the processes of contextual facilitation happen *after* the first phases of the processing of the target word.

Thus, as elements develop along the syntagmatic axis there is an automatic rejection of the paradigmatic possibilities at the level of phonemes, morphemes, lexemes, combinations of lexemes; all that according to phonological, structural, grammatical, semantic and contextual laws which lead on to the laws governing behaviour in society.

Perception seems to work in a globalizing manner, scanning data and restructuring them on different planes (the more elements are grasped at one time, the fewer the paradigmatic elements at work). And if there is a dysfunction at the highest level we shall drop to the following one, and so on in succession. It is a question of conceiving the "whole", in the Gestalt manner, as an entity in itself, different from the sum of its parts but at the same time allowing for the breakdown of the parts to build new structures with them.

Boundaries between words can sometimes create problems for perception. During the First Congress of European Dental Prosthesis Experts held in Paris in January of 1983 a French speaker, stopping at one photographic slide referred to it as /sit dɔnœːʀ/. The interpreter into Spanish translated it into "*lugar privilegiado*" having understood "*site d'honneur*" as he was trying to guess at top speed the reason for this designation. When, a few seconds later, he heard the speaker refer to "*le site receveur de la greffe*" he realized at once he had made a mistake; it was "*site donneur*" and not "*site d'honneur*". The opposite term outlined the semantic field and the boundaries between words. In a brief aside and by using a certain tone in

honorary site

the recipient
site of the graft
the donor site

his voice the interpreter told his listeners that he had made a mistake.[5]

Boundaries between words can be as difficult to perceive as boundaries between objects. Merleau-Ponty[6] points out that our perception of a half submerged hulk of a ship on the beach can be organized in different ways as we approach it.

> "How come I did not realize that these masts were part of the vessel?" he ponders. "They were, however, of the same colour and blended in well with the superstructure".

This brings up the sometimes painful problem of interaction, when a part must be modified in the light of the whole.[7]

If we walk down the Rue Ulm towards the Seine, in Paris, and look up, we shall see a bar above the Pantheon. If asked what we are looking at, we would certainly not answer "a bar" but a "cross". Perception is the beginning of knowledge but often knowledge is what permits the adjustment and completion of perception.

I dare say that what makes interpreters' "simultaneous" work feasible is their tendency to work "from above" encompassing from the very outset the largest possible number of elements of a varied nature in a process of perceptual integration. This explains why some interpreters can give the approximate total of a sum of various digits in a few seconds after barely glancing at a sheet

---

5 *The possibilities of self-correction for an interpreter are comparable to those available to radio announcers. E. Goffman makes a very interesting analysis in* Radio Talk. *(Forms of Talks, Philadelphia, Pennsylvania Press, 1981). He proposes a classification for the types of errors ("influences, slips, boners and gaffes") and makes an analysis of the strategies used for self-correction. For instance: "… an eight **minute** walk from the Kaverfork Station, not an eight **mile** walk, as I believe I said yesterday (laughs)".*

6 *In* Fenomenología de la percepción, *Fondo de Cultura Económica, 1987. Page 18.*

7 *Rudolf Arnheim,* El pensamiento visual, *Buenos Aires, Editorial Universitaria, 1971. Page 209.*

full of numbers.[8] And others solve problems such as this one in a few seconds.

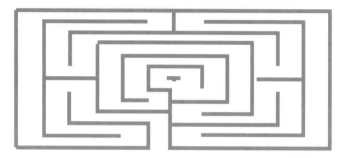

But the interpreter must keep the "doors of perception" fully open for, if he does not, he could wind up inventing his own speech with no respect for the original.

It would seem, then, that although interpreters must cover the maximum possible number of elements to react quickly and even though they consequently work "from top to bottom", they must also keep a permanent control "bottom up".

In the accomodation of these two movements we find the "control and command" which produces the best possible interpretation. We also find, by contrast and all of a sudden, the two extreme cases of poor interpretation: literal "word by word" translation and a speech of one's own.

I especially recall two exercises from my first course on interpretation:[9] in the first one, we had to invent a story using a list of unrelated words; the second consisted of memorizing the license plates of automobiles in the street. The first aimed at strengthening imagination and logical think-

---

8 *"There are two ways to estimate an amount: counting and measuring or by scanning a perceptual structure".* Arnheim, El pensamiento visual, *Buenos Aires, Editorial Universitaria, 1971. Page 209.*

9 *In Buenos Aires with Emilio Stevanovitch.*

ing; the second at developing accurate perception and recall. Although certain European schools have traditionally refused to include mnemonic and perception exercises in their courses, this type of exercise can help develop some of the abilities essential to interpretation.

In other fields, the multiplicity of operations carried out without our conscious or voluntary participation in such short spans of time permits us to: 1) understand why a computer must perform over two thousand binary operations to translate the simplest sentence, and 2) postulate with Jastrow[10] that the brain works much faster than fast computers.

Summing up, then, the experiment designed by Seguí had detected, *inter alia*, the automatic activation of the semantic network. It is therefore, plausible to think that a similar activation happens at the level of phonemes, morphemes, lexemes and groups of lexemes. This activation would be the result of waves of associations or in the technical jargon of cognitive psychology, "spreading activation" by similarity, opposition and contiguity, or a combination of these. The incorporation of new parameters can produce an interruption or deviation of these associative chains. The confluence of the syntagmatic and the paradigmatic axes yields fast automatic selection providing structured units of different kinds.

The perception of just one element produces the simultaneous propagation of associative chains at different levels. Only a few of this multitude of reactivated elements will be brought to the threshold of consciousness. Very few will eventually emerge; very few will be made conscious. Recovering these networks of associations is perhaps, among others, the silent purpose of writers, artists and poets.

---

10 *In* Àu-dela du cerveau, *Paris, Mazarine, 1982.*

Perception and Memory

As we already saw in chapter 6, analysis suggested the existence of two axes in speech which the interpreter learns how to handle: the simultaneous and the successive ones. The first permits relationships between perceptions of a different nature whereas the second allows for the association of present or absent elements. The first entails *perception* and the second, *memory*.

We had also shown the existence of two other axes similar to the two already mentioned but which operate below the threshold of our conscience. The union of the syntagmatic with the paradigmatic axis performs an ultra fast filtering job to provide us with *automatically* structured units .

What preceeds leads us to place emphasis on these four axes of overlapping functioning and multiple effects: two can be handled consciously; two function on their own.

Conscience works in specific space-time conditions accepting only certain speeds. The subconscious, working at considerably higher speeds, provides some already structured units. Voluntary processing is slow but allows for mistakes to be detected and corrected. Unvoluntary processing is considerably faster but cannot be easily modified.

Perception, memory and knowledge are closely interwoven. The manner in which their interrelationships are linked is the subject matter of Cognitive Psychology. It is not our purpose to reinvent the wheel here.

*What is new in what we are saying is that, the voluntary and conscious decisions we make when speaking or seeing are based not only on linguistic or visual automatisms of which we **can** be conscious, but also on the elections and selections our unconscious processing performs beforehand at full speed in order to provide us with structured units. In other words: there are conscious and non-conscious acts of memory and perception. The latter constituting, paradoxically, the foundations of many of our decisions.*

Obverse and Reverse

There are two fundamental and inseparable mechanisms for good interpretation: "anticipation" (using foresight, hypotheses and scenarios) and "verification". These happen at all levels (at the phonemic, prosodic, lexical, semantic, pragmatic levels) although when the mechanisms work properly, it is the pragmatic or semantic ones we are only aware of. This notion is important for, as we all know, when we speak we are conscious of only a part of what we say. Different perceptual and linguistic processing occurs, therefore, simultaneously at different levels and without our being aware of all of it. For example, as we saw, we are not aware of the phonemes we use, of the other meanings a certain word may have, of some of the associations the chain of words we use can produce, etc.

If our hypotheses about what we have heard are confirmed, we continue on the same track without problem. If, on the contrary, our hypotheses are not confirmed, we can suddenly find ourselves in a "vacuum". What allows us to proceed is nothing less than the disintegration of a "whole" at a given level and the restructuring of elements into a new "whole".

❖   ❖   ❖

Interference

*Of how interference
between two
languages operates
by the same rules of
articulation as slips
of the tongue.
Two classifications.
Three conclusions.*

I shall call *interference* the unintentional influence of certain ideas, elements, beliefs, systems of beliefs and rules, etc. over other ideas, elements, beliefs, systems, rules, etc. Interference often produces interruptions and wastes time and energy – things do not get done; results are only partially or simply not achieved. The more aware we are of these influences, the clearer our thoughts become.

Interference can exist outside and inside ourselves.

Language often reveals the existence of interference both from within and from without and it is language that we will use once more to lay bare the mental and emotional mechanisms underlying it.

Interference in Production and Reception

We can distinguish between interference in production and interference in reception.

Basil Thomson's cartoons in *"The Buenos Aires Herald"* already quoted offer some funny cases of production interference: "Between no more and drink a chair" is a good intentionally humorous case of what unintentional transfers between languages can produce (see page 171).

Some of the illustrations in the following pages also aim at making us smile thanks to some of these interferences (both in production and in reception).

The presence of the interpreter becomes interesting in the cases of lapses in reception. As we have already seen, quite frequently people understand something different from what is being said. In everyday life we do not bother with these unimportant misunderstandings, which can be dispelled as the

conversation proceeds. But often interpreters cannot avoid them and, unless they save face by remaining silent, they draw attention to themselves.

It was thus possible to hear an interpreter speak of "Jewish prudence" when the speaker referred to "jurisprudence". In another case, an interpreter revealed, in spite of himself his innermost thoughts when speaking of "the Secretariat's fear of competence" instead of the more customary "sphere of competence".

Crossovers from one meaning to another within the same language often make us smile because we quickly see, so to speak, the origin of the mistake.

However, when the interpreter transfers them from one language to another, the risk of misunderstanding is much greater.

The similar sonority in French between "*des hotels odieux*" and "*des autels aux dieux*" may give place to some humorous misunderstandings. But the same mistake – the same interference – becomes a gross distortion when expressed in another language.

Interference and Slips of the Tongue

Psychologists and psychoanalysts were perhaps the first to draw our attention to the significance of slips of the tongue, spoonerisms, etc. They were at least the first to interpret them. We will keep their terminology for these phenomena. We will even soon borrow an interesting classification from them.

A beautiful young Argentine in Paris during one of her first mundane outings. After having observed a harp and an organ in the living room, she could not skip the interference.

But we will propose a different viewpoint, starting with language itself, which has been and still is our main subject.

Learning a language consists, among other things, in acquiring a number of automatic reflexes. Learning a second language entails temporarily setting aside a series of automatic reflexes from our first language and acquiring others. Anybody who has learned a second language is surely familiar with the problem of interference, transfers, contaminations and leakage from one language to the other. Interference can occur at a number of levels:

1. Phonological

When a Spanish speaker who wants to say "very good" says /beri/ instead of /veri/, he is transferring into English a Spanish phonological rule which stipulates that /b/ and /v/ can be used interchangeably since /v/ in this language works as an *al-*

*lophone** of the phoneme /β/ and is not therefore significantly different.

The Spanish phoneme /β/ is spelled "v" or "b".

2. Prosodic

A Frenchman who uses the following intonation in order to learn whether Tom will accompany him or not:

is applying a French intonation pattern instead of the normal English one for these cases:

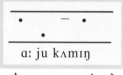

Are you coming?

3. Structural

The Spanish speaking student who says: "I want that you do this" instead of "I want you to do this" is copying the grammatical structure of the subjunctive in Spanish.

4. Morphological

If somebody translates "*a scientist*" as "*un cientista*" instead of as "*un científico*" which is the correct version, it is because he has most probably followed this train of thought: "*ist*" a suffix which in English indicates a specialist, as in "dentist", "biologist", "chemist", "ophthalmologist", "oculist", "radiologist", etc. "*Ista*" is a Spanish suffix with exactly the same meaning, as in "*dentista, oculista, electricista, maquinista, etc*". The student therefore translates "*ist*" as "*ista*", applying one of the principles which holds good in both languages. But he makes nevertheless a mistake for, even though the principle is valid in both languages, the conditions in which it applies, vary. "Dentist" is translated as "*dentista*" but "scientist" must be translated as "*científico*", "ophthamologist" as "*oftalmólogo*", "chemist" as "*químico*", where other suffixes occupy the space, so to speak.

5. Semantic

An Italian, angry at something he has just heard, shouts in French: "*Chandelle, chandelle!*" perplexing his listeners. He has surely opted for the following "hidden" course:

In Italian the word "*bugia*" has two meanings:

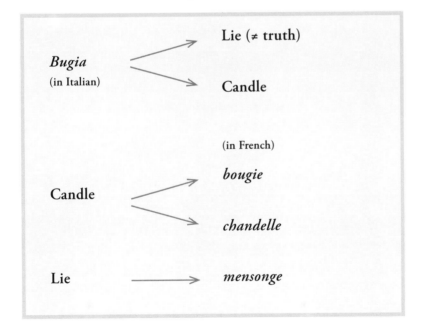

He means "*mensonge*" (lies) but when seeking the word, to little avail, and knowing that an untruth does not translate with the same signifier into French and Italian he rejects "*bougie*" and prefers its synonym in French "*chandelle*".

Or, as in the case of a Latin American delegate who, when giving an Englishman his card instead of "*here is my card*" says "*here is my target*". His mispronunciation of "*target*" [t̪arxet̪] is phonetically very similar to the Spanish "*tarjeta*" [t̪arxet̪a] (which means card). In a certain way, we might say that he has expressed himself accurately since, undoubtedly, his "*target*" /tɑːgɪt/ (aim) was to make himself known.

In all these cases there is an attempt to copy procedures from the mother tongues. It is interesting to note that big efforts are made to apply rules or principles, which would be hard for most people to identify, let alone explain. In other words, *the principles governing the functioning of our mother tongues are so strongly imprinted that we tend to use them in new situations without even realizing it.*

When learning a new language, most of us were once surprised at meeting a "**false friend**", one of those words resembling a word in our own language so much that we falsely assumed it meant "*the same thing*". For example: the word "actual" in English is graphically identical to the word "*actual*" in Spanish. The first is an adjective meaning "real" whereas the Spanish adverb means "at present".

Errors are easily committed due to identification or projection, forgetting that even if an isolated element seems identical (such as *phoneme* / ß / or suffixes "*ist*" and "*ista*"), its articulation and combination with the rest of the system can completely alter its meaning.

Translators and interpreters are very wary of the dangers of such transfers. However, they are never totally immune from them, especially in cases of information overload, annoyance, fatigue or over excitement. As in any language environment, these are precisely the conditions which most often cause "lapses", or slips of the tongue.

We shall keep the previous classification and apply it to the various lapses, which can occur at different levels within the same language.

1. Phonological

Replacement of one phoneme by another.
I.e.: **"a cuff of coffee"** instead of **"a cup of coffee"**.

2. Prosodic

When someone asks a question in the form of a statement or vice-versa or when someone says **"I love you"** indifferently or aggressively.

3. Structural-Syntactic

When structures are altered.
i.e.: - "I you give". (*"Je le te donne"*)

4. Morphological

When one morpheme is substituted by another.
i.e.: *"biologista"* instead of *"biólogo"*.

5. Semantic

Complete alteration of a word, producing an entirely new meaning.
i.e.: **"We now bring your Mr. Keene, loser of traced persons"**.

The classification of slips of the tongue into 1) inversions, 2) anticipations, 3) prolongation or echoes, 4) confusions and contamination and 5) substitutions, as proposed by Meringer and Mayer[1] does not contradict the classification we have just proposed. On the contrary, the two classifications can be seen to complement each other.

---

1 *Quoted by S. Freud in* Introduction à la psychanalyse, *Paris., Payot, Page 22.*

1. Inversions

a) **At phonological level.**
Transposition of one phoneme.
i.e.: "troothbush" instead of "toothbrush".

b) **At structural level.**
Reversal of the correct order.
As when someone says: "It of slipped out my hands."

c) **At morphological level.**
Transposition of one syllable without change of meaning.
i.e.: "serenpidity"– "serendipity."

d) **At semantic level.**
Transposition of a lexeme.

i.e.: "The Milo of Venus."
Reversal of a phoneme or morpheme creating a new meaning.
i.e.: "Queer old Dean" instead of "Dear old Queen."

Some inversions can happen at a number of levels at a time. "Flesh crean water" is a case of phonological inversion "flesh crean" instead of "fresh clean"; and of morphological and semantic confusion since even though "crean" means nothing, it can be associated with "cream"; and the word "flesh" is an English noun used surprisingly instead of the adjective "fresh".

a) **At phonological level.**

2. Anticipations

"A cuff of coffee."
"A sorn in my thide."

b) At prosodic level.
" `What will you do? "

3. Prolongations or echoes

a) At phonological level.
"Bring us thee treas."

b) At grammatical level.
"With whom are you going with?"

4. Confusion and Contamination

a) At phonological level.
"A cuff of coffee"
"A Spanish speaping hotel"

b) At phonological, grammatical, structural and semantic levels.
"Close the keyrobe."
(Close the wardrobe and give me the key).
"Donne moi ton conseillon" (Give me your advision).
(Give me your advice and your opinion).
In these last two cases, a contraction of elements produces a correct grammatical structure.

5. Substitutions

a) At phonological and semantic levels.
"I put the samples in the mailbox" (*Briefkasten*)
When what was meant was: "in the incubation vat"
(*Brutkasten*).

Of course, in ninety per cent of the cases the interpreter will supply the missing phoneme, re-establish the correct word order and make any other necessary changes without a second thought and in some cases without even realizing he is doing it. Freud[2] himself admitted that not all lapses are of equal importance and that some are even "insignificant".

> "The simpler "lapses", the most frequent and insignificant ones are those which consist of contractions or anticipations which appear in the less striking and apparent parts of the speech."[3]

Working under time pressure, interpreters do not normally reproduce or explain lapses, except in two types of situations: 1) where the contradiction is flagrant to the point of causing a reaction in the room, as when the president of the Austrian House of Representatives wanted to start the meeting but declared it adjourned; and 2) when certain elements in the situation suggest that the "slip" may be significant. For instance, if someone who denies having committed a crime asks for "a cuff of coffee" the infiltrated term (cuff-handcuffs) may turn out to be very meaningful in context. In the same way, if the floormaid of a hotel where a crime was committed declares that she has seen or heard nothing and then refers to the "Spanish speaping hotel" where she works, it may well be of interest to uncover the train of thought which made her go from "speaking" to "speaping", the sound association between the two words and the initial meaning of the last word: "peep" = spy.

Whether through substitution of one word by another of opposite meaning or through the sound transformations which mask a word, lapses become an indication of interference between two or more intentions.

---

2 Ibidem. Page 55.

3 Ibidem. Page 51.

Following a path diametrically opposed to that taken by Freud to explore the unconscious, a comparison of the transcripts or recordings of conferences – in particular, at those "places" where the interpreter seemed to say less or more than the speaker – allowed us to detect divergent signals in speech. We saw how interpreters are disturbed when such signals occur, especially when they contradict their hypotheses about the speaker's intention and motivations.

The interpreter's omission of "**nonetheless**", for instance, surprised us at first. We were then able to see that in real time and at great speed the interpreter had sensed the incongruity; that had led her to exclude the word. We then tried to find an explanation for the less than cogent inclusion of "nonetheless" by imagining a hypothetical dialogue the speaker could have established with himself concerning the advantages, or lack of them, of the electronic office.

> "The disturbance – says Freud[4] – can have as its origin a current of ideas which would have concerned the person shortly before … it is a true echo and not always and not necessarily the result of words which may have been uttered."

From what we have said so far, we can draw the following conclusions:

1. Interference between languages or within one language functions according to the same laws of articulation.

2. Interference between languages is governed by phonological, prosodic, structural, morphological, syntactic and semantic rules belonging to the speaker's first or predominant language.

---

4 Ibidem.

3. Failed acts, lapses, interference and divergent signals are closely interrelated phenomena which show, paradoxically, that the *absence* or the *presence* of one element can signal a struggle between opposing forces and tendencies.

4. When, on the contrary, forces converge and ideas flow in the same direction, when no outward or inner struggle exists, when no attempt is made to conceal or deceive, understanding easily occurs and discourse, dialogue and interaction flow.

5. When information flows to and fro without interference, the speakers' credibility increases and trust prevails.

Learning a second language (a third or a fourth for that matter) implies, as already said, leaving aside a number of rules and automatic reflexes and acquiring others. We must expect interference from our first language to last for quite a long time. Learning, training, repetition and practice will prove fundamental in eradicating errors.

The important point is that it does not suffice to learn new phonemes, structures and words. It is also necessary to learn how to prevent the previous system from infiltrating and influencing the second. In other cases, to be able to learn something new, it may even be necessary to unlearn *certain automatic responses or habitual thinking patterns.*

Our capacity to learn something new – a new language in this case – sometimes depends on our capacity to leave other knowledge on stand-by.

Changing our Viewpoint

The concept of *interference* allowed us to embrace a number of phenomena.

We distinguished between production interference and reception interference.

When the phenomena are detected between two languages, we call them: transfers, leakage, etc.; when they occur within one language, we call them lapses or slips of the tongue.

I used a grammatical criterion to classify cases of interference between two languages. (The better the speaker speaks the foreign language, the easier it will be for the bilingual to detect the transfers). We enriched our classification with a psychoanalytical taxonomy of lapses proposed by Meringer and Mayer.

More Cases of Interference of Different Types

Let us now enlarge our view with some slightly different cases. If somebody gives an order, and somebody else interferes with it, the order may not be fulfilled. If somebody gives an order, and the instruction is carried out, time is necessary for the effects to feed back into the system. If somebody interrupts the flow back, the feedback information may never reach back to the person who gave the order.

Interferences divert attention and undermine action. As we saw in some of our examples, double binds and other types of divergent signals may paralyse us or delay our response.

When a system (any system: the human body, a working team, a gym team, a financial system, etc.) works harmoniously, circulation (of energy, information, blood, money, etc.) flows with no interruptions, bottlenecks or short-circuits. Information flows forward and backward. The system works and is healthy.

As we said, interferences can happen between two languages (transfers, false friends, contamination, etc.) or within one language (slips of the tongue, etc.), but there is yet another type of interference: the kind that occurs when we take a wrong script or when we strive to apply the same rigid scheme to different situations without accepting the free interplay of variables. This can block or prevent understanding. This can affect both reception or production. "Scenarios" facilitate *understanding* since they provide an overall vision of the forces in action. But, paradoxically, they can also impede comprehension when the overall view is inappropriate, or when it is too rigidly stereotyped, as was shown by our example concerning "**prostitutes**".

There are more examples: In 1969 (before the United Kingdom joined the European Economic Community), an interpreter mistook a Dane for an Englishman and understood nothing of his defence of the interests of the community. He had made a mistake in the cast distribution of his scenario and was not sufficiently pliant to change it while still on the track.

At the end of a meeting, an interpreter, anxious to be home as soon as possible, undersood that the Angolan chairman asking delegates to turn in their "*bilhetes*", was referring to "airline tickets". What the chairman had really meant was "notes" with remarks and comments on the main issues of the meeting. Wrong scenario! The interpreter, victim of interference from another language, changed the meaning by changing the script.

A student seeking to enrol in a school of interpretation was rejected for translating:

> "... the soldiers were cared for in the military emergency hospital to enable them to return ... *to their homes*" instead of "... *to the battlefield* as soon as possible".

His script was not only plausible and probable but also more humane than the one imposed on him. This coincides with the results obtained by Chernov when proving the existence of mechanisms for probabilistic predictions (see page 71).

When in the booth we hear something unexpected such as a foul word in the mouth of a prelate or a philosophical quote from a boxing coach we instinctively look at our colleague to assure ourselves that we have heard properly. We tend to seek confirmation when what is perceived is very surprising. When an element seems utterly disruptive or unexpected in relation to the basic parameters of the scenario, we try to confirm or invalidate our own perception.

But there is a big difference between the various cases of interference in the scenarios mentioned above. In their vast majority, the subjects heard correctly and could have easily repeated the words even though they had misinterpreted them or could find no logical explanation for them at all. By contrast, in the case of "*prostitutes*", the interpreter could not make out the word. I had just heard a noise. Interference therefore occurs at different levels.

Vernon reports an experiment[5] in which he showed subjects a set of playing cards with the colours reversed: hearts and diamonds were black and spades and clubs were red. Some subjects noticed the incongruence immediately; others did not realize it. Yet others found a compromise solution: they thought they had seen purple clubs and grey hearts. Others showed that the perceptive apparatus may break down: they did not know what they had seen. Some were not even sure of having seen a playing card.

When we hear words whose meaning we know yet cannot manage to understand, it is probably because we have not detected elements in the scenario that we need to perceive the "whole" (the unity), or because certain knowledge creates a problem, because certain elements have been poorly structured or because there is a need to change the point of view.

When, on the contrary, we feel we have not heard, or have heard just "noise", or when we understand something differ-

---

5 *In* Psicología de la percepción, *M.D. Vernon,* ,The Psychology of Perception, *London, Penguin, 2nd edition, 1971.*

ent from what the others have understood – and this happens a number of times – when the perception of the "whole" gets really scrambled, the problem probably lies within ourselves.

Once the subconscious has blocked perception, as in the case of "*prostitutes*", it is the *absence* of one element that becomes *significant* (as when there is a "blank"). In the case we shall now look at it is the *presence* of an element from which the subject is unable to free herself and which engulfs her like a "black hole" that becomes indicative of *deep personal interference*.

The following example is taken from a novel by Argentine psychiatrist Emilio Rodrigué.[6] During a conference on psychiatry in Buenos Aires a young interpreter involuntarily becomes the centre of the experiment when she is asked to translate the *description of an experiment* in which a subject had been asked to repeat uninterruptedly the word "*papá, papá, papá, papá, papá …*". Unable to detach herself from the associations, recollections and reminiscences the word "*papá*" (dad) had evoked in her, the interpreter goes on calling out the word from her booth with increasing loudness.

This fictional episode of her breakdown triggers the conflict in the novel and marks the beginning of the character's long inner quest. It is an example of deep personal interference.

According to our previous classification, we had seen that interference occurred at different levels: phonological, prosodic, structural, morphological and semantic. Two more must now be added to the list: at the pragmatic level and in the deep unconscious.

There can also be interference in concatenation of ideas or acts and when ideas and actions are assembled. They can be logical or emotional.

---

6 *Emilio Rodrigué*, Heroína, *Buenos Aires, Sudamericana, 1969. (Raúl de la Torre later turned it into a film).*

Comparing Examples

We will now go back to some of our examples from the interpreting world and consider them from this new perspective of interferences. The examples given in the chapter on divergent signals could easily be considered instances of interference (see pages 104, 108 and 111):

1. The presence of "nonetheless" would have been an interference in the logical sequence of a speech within the perceived scenario;

2. "I don't want to skip time-sharing; everybody knows what that is" indicates a lapse, showing how two opposite intentions crisscrossed half way.

3. The filtration of "I'm sorry" quite probably indicates interference at the pragmatic level (or at the level of script).

In fact, the *same* phenomena will be given *different* names depending on the *standpoint* adopted; *divergent signals* for the observer who manages to detect them from the outside; *interference* for the subject who is feeling the impact inside.

Staying within this perspective (of the subject as a *conscious* or *non-conscious producer* or *receiver*), knowing what we know about the paralysing effects of contradictory signals for interpreters, listeners, and even animals,[7] it is easy – and dismaying – to deduce that confusion and inaction can be voluntarily brought about in a group of human beings. Their reactive

---

7 *Along the same lines of the classical experiments conducted by Pavlov on experimental neurosis, Bateson demonstrated that a dog that learned to discriminate and react specifically to two conditioned alternative stimuli, a circle and an ellipse for example, could literally "go insane" if the orders got mixed by flattening the circle and making the ellipse round.*
G. Bateson, La nature et la pensée, *Paris, Seuil, 1979, page 126 and* Vers Une Ecologie de l'Esprit, *l and 2. Paris. Seuil, 1977 and 1980.* (Steps to an Ecology of Mind*).*

capacity can be delayed if they are confronted with divergent signals *without their knowing it*. (These can be of any kind, linguistic and also visual or kinetic). In other words, as long as the conditions of the collision and the divergent signals have **not** been identified, the subjects will be the victims of manipulation, for their actions, thoughts and feelings will have been interfered with at least momentarily.

Actions, thoughts and feelings of groups of human beings can be interfered with and they can thus become the victims of manipulation, if they cannot accurately perceive the collision between diverging signals, with a clear awareness of what collided with what, where and when.

To sum up then: The broad concept of "interference" has allowed me to identify a number of *similar* phenomena that can occur in speech, either within one language or between languages. What was called "divergent signals" before is seen to be a case of interference. We call them "divergent signals" when we perceive them as coming from "outside" ourselves and "interference" when we perceive them as coming from "within" ourselves. If interferences are deliberately induced in groups of people through the use of divergent signals – on purpose – and subjects remain unaware of this, their reactions will be delayed and their behaviours influenced. This is a form of manipulation.

❖   ❖   ❖

CHAPTER 18

Misinterpreting

Of humility as a "must".
Not only can we make mistakes, we do make them sometimes.

When we cannot hear correctly, when we are misinformed or when we make wrong inferences, we misinterpret. Misinterpreting is a fact in language exchanges which should make us modest and increase our carefulness in our use of language.

Interpreters or translators often prefer to remain silent rather than use the wrong word or expression. But even silence – or gestures – can be misinterpreted.

Certain mistakes lead to bewilderment on the part of delegates because they seem to have no underlying logic. These mistakes are the result of random distractions, absent-mindedness or stress.

In other cases, as we have already seen, we can detect the *hot spot* of confusion and explain the *type* of mistake. These mistakes have a certain logic.

But what happens when a mistake is such that communication is affected or impaired? When the interpreter misinterprets something important and says something which does not correspond to what the speaker said? What happens when he skips a sentence that later turns out to be fundamental?

If the interpreter is "in command" and aware of what has happened, he can correct himself in several ways, either adding something or changing the tone (as a radio speaker may do); he can use several strategies to gain time and hide the difficulty or he can simply skip the troublesome bit and go back to it during the coffee-break.

At other times though, the interpreter is aware something has gone wrong but is unable to pin it down. Working in pairs or in a team proves extremely helpful in such cases. If the problem is due to a special accent or lack of empathy with a speaker, another interpreter may take over.

What happens in most cases is that an awful sensation fills the booth and sometimes even the room where the meeting is being held. This does not happen often among professional interpreters, but it does happen occasionally.

In most cases, things are set right behind the scenes. No meeting I have attended was ever openly interrupted to acknowledge a mistake of this sort. Both at the conference hall and in the booths, the response is physical, emotional: much happens behind the scenes. Frenzied movements may be seen between the secretariat, the auditorium and the booths as fear, uncertainty and anguish prevail. The important thing then is to pinpoint the hotspot of trouble and *understand* what went wrong.

But generally, as former colleague and military officer Ekvall[1] says,

> "Whenever a mistake is made it gets into the bloodstream of the discussion, infecting issues until at long last argument, explanation and the piecemeal unscrambling of cross-purposes get it isolated and finally neutralized. Such a process takes time; frequently the initial damage is never entirely repaired".

This happened in the case of the misunderstanding he reported between Spaak and Chou En-lai during the 1954 Conference (already quoted in chapter 2).

Most of the time, though, slight errors and misinterpretations go unnoticed, covered up by the fluency and speed of a professional interpreter. If they are noticed, they often do not seem worth correcting. In some cases, these trivial mistakes act like an invisible hand, steering communication along a *slightly* different course. It is *almost* the same, but not quite! As if the waters were shallower or darker … Not much

---

1 *Robert B. Ekvall,* Faithful Echo, *Twayne Publishers, New York, 1960, Library of Congress Catalog Nº 6015421.*

can be done then. More often than not, it would be just as distracting to interrupt discussion each time an interpreter misunderstood something or used a wrong word.

Back in 1960 Erkvall wrote:

> "As yet, no system for the effective monitoring of interpretation with built-in arrangements for interrupting the meeting in case of significant error and setting the record straight, has been devised for international conferences."

> "(...) Like many linguists serving on the UN staff and in the language division of the State Department in those early days, I am gravely concerned over the lack of such a device, system or procedure. Such arrangements, even if unwieldy, would guarantee the best possible performance for specially difficult negotiations or complex political situations."

To the best of my knowledge, this is still true nearly half a century later.

If what matters is *understanding*, no efforts should be spared to ensure it. We should repeatedly check and confirm that *our* interlocutors *understand* one another even if they do not *agree* with one another.

If officials, diplomats and authorities became more knowledgeable about how our "minds" work and how language functions, if we became aware of the inherent difficulties for correct *understanding* and *interpreting*, we could take some precautions when in tough or delicate situations: we would not mind, for instance, going more slowly when the items on the agenda are important. Officials – and interpreters – would make a point of focusing on clarity, brevity and transmission. Linguists – together with lawyers and diplomats – could do a lot to clarify the preparatory work for treaties and international agreements. If the political will existed, there would often be no need for endless meetings to discuss where to place the commas in a treaty. Ambiguities could be clarified and nuances could be introduced at a less exalted level. But of course, ambiguity and confusion, lack of precision and focus, are sometimes used by some politicians *on purpose*.

One piece of advice and two suggestions, then:

When what is at stake *matters*, we should ask for a "repeat" even at the cost of interrupting the flow of the meeting. Both interpreters and delegates should go slowly, making sure they understand and, if in doubt, asking for confirmation of mutual understanding.

Even in conferences with *simultaneous* interpretation, interpreters should be permitted to ask for a "repeat".

In *consecutive* interpeting, interpreters sit by their ministers or presidents and can listen to their counterparts translating. In this case, they could give early warning that a mistake has been made, not by openly correcting the other interpreter, but by suggesting that the minister or president ask for a "repeat".

These moments in consecutive interpreting are also unique in that, "sensitive to nuance and atmosphere, the interpreter hears everything twice" and can thus "match stray pieces into a pattern and pass the pattern to his principal". As a neutral observer, he can provide good help. But there is a risk in these exceptional cases. As Erkval put it:

> "If ever his principal queries him for those impressions ... he is no longer acting as an interpreter but – for an instant – as an advisor ... Better to be an echo ..." – *he thinks* – "even if more nerve-racking ... "

Although it is difficult for our rational mind to admit, misunderstandings are an integral part of normal communication. To admit it implies to accept the nature of things. It does not imply accepting misunderstandings as such and doing nothing about them. On the contrary, it helps us to be on the look out for errors. Going more slowly and not being ashamed of asking when we are unsure can also help.

Instead of trying to save face by pretending that nothing has happened, interpreters should face problems in communication in a professional manner. This is not easy since incidents are erratic, and their importance is difficult to predict.

Neurologists and psychologists have established relationships between behaviour and some brain circuits. They know, for instance, that confusion and ambiguity produce anguish, stress, sometimes fear. Boredom produces fatigue, inattention. The "joy" of dolphins when they *understand* the instructor's instructions has also been remarked by ethologists, for example.

In those awful moments the interpreter loses control, when he feels in "the dark" unable to understand what is going on, unable to decipher what he is hearing … it would seem as if the rational calm control of the cortex came to a halt, and he or she may feel like an animal in danger where the options are "fight or flight" … As if the cortex had been short-circuited by the more primary functions of the amygdala in the limbic brain.

In my career of 30 years as an interpreter, I remember just a few instances where I was assaulted by this sensation. The sensation of uneasiness was so strong that I would not like to have to go through that again. I thank my colleagues who helped me out in those cases, as I have, in my turn, helped out other colleagues in some others.

Trust and confidence are essential among professional interpreters, especially at moments like these when prestige, career or economic welfare may be at stake. Fear or competitiveness may cause interpreters to undermine their own or each other's efforts. Moods, attitudes and energy make all the difference in a booth. I remember my mentor Emilio Stevanovich saying in the old days:

> "I'd rather have two good interpreters in a booth rather than two stars. The two good interpreters will cooperate and results will be better, stars will tend to compete."

Or that other colleague who, for years, organized the interpreting services for the royal conferences in Morocco and who always had in her team an old American interpreter based in Geneva not only for her language skills but also for her energy. "Most delegates love her, teams work better and more harmoniously when she is around. We always get compliments when she is there".

Mood influences our behaviour and behaviour, in turn, influences our mood. This is especially true in the confined space of a booth. At the very moment the interpreter is at the peak of his performance and wants to go on excelling at his job, his booth colleague may start fidgeting to get the microphone back. An unspoken duel then takes place adding stress to an already stressful situation. At other times, an interpreter may send a colleague out for water so as to be left by himself. The availability of a colleague in the booth is fundamental. It is also important to trust your colleagues and let them do their best.

Focusing on misunderstandings reveals our fragility. Few people like to expose their weaknesses. To my mind though, it is better to reveal them than to conceal them. Becoming aware of our weaknesses helps us to cooperate in finding ways to avoid problems. Our egos may suffer but our margin of safety improves.

In the mid-1970's, I started my research as a synthesis of many ideas "in the air". Soon, however, I was tentatively questioning one of the axioms that most interpreters lived by: that *interpreters do not interpret what the speaker says but what he means*. It seemed to me that "interpreters only interpret what they *think* the speaker means".

That slight change produced turmoil among the academic community. I admit I did not realize then the scope of my questioning. Until then, the small but prestigious French academic interpreting circle seemed to have got along with the formula and everything it entailed. Was I daring to say that international exchange and interaction was based entirely on people's perceptions? Did I realize that a serious and long-standing international system such as this with its conventions, agreements, and treaties could not depend on the *fragility* of somebody's perceptions? Interpreters knew what speakers meant because they were clever, cultivated and well read. Why else would they be hired for the job?

There was, of course, one more step to go: it was not the *interpreter's fragility* that was being laid bare but the *whole human race's*; the difference in approach did not point to the interpreter's limitations but to the limitations – and potential – of us all as human beings.

Once we become aware of the subtleness, richness, variety and limitations of our perceptual and cognitive processes, which underpin all that we know, feel, say and do, we will be able to work in a more relaxed manner with others – peers, superiors and subordinates – thus improving the quality of our work, and most importantly, of our lives.

Admitting we can make mistakes makes us more tolerant. Tolerance, in turn, improves our chances to detect and correct them.

❖   ❖   ❖

CHAPTER 19

Words in Action

Of interpretation, theatre and life. Of what we do when we speak.

As I already mentioned in chapter 18, back in the seventies I enrolled in an actor's course in Buenos Aires, with well-known Austrian-born actress Hedy Crilla and director Julio Ordano. My intention was not to become an actress myself, but rather to experience what actors do to convey emotions and meaning.

The following exercises, all taken from those acting lessons, provide a type of training whose effects go beyond the interpretative framework of interpreters and actors.

In the first exercise, drama students were asked to invent, collectively, a brief text and say it while adopting different attitudes which would considerably change the meaning. For instance, let us say the sentence was: "*Yesterday morning I got up at eight, prepared breakfast and after turning on the radio went for the newspaper and the mail ...*". We first evoked an everyday situation and we had to do this as quickly and as intensely as possible: we had to "see" who we were speaking to and why. But then, the situations to imagine were supposed to vary a lot. All the acting students were on stage and in turn repeated the *same words* producing an array of *varying meanings* according to the different characters and plots invented: a woman cuddling her baby or arguing with her husband; a judge sentencing a criminal; a circus clown in mid-show; a popular singer enthralling his public with a song; a garrulous neighbour passing on gossip, or a politician addressing the nation.

In the "*Checo*" exercise, the purpose was to convey meaning through the simple emission of unintelligible sounds. Now, it was a matter of enunciating existing English words cogently chained together but emptied of their meaning. A new content, created in our imagination, had to be given to these stark configurations, which had to be viable in voice, inflections, gestures and silences. In Austin's terms, the "*Checo*" exercise was a *phonetic** act with a certain *illocutionary** strength which depended on the speaker's intention. This new exercise aimed at transforming a *phatic** *act* into a simple phonetic act by coupling it with an illocutionary force (called *"attitude"* on the stage) which depended, here again, on the choice made by the character.

It was not at all easy. Sometimes, we lost the thread and forgot what followed, or we said the text properly but the sub-text disappeared. Most of us would have accepted until then that there is no gap between what is said and what is thought. My immediate reflex as an interpreter was to imagine how difficult it would be to interpret a speech such as this one, where there seems to be no relationship between the words that are heard and the images created by the speaker, where voices and gestures evoke feelings or meanings other than those initially suggested by the words themselves. But once the matter is given careful thought, I wonder whether in fact the exercise we have described is simply an extreme case of what somebody called "the absence of the speaker from his speech." At large medical congresses there is usually a section called – ironically? – "*Communications*", where professionals from different countries strive to utter a maximum of words in a minimum of time. The only thing they really manage to *communicate* is that they have been present and that they *have spoken*; because of the way it is presented, content would seem to be of no importance at all[1].

Another exercise consisted in taking a text (the most popular one was from *Tartarin de Tarascon* by Alphonse Daudet, a passage full of life and colourful rich images) and, first of all,

---

1 *Our colleague and present translator of these pages, Enrique Robert, reports that during a medical congress held in Santiago, Chile, a well intentioned technician put a red light on the lectern to tell the speakers they were going too fast but neglected to explain it to them. The speakers, on seeing the red light come on, thought their time was ending and went on reading at twice the previous speed!*

saying it *objectively*, which in Hedy Crilla's jargon meant reading the text in a neutral tone, producing a sequence of sounds that were continuous, flat and monotonous. A supposedly "objectivity" effect was achieved because the person delivering it did not feel committed to what he was saying.

We were then required to take over the text, and let the text take command of us. The students searched for elements in their past powerful enough to awaken the appropriate feelings and motivation. When, for instance, had they felt like shouting for joy in the streets as Tartarin had done in the quoted passage? It was better not to intellectualize; it was better to let oneself be carried away, associate freely, evoke sensations and feelings. Once a clue was found, some would want to jump, others to run, turn a cartwheel and did so until a feeling of happiness ensued; the strength and excitement needed to convey the vital and colourful images of the text. Details depended on everyone's imagination but the more clearly the details were outlined, the better the performance would turn out. And it was not only a question of *seeing* what was being said but also of *feeling* the texture, the weight, the smells, the heat and the noise in the street, the feel of a breeze in your face ...

Experience showed that when one of the acting students could picture what he was about to say, he would quite naturally use the right intonation and his gestures would be spontaneous. As a consequence, the audience would be caught up by his performance.[2] The more involved he was in the emotions and visions to convey, the better he captivated his audience.

The objective of this exercise was threefold: 1) to search one's personal history for emotional experiences which could be assimilated to the text; 2) to become aware of one's senses and sensations, and 3) to create a new situation based on the

---

2 *"To hear is to see what is said, to speak is to extract visual images. For an actor, a word is not merely a sound, it is the evocation of an image ... Therefore, do not speak to the ear but rather to the eye of your stage companion".* Stanislavski, La construcción del personaje, *Madrid, Alianza, Pages 145 and 181.* (Building a Character, *Theatre Arts Books, 1989)*

text but interwoven with personal elements. The ultimate objective was to train students to reactivate promptly a set of feelings, sensations and images starting from a signal-stimulus.

The third exercise devoted to training 1) memory, 2) associative capacities and 3) imagination, had the same aim: *to facilitate the retrieval of a complex whole starting from a very simple signal.*

To begin with, it was necessary to find relationships in sound similarity between numbers from *one* to *ten* and ten separate words. For instance:

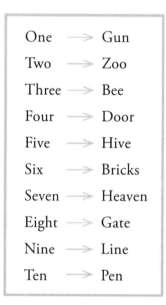

One	Gun
Two	Zoo
Three	Bee
Four	Door
Five	Hive
Six	Bricks
Seven	Heaven
Eight	Gate
Nine	Line
Ten	Pen

Once the list was memorized, nouns were called out at random and we had to link them through the expression "is in" into short, mostly meaningless sentences, which we had to memorize together with the order in which nouns had been given. The memorized list operated as a mnemonic support. For example:

1. The horse is in the garden.
2. The sun is in the icebox.

3. The butterfly is in the shoe.

4. …

5. …

6. The cloud is in the bathtub.

and so on.

An elaborate image of a horse in a garden had to be created and then linked to the word *gun* to remember that it was phrase number *one*. (For example, a cowboy on horseback shooting his gun into the air in a garden full of beautiful blue roses and yellow daffoldils). Someone then called out the numbers and we chorused the corresponding phrases. If we had managed to perceive colours, smells, movements, textures, sensations and feelings, so much the better: the ease and speed with which we retrieved the images later on was directly proportional to the richness of the experience. The procedure was as follows:

Six ⟶	bricks ⟶	triggering of the complete image ⟶
		i.e.: bricks falling in a tub where a chubby, smiling child is having a bath playing with water and using a sponge with the shape of a cloud.

As a complete image was thus triggered we were able to answer "The cloud is in the bathtub" without the slightest hesitation on receiving the signal-stimulus: "six". Visualization of speech was thus encouraged, and used as a starting point to include all the other senses as well. The challenge was to find strong links, *however absurd*, between the various elements.

Upon hearing the number "two", most of us answered immediately "The sun is in the icebox" thereby showing that we had correctly performed the mnemonic exercise and that there was coincidence in the end results. But if asked to describe each image, we would have found enormous differences from one person to the next. There would have been, of course, common denominators but the way in which elements were assembled would have shown considerable variations. This is our secret garden: our individual space for imagination and creativity.[3]

This exercise prompted associations, first at the level of sounds (*ten = pen*), then between sounds and images and last but not least between images among themselves in order to create new ones. This web of associations was woven in such a way that a sound or a visual signal triggered the *instant* retrieval of the constructed image together with the sentence in question. We retrieved both the process and the result at the same time. *The lion from its claws.*

These exercises were inspired by Stanislavski, who had set out to solve a major problem: how to obtain inspiration on demand? What can actors do to enact a role, to truly identify with their character and move their audience? And move them, moreover, at specific times of the day or night several times a week? The challenge was great and implied finding a path to subconscious creativity; finding the access gate, or the magic key. No more, no less.

We should point out that if Stanislavski attained his aim and his teachings promptly became "the" most famous acting method in the world, his exceptional intuitions and the result of his research have not, until this very moment and as far as we know, been applied outside the theatrical environment.

A trivial incident during one of his rehearsals brought about some unforeseeable consequences and showed him the

----

3 "We still have one fundamental faculty left of the human brain. All we need to know is how to use it. It is the ability to imagine, to elaborate on the basis of experience ... a new structure, a set of relationships of the memorized facts". H. Laborit, L' aggresivité détournée, *Paris, Union Générale d'Editions, 1970. Page 130.*

path to follow. The incident was as familiar and as revealing as the apple falling from the tree was to Newton.

During a rehearsal of Tchekov's *Three Sisters,* there was a moment when all the actors came to a complete standstill, unable to see the point of what they were doing. During this *impasse,* someone started scratching on the bench where they were sitting. The noise reminded Stanislavski of the scurrying of a mouse and this, in turn, unearthed a series of repressed memories which allowed him to frame the actors' performances anew. Later, he invented dozens of exercises whose purpose was to open "the doors of perception" of the young actors, and help them to recall emotions and scenes from their past through the use of sensory associations. In this way they learned to tap into creative forces which they could immediately apply to new situations. The concept of "emotional memory" so dear to Ribot had deeply marked both Stanislavski and Freud.

If we compare the processes set in motion by the last exercise with those of the "scratching noise" incident, we shall see that they do not differ much.

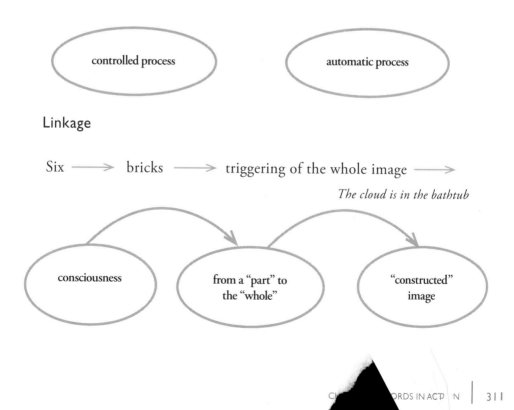

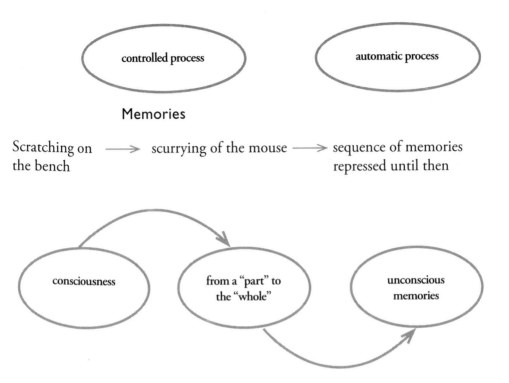

The purpose of the exercise was to try and obtain an automatic and complex response to a signal-stimulus. It aimed at *linking* the process of *controlled* association of memories to a process of involuntary association, by mirroring, so to speak, the very rich network of unconscious contacts and irradiation.

The *conscious* association of one sensory perception *at the present time* with another from the past (as the memory of a sound, a smell or a colour) may allow us to recall other perceptions that had been simultaneously perceived in the past.

As Laborit said:

> "From the most violent feeling to the most subtle of emotions, everything is based on the shifting of electrons, on the transmembrane exchange of some ions".[4]

4 H. Laborit, L'aggressivité détournée, *Paris, Union Générale d'Éditions, 1970, page 11.*

An emotion is the reaction to a situation, person, object or internal event (e.g. dream, memory) that involves changes in cognition, physiological arousal, motor expression, and/or subjective feeling. At the outset, there is nothing but a slight movement: something, literally, moves inside in order to respond to a stimulus (a gesture, an act, a look, a shout, etc.)

An equivalent sensorial signal can reactivate in our memory the same movements the original signal had produced in our bodies. It is the same mechanism according to which a specific smell can trigger a set of actions in mammals because of the associations stored in its memory.[5]

It is through associative chains that we uncover and recover repressed memories. When doing so, *something* that was blocked gets liberated and nervous tension is reduced. When nervous tension goes down, interferences vanish: whatever was blocking recedes, paralysing forces and fears can be let go of and creative forces come into play. These were, *inter alia*, some of the findings of Sigmund Freud and of Constantin Stanislavski.

The experiments described above[6] proved the existence of *automatic facilitation processes* – semantic priming for some – which are apparently the result of spreading activation in our memory from a word in the person's internal lexicon to other words differently linked to it. (**bank = credit institution; bank = edge of river; /bæŋk/ → /bænd/, /bæŋ /**, etc.). In the same way, the word "**man**" would facilitate the processing of the word "**woman**" and vice-versa. If the brain can spontaneously retrieve an entire network associated to one "access signal-word" through links of sound similarities or through associative conceptual links, *it seems that not only the same principle applies to feelings and sensations but that we can, moreover, learn how to manage them.* This would

---

5 *"Linkage is basic to the creation of conditioned reflexes and to the functioning of mnemonic techniques."* H. Laborit, ibidem, page 34.

6 *See chapter 15, page 247.*

be, precisely, one of the purposes of training actors: to help them make personal links between certain emotions and certain signals and find the means to recover the emotions by stimulating the signals. It would also seem that, like a super computer, *our brain can, in real time, command all these levels at the same time.*

At the beginning of the 20th century, Freud underscored the importance of the functioning of the unconscious and developed the psychoanalytical method which enabled a patient to recover and recreate his past through speech: the past becomes present, and dreams become reality, not because of the verbs used but rather because of the primacy, intensity and force of the feelings and emotions which have been preserved – intact – in some recess of body-memory-and-mind. A mere word can set the most amazing chain of emotions and reactions in motion.

At the same time, in Moscow, Stanislavski developed a new system for the training of actors: it was no longer a question of learning a text "by heart" and then performing it. The actor needed a sub-text of his own, which would irrigate the words and the silences in the text like an underground stream. In order to achieve this, he had to train and develop his "emotional memory" and keep in mind the "super-objective" of his character within the context of the play at large. A sound, the texture of a cloth, a special smell can trigger a surprising series of sensations, emotions and images.

At the same time, in literature, James Joyce created the "stream of consciousness" where free association was the only governing law. And Proust discovered, to his own amazement, the effects of his "*madeleine*".

The exercises here described, conducted daily by actors and acting students all over the world, prove that thanks to personal associative work and sensorial research, chains of images, feelings and sensations can be established susceptible to being recovered as a whole by means of a trigger-signal. A simple brief signal can trigger the unravelling of a thread taking us right to the heart of the labyrinth. This is tantamount to saying that it is possible, after a certain amount of training,[7] to repeat, at will, the surprising phenomenon felt and described by Proust with his "*madeleine*".

Of course, these techniques may become jaded by repeated use and it may be necessary to find new ways of triggering the same emotions. To avoid getting into a rut, some actors develop games to surprise their partners onstage. By shifting, for instance, the stress or changing the emphasis in a declamation so as to disconcert their partners (through the activation of a different pattern) and force them to be present at all times.

Outside the theatrical world, these ideas can prove useful for developing imagination, memory and creativity. We must point out, however, that if the process is reversed and the same ideas are applied without the active and conscious participation of subjects, we may find ourselves in a completely different field, following the tracks of conditioned reflexes: the field of manipulation.

Indeed, the mechanisms of association described here are similar to those underlying conditioned reflexes. Stanislavski (1863-1938) and Pavlov (1849-1936) lived in Russia at the same time. It should come as no surprise to learn that they knew about each other's work. Pavlov experimented on animals and Stanislavski worked with human beings. But the main difference is that subjects are passive in Pavlov's experiments whereas they are active in Stanislavski's. If a group of human beings were encouraged to make certain associations – without their being aware of the implied links – they would be treated as dogs were in Pavlov's experiment and conditioned reflexes could thus be induced.

Saying is doing, for, as Austin states, when we speak we perform acts such as making promises, giving orders, etc. But

---

7 "... *this system is not like "a ready to wear" garment that you can buy in a store nor is it like a book of recipes where all you need is the page number to find the appropriate instructions. Absolutely not! It is rather a way of life in which you have been raised and educated for years*". C. Stanislavski in La construcción del personaje, *Madrid, Alianza Editorial, 1975, page 332.*

our incursions in the world of the theatre let us go even further and state that we do much more: we evoke memories, we awaken emotions and feelings, create images and change relationships among people.

And if saying is doing also in this sense, speech acts belong – and must consequently be studied – within the framework of an *action theory* which requires a thorough knowledge of the perception of acts and of the various networks of social relationships which exist or may exist among all of us in our simplest daily interactions.

❖   ❖   ❖

CHAPTER **20**

A Cross-Cultural Approach to the Sign

Of Semiotics,

Linguistics,

Semantics, and

General Semantics.

Of polysemy

and the quest for

invariance.

The development of certain ideas or concepts often prevails in certain cultures and not in others and it sometimes takes many years for a given concept to be translated and fully understood and accepted in other contexts.

We shall focus now on the *sign*, a very useful concept in the linguistic and semantic fields.

Two disciplines have focused on the sign concept in the Anglo-Saxon world: semiotics and semantics. According to the *Encyclopaedia Britannica*, these disciplines are defined in the following manner:

Semiotics is the study of signs and sign–using behavior, including the use of words (linguistics), of tone of voice, tempo or drawl (paralinguistics), of body motions and gestures (kinesics). The term was introduced in philosophy at the end of the 17th century by John Locke. It became more widely used as a result of the work of the U.S. logician and philosopher Charles Peirce and later (1938) by behavioural semanticist Charles Morris.

Semantics is the study of meaning which may be approached from a philosophical or logical point of view emphasizing the relationship between signs, or words, and their referents and including such concerns as naming, denotation, connotation, and truth; or regarded from a linguistic point of view, focusing on such topics as changes over time in the meaning of words and the interrelationship of language structure, thought and meaning.

There is one more discipline whose treatment of symbols and structures is worth mentioning here. *General Semantics* can be considered a neuro-semantic, neuro-linguistic discipline; a systematic method for evaluating and improving how individuals integrate their verbal world (language and symbols) with their non-verbal world.

In the Latin European and Latin American world, the concept of sign spread thanks to Swiss linguist Ferdinand de Saussure (1857-1913). The publication by two of S aussure's students, Charles Bally and Albert Séchehaye, of Saussure's lecture notes and other materials as *Cours de Linguistique Générale* in 1916 (Course in General Linguistics, 1959) is frequently considered the starting point of 20th century linguistics.

Saussure contended that language must be considered as a social phenomenon, a structured system that can be viewed *synchronically* (as it exists at any particular time) and *diachronically* (as it changes in the course of time). He also introduced two terms that have become common currency in linguistics – *parole**, or the actual *speech** of every individual person, and *langue**, or the abstraction of a systematic structured language, such as English, existing at a given time within a given society. His distinctions proved to be mainsprings of 20th century linguistic research and the starting point of structuralism.

The *sign* – a fundamental notion in modern linguistics – is made up of *the signifier* and *the signified* as defined and described by Saussure.

Signifier: the acoustic image, the sensorial part of the sign

Signified: the concept or mental image

What Saussure remarked was that in the continuum of sounds and of ideas we detect and distinguish units, those

units constituting *signs*. What the sign unites is not a thing and a name but rather an acoustic concept and an image. In Saussure's classical definition there must be a relationship of balance or symmetry between both parts.

Taking up Saussure's dichotomy between *langue* and *parole*, and his concept of *sign*, and combining it with the concept of *polysemy* from French linguist Maurice Pergnier, we find a new dichotomy *within the sign* which may prove interesting from a translator's point of view and from a cross-cultural perspective.

Pergnier points out that Saussure's signs exist in "speech" (*parole*), in actual discourse, where for example, we may distinguish the word "**bank**".

As in the "**banks** of the Paraná River sung by Spanish poet Rafael Alberti" (meaning "slope, elevation in sea or river bed").

Or as in "I've opened a checking account in the **bank** next to our shop" (meaning "establishment for custody of money").

But, at the level of the abstraction we call "language" (*langue)* we should perhaps look for a different kind of **sign** where instead of the **referents** (slope, money agency, etc.) we would have **the semantic "knot"** or "value" of the word. For ex: in the case of *bank* we might say that this is: **raised surface providing safety**.

in "speech"   in "language"

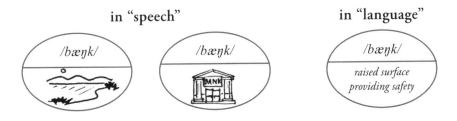

On Polysemy

Having placed "polysemy" at the very core of language mechanisms, Pergnier shows through different examples that polysemy is not only far from anarchic; it is "the manifestation of a structural order not immediately perceptible but which can nevertheless become apparent thanks to scientific analysis. He distinguishes then between "referent" (*désignation*), i.e. the symbolic rapport or link between a signifier and one of its concepts and the "meaning" (*signification*) defined as the "value" the sign acquires from its relationships and differences from other words. The common core of meaning linking the different denotations of a word is known as its *linguistic invariant*.

To make the list of the "referents" (*désignations*) of a word is not an especially difficult task. To try and find the "linguistic invariant" presupposes, on the contrary, a theoretical conscious effort of a higher order: one has to determine through which trait or traits every referent is distinguished from the other possibilities in a paradigmatic chain; when in several paradigmatic chains, we succeed in finding the *same difference* we will have found the *linguistic invariant*, the *value* or intrinsic semantic knot.

Let's take another example:

The word "**band**" may refer to: **strap, iron band, plastic band, etc.; music band, dance band, Band of Hope, etc.**

Its *value or semantic knot* could be considered to be: **something "binding", uniting or connecting people or objects together.**

I break the flow of our narrative to tell you, the reader, how difficult it can sometimes become to write a book while working at the same time and having a husband, a household and friends to attend to. I meant to finish this chapter today but there have been too many calls and interruptions. With a bit of luck, I shall finish it tomorrow! But in any case, I was glad to have news of so many dear people around.

E. J. called to let us know he was organizing a collective exhibition in a gallery not far from home in order to help one of his friends, an artist who had just lost all his work – both pictures and sculptures – when his atelier caught fire.

Sarita dropped by and I was happy to confirm she is the very picture of health! I'm so glad to see she is completely recovered after surgery.

Anita came by with my little nephew for whom I had a surprise: a beautiful picture-book and some colour pencils for him to colour it. She brought along her holiday pictures and we had fun going through all of them and remembering the good time we had had together the previous summer.

If readers have not yet realized that this digression was simply intended to produce an apparently spontaneous act of communication so as to use the word "**picture**" in different possible collocations, the aim has been achieved.

The English word "**picture**" has several **referents**:

> Picture: painting, drawing as work of art.
> Picture: a perfect type, the image.
> Picture: scene, total visual impression produced.
> Picture-book: containing pictures.
> Picture: photograph.

Its **meaning** or *linguistic invariant*, value or intrinsic *semantic knot* according to Pergnier, would be: image, scene, something to be seen or watched.

> Picture: scene, something to be seen or watched.

Now, what do we translate then? *Reference* or *meaning?*

There is no doubt that what we do is look for the equivalent referents.

Let us take our examples and translate them into French to grasp these differences better:

Johnny called to let us know he was organizing a collective exhibition in a gallery not far from home in order to help one of his friends, an artist who had just lost all his work – both **pictures** and sculptures – when his atelier caught fire.

*Johnny a téléphoné pour nous faire savoir qu'il était en train d'organiser une exposition dans une galerie pas loin de chez nous afin d'aider un de ses amis, un artiste qui a perdu la totalité de ses oeuvres – **tableaux** et sculptures – lorsque son atelier prit feu.*

Sarita dropped by and I was happy to confirm she is the very **picture** of health! I'm so glad to see she is completely recovered after surgery.

*Sarita est venue me voir et je suis très contente d'avoir constaté qu'elle est **l'image** même de la santé. Je suis heureuse d'apprendre qu'elle s'est complètement remise après son intervention chirurgicale.*

Anita came by with my little nephew for whom I had a surprise: a beautiful **picture-book** and some colour pencils for him to colour it. She also brought along her holiday **pictures** and we had fun going through all of them and remembering the good time we had had together the previous summer.

*Anne est venue chez moi avec mon petit neveu pour qui j'avais une surprise: un beau **livre illustré** et des crayons en couleur. Elle a aussi ramené ses **photos** et nous nous sommes bien amusées en les regardant et en nous rappelant les bons moments passés l'été dernier.*

The same English word *picture* was translated into French by means of four *different* words: *tableau, image, illustré (livre) et photos.*

Let us compare both versions:

Picture: painting, drawing as work of art.	tableau
Picture: a perfect type, the image.	l'image, le paradigme
Picture-book: containing pictures.	livre illustré
Picture: snapshot, photograph.	photographie

If we take the first referent of the French word **tableau,** we will see how its semantic core differs from the semantic core of its equivalent in English.

Tableau: ouvrage de peinture exécuté sur toile, sur bois, etc.	picture, painting
Tableau: châssis de planches assemblées et peintes en noir pour écrire – tableau noir	blackboard
Tableau: subdivision d'un acte dans une pièce de théâtre	scene
Tableau: liste de personnes prévues pour un avancement	board
Tableau: panneau destiné a recevoir une inscription, une annonce.	table, chart – departure indicator
Tableau de prix: liste de prix; tarif	price list

We should remark two things here: **picture** and **tableau** refer to "a painting made on canvas, tissue or wood" both in English and French, but the other referents of the words *picture* and *tableau* vary and cannot consequently be translated by the same word. Polysemy does not correspond from language to language.

And whereas the English *linguistic invariant* (or *meaning* according to Pergnier) is

> **"image, scene, something to be seen or watched",**

the French *linguistic invariant* would be

> **"that which allows to show something, to capture other people's looks"** – *qui sert à exposer quelque chose au regard.*

The difference is subtle but it is there.

This quest for *variants* and *invariants* has been vital not only in the linguistic field but also in other disciplines.[1] It was one of Alfred Korzybski's subjects of concern and it is one area especially dealt with in General Semantics. Argentine-born writer Jorge Luis Borges seems involved in the same quest.

Let's take another example, from English into Spanish, this time, to see how the *same* English word can have different Spanish equivalents according to the designated referents. The same holds good in the other sense as well.

Eng. "bank"   Sp. "*banco*"   Eng. "glass"   Fr. "*glace*"

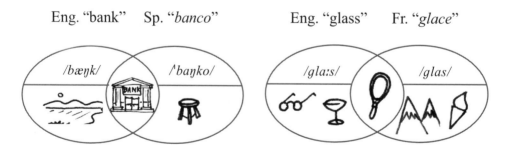

---

1 For a rough approach, see chapter 22, page 353.

What is even more surprising is that even while taking the *same* referent (let's say between a branch of the CitiBank in Boston and a branch of CitiBank in Cochabamba, Bolivia) meaning may differ as a result of the different relationships each bank has with neighbouring institutions in the two cultures (for ex. with the Federal Reserve/ private banking/ insurance companies/ tellers at supermarkets/ electronic banking/ etc. and with *el Banco Central/ Ministerio de Hacienda/ banca privada/ aseguradoras/ cajeros en supermercados/ banca electrónica/* etc).

The *same* type of institution may show big *differences* across *different* contexts or historical periods.

Thus, as reported to me by former American diplomat and cross-cultural writer Glen Fisher,[2] the newly appointed CitiBank manager in Cochabamba in the early seventies discovered there were big differences between American and Bolivian banks. As a cross-culture expert, he decided to draw a comparison between banks in the two countries regarding their objectives, owners, customers and attitudes. *Differences stemmed from the different* cultural backgrounds and the *different* network of relationships between banks and other institutions in each society.

	American Banks	Bolivian Banks
Objectives	Profitability	Unclear : government and private interests mixed up
Owners	Share-holders	Government + certain families
Customers	Everybody	Restricted to certain commercial transactions
Role	Counsellor, advisor	Partner in a few cases
Attitude	Respect, trust, security	Fear, distance No contact whatsoever

2 See Fisher, Glen, Mindsets. The Role of Culture and Perception in International Relations, *Yarmouth, Intercultural Press, Inc., 1988. And* International Negotiation. A Cross-Cultural Perspective, *Intercultural Press, 1980.*

The analysis of the new director was no theoretical exercise: he had observed that *collas*, the Indigenous women, handled money at the local markets. His analysis enabled him to attract a new segment of the market which had so far been overlooked.

In the first chapter of this book, we took the sentence **I've bought the paper** and gave it very different meanings.

Now, as if splitting atoms, I have chosen one word (bank) – just one of its possible referents (financial institution) – and I have shown how part of its meaning also varies when it is placed in different geographical or cultural contexts.

❖   ❖   ❖

The Inner Interpreter

"... that kernel of myself that I have saved, somehow in the central heart that deals not in words,
traffics not with dreams and is untouched by time,
by joy, by adversities".

Jorge Luis Borges
(*Obras Completas*, page 294)

Part IV

LOOKING INSIDE

S o far we have considered speech and words as objects or events existing in a space "outside" of ourselves. I will now propose a drastic shift of attention and turn 180 degrees: we shall delve inside.

CHAPTER 21

The Inner Interpreter

Of the importance of introspection. Becoming aware of how our brains work may have an impact on our behaviour.

All living creatures are continually exposed to intra and extra-corporeal stimuli but only we, humans, can put those sensations into words and communicate to others what we feel both physically and emotionally.

On the other hand, out of the endless number of stimuli that bombard us simultaneously – visual, tactile, auditory, olfactory and taste – we only become aware of some of these, i.e. we select some of them, elaborate them and transform them into sensations. The same happens with stimuli produced by processes within our own bodies.

Now, how does this selection occur? What sets this process in motion? How are stimuli turned into sensations that we can then "decode" and translate into words?

I will be bold enough to take the interpreter's case and use it allegorically. Let us imagine for a moment that there is a witness within us that silently perceives, observes, records and interprets – a witness who can stay silent and calm. Let us call that witness our *inner interpreter*. Deep inside, this inner interpreter witnesses how thousands of perceptions of a different nature are permanently being selected, processed and combined. The inner interpreter then translates perceptual units of one sense into the other senses, and also instincts, feelings and emotions into ideas, actions and thoughts.

Out of an enormously rich variety of elements of all sorts that bombard us, the *interpreter within* will select and present some organized "units" which he will eventually translate again, if necessary.

As Argentine writer Jorge Luis Borges wrote in Spanish depicting the fruit "*naranja*" back in 1926,[1]

> "We feel a round shape by touching, we see a heap of light at dawn, a tingling fills our mouth with joy and we melt those three heterogeneous things into what we call an orange ."

Is it surprising to see in a scientific video[2] that the reconstruction of the process in the brain literally follows Borges' poetic and intuitive description? We can see in the computerized simulation of the video how the "feel", the "colour", "the taste" come from different brain areas and are synthesized in the unifying "word".

It was even more exhilarating to me to find in Jeff Hawkins' recent book *On Intelligence*[3] (2004) some descriptions of *brain functioning* that fit my own tentative descriptions of *language functioning* (as revealed when we speak under pressures of time-space). Hawkins' hypotheses on the neocortex processes encouraged me to develop these ideas a little further.

"When we assign a name to something – says Hawkins – we do so because a set of features consistently travel together" like in Borges' *orange* "the rich glow at dawn, the roundness and the tickling filling our mouth with joy ..."

Let us imagine then some of the processes that *may* take place when we are babies. I use the word *imagine* since what follows is naturally based on inferences. When babies are born, they abandon the warm, liquid, sonorous, intimate environment of the womb and enter a dry, airy and probably (for them) chaotic environment full of new and indefinable

---

1 J.L. Borges, El tamaño de mi esperanza, *Buenos Aires, Proa. 1926, Seix Barral, 1993.*

2 Discovery Channel, 1997. Series of three videos, The Brain – Our Universe Within, *VHS 24238/39/40.*

3 Jeff Hawkins, On Intelligence, *New York, Times, 2004.*

sensations. Little by little – through experience – they start getting used to their new habitat and they start recognizing *similar* tones and pitches of a voice, *similar* smells and tastes, etc., across different situations. *Similar features* that seem *to travel together*. They can probably then start identifying some *similar* elements within the ever-*changing* ambiguous uncertain unknown environment. Let us suppose that at some given point in time, the baby starts making *connections* between different types of sensations: what he/she feels, tastes, sees, touches, hears. The baby will then eventually isolate different traits and will link them to certain sounds repeatedly heard simultaneously with those sensations, making an internal connection between – say, "mom", and the array of normally pleasant protective nourishing sensations associated with mother. And the same is true for other external objects in his or her "world".

Connecting, linking, binding, associating, relating is perhaps one of the very first mental activities we engage in. This activity presupposes other "previous" activities such as perceiving, observing, comparing, distinguishing, discriminating, identifying and recognizing *similar* patterns which implies discriminating differences and recognizing *similarities* between the elements. Repetitive exposure surely counts. When babies – playing with the sounds – acquire their first words, they learn the *result* of the experience and ALSO the *process* through which the result was obtained. This means that when we learn how to relate A to B, we simultaneously learn how to relate A or B to something else, say C or J, even when the related elements belong in different levels or to different fields.

What enables us, as babies, to create the link, to bind two different elements together is our own experience. *This life experience*, through different processes, is eventually abstracted and synthesized. Let us remember here that *synthesis* is the process through which separate parts constitute a complex whole as when two or more elements in chemistry are synthesized into a chemical compound.

Synthesis paves the way for order, for hierarchies, priorities and levels. From this point of view, it becomes the opposite of *confusion* which dispels, tangles and flattens hierarchies, priorities and levels.

The *results* of this will be twofold for the baby: 1) "in the reality out there" an individualized *entity* (or *unit*) will have been selected out of the continuum of sensations and perceptions on the move, and an object – for example, a nursing bottle – will have been recognized by the baby's brain. And at the same time, 2) a *word*, a *sign* will have been created which will enable the child to refer to *that* nursing bottle or to *any* nursing bottle in the world, be it *present or not*.

A concrete *life experience* gets thus transformed into the bar or relationship between the *signifier* and the *signified* in the linguistic concept of the *sign*, according to Ferdinand de Saussure's intuitions.

Our imaginary itinerary leads us to conceive the *symbolizing capacity of man* (*thinking, reasoning, imagining*) as an ever-growing continually self-organizing network of relations. Man's *capacity for abstraction* allows for an internal organization and re-organization of levels of relations in which his *capacity for synthesis* plays a fundamental role.

In these simple acts babies perform when learning their first words, there seems to be a blissful seed: the baby is learning to make a connection, a *bond* between certain sounds and other perceptions. As a consequence of this relationship established between some tangible and intangible elements, a "word" will be born. The wonderful part of all this is that it is not only a word: the word mirrors the entity co-created outside. As babies identify entities outside of themselves, they simultaneously incorporate *names* that will enable them to bring back these entities whenever they wish, as magic Abracadabra! in a conjuring trick.

There is movement, action, life; discovery and wonder and pleasure in such a simple act as that of a baby learning to talk. There is *creativity* involved. As when an adult finds the right word and the right sequence and the right means to translate his feelings/thoughts/ideas/emotions and put them into words. Or when, passing from one language to another, the translator translates, turning a certain network of relationships (of shapes and sounds, and signifiers and signified) into a different network of relationships in order to preserve a certain *similitude of values, relations and beliefs*. A certain alchemy seems to be at work to succeed the "pass".

"Public speech", as George Steiner says in *After Babel*, "is only the tip of the iceberg".

From the public arena where we started, we are now daring to delve inside, exploring the private area where our *inner interpreter*, "the witness" or "the observer" lives in that intimate space, the "free-will" zone, the secret garden of poets and mystics. *Le jardin secret dont parlait Voltaire*. The cognitive space where perceptions, feelings, and language meet to help us co-create "our" world.

How we select, choose, combine and integrate elements from the environment to constitute entities and internalize them is difficult to describe. The "filtering" process involved we call "abstraction". We sift elements: some stay, some go.

Since we do not yet have instruments at our disposal to picture the process within, we can only explore the field following the intuitions of certain visionaries who dared to leave the beaten track and defy the "normally accepted vision of the world".

Fortunately, the abstracting process seems to keep recurring at different levels as a mantra or a mandala or as a pattern repeating itself. In this manner, even at the physical level, a very concrete "abstraction process" occurs even before the baby is born. Its description can help us visualize other abstracting processes. Foetuses feed through the placenta. The placenta filters what it needs from the blood. Whatever is not needed, proceeds. In the same way, our nervous systems select certain things and discard others.

Attention – Focus
The Scientific Orientation In Everyday Life

Since we are taking a look inside, *attention* must be paid to attention itself.

To some spiritual teachers, attention is the key to the spiritual road.

What do we choose and decide merits our attention?

According to the Oxford Advanced Learner's, *attention* is the action of applying one's mind to something or somebody or noticing something or somebody; special care or action; kind or thoughtful act.

Attend is to apply one's mind steadily; to give careful thought.

Tend is to take care or look after; be likely to behave in a certain way or to have a certain characteristic or influence; to take a certain direction.

A very subtle internal movement, an imperceptible attitude seems to underlie the direction we give to our attention.

"Attention is an exceptional state which does not last long since it contradicts the fundamental characterisitic of psychic life: change" said Ribot.[4] And he quotes Maudsley saying:

"He who is incapable of governing his muscles is incapable of paying attention".

Also in the 19th century psychologist William James wrote:

"volitional effort is effort of attention … effort of attention is thus the essential phenomenon of will".

In the 21st century, other researchers point in the same direction. After having obtained some success in the treatment of patients with obsessive-compulsive disorder, psychiatrist

---

4 *Théodule Ribot*, Psychologie de l'attention. *Paris, Alcan, 1916.*

Jeffrey Schwartz[5] contends that attention gives the brain the power to reshape itself.

"Attention can sculpt brain activity by turning up or down the rate at which particular sets of synapses fire. And since we know that firing a set of synapses again and again makes them grow stronger, it follows that attention is an important ingredient for neuroplasticity".[6]

From the very outset of this book, either explicitly or implicitly, I have emphasized the importance of *paying attention. Attention, focus, concentration*. Paying attention to people, speakers and listeners, to their history and background. Listening for implied and hidden messages. Observing the tangible and the intangible; observing closely forms, shapes, figures, details and backgrounds, contents, histories, relationships, actions and essence. Listen to what someone is saying, and how he is saying it, and to whom. Look at where he is sitting, who is sitting by his side, in front and behind him. Notice how people treat him, how he walks, what he eats, if he smokes.

These and many other data will enable the interpreter to formulate hypotheses about the speaker's intent, about the consistency of his speech and the veracity of his words. Observation will foster prediction. Prediction is necessary to interpret and to act.

"Correct predictions result in understanding; incorrect predictions result in confusion and prompt you to pay attention."[7]

---

5 *Jeffrey Schwartz and Sharon Begley,* The Mind & The Brain – Neuroplasticity and the Power of Mental Force, *New York, Harper Collins, 2002.*

6 *Neuroscientist Ian Robertson of Trinity College Dublin as quoted by Schwartz in* The Mind and The Brain, *New York, Harper Collins, 2002.*

7 *Jeff Hawkins,* On Intelligence, *New York: Times Books, 2004.*

Then the interpreter will check the hypotheses against the new data gathered through the experience of the meeting and the contact with speakers and through the discourse itself. Some of such hypotheses will be confirmed, others rejected and/or transformed, and new ones will be elaborated.

What we would like to add at this point is the need for the interpreter – any speaker or human being for that matter – to also pay attention within. Pay attention inside, to what *he/she* is feeling, sensing, thinking, wishing.

Throughout the 20th century we have mostly been taught in the Western world to pay attention to the *outside* world, to rely on our senses, to demand verification, to expect "objectivity". There is nothing wrong with that provided we do not forget to revise our own assumptions and beliefs underlying our search for "objectiveness". Looking inside ourselves may prove fundamental. It is perhaps the interweaving of the observations from within and from without that provides us with our more reliable tools in life.

Some of the humblest human beings I have met are scientists. Those at the frontier of knowledge know better than others about the precariousness and the partiality of their own views.

This healthy unpretentious scientific approach, respectful of the mysteries of the universe and conscious of our limitations and potentials could easily be applied by all of us in our everyday lives. Indeed, Wendell Johnson[8] has suggested four basic steps to what he calls "the scientific method in everyday life":

1. asking clear answerable questions,
2. observing,
3. reporting as accurately as possible and
4. revising assumptions and beliefs in light of the observations made and the answers obtained.

---

8 *Wendell Johnson,* People in Quandaries – The Semantics of Personal Adjustment, *USA, Harper and Bros, 1946, 4th printing, International Society for General Semantics, 1989.*

We could also translate this "scientific method" into the four following steps: 1) observation inside and outside ourselves using all our senses, 2) experimentation, 3) testing, verifying, 4) formulating hypotheses again.

This came easily to me since, as an interpreter, I was used to following quite a similar path at work: 1) the clear answerable questions being the simple questions I should always ask: who is saying what to whom, when, where and for what purpose. 2) observing, 3) my "version" became my own – hopefully accurate – real-time reporting in a different language, 4) I had to revise my own assumptions, hypotheses and beliefs in the light of what I had heard, seen and translated.

I said that one of the aims of this book is to succeed in bringing about a shift in attention, making you, the reader, focus on things or aspects of things you would not normally have considered – both externally *and* internally. The first shift, then, is to pay as much attention to what is happening inside you as you do to what is happening outside of you. And in so doing, try to navigate through your own feelings and emotions, distinguishing them from one another and evaluating them instead of simply being carried away by them.

Being able to redirect our attention and shift its targets implies being in command of our own selves.

❖ ❖ ❖

CHAPTER 22

On Variance and Invariance

Of how we navigate in an ocean of differences, trying to abstract from them something that remains stable, unchanging.

If you look up the word *life* in the Encyclopaedia Britannica, you will find: phenomenon almost impossible to define or to explain in all of its *varying* aspects.

Variety, diversity and multiplicity characterize *life* to such an extent as to make any attempt to define it or to explain it almost impossible! Every creature in nature, humans included, every plant and animal vary from one another and also change themselves as time goes by. Even rocks do. What ensures each unit then, each entity? Even elements like water, earth, air and fire that have fixed properties as defined by modern chemistry, constantly vary. We have known since Heracleitus that *we do not set our feet twice in the same river.*

How come then, among so much variety and so many individual differences, humans are able to identify units, to group and classify them, and to establish hierarchies? How come we manage to understand and agree with one another?

The *abstracting process* that takes place to ensure the passage from variance to invariance seems to play a fundamental role. Evolution seems to follow a path ensuring the passage from variance to invariance and back. Neurobiologist Hawkins[1] says:

"Nature solved the problem of variation in a very clever way, the cortex creates invariant representations".

But let's go back for a minute to the realm of concrete everyday life full of the most incredible and almost endlessly rich array of auditory, visual, tactile, olfactory, kinesthetic perceptions of all kinds. What prevails here is the *unique* physical sensuous indi-

1 *Jeff Hawkins,* On Intelligence, *New York: Times Books, 2004.*

vidual *experience*. Alfred Korzybski[2] gives a great importance to this experiential level – which he calls "extensional" and which he contrasts with the "intensional" level – higher up in the abstraction process. Because everything constantly changes at the extensional level, he suggested (back in 1933) the use of "indexes" to show differences within classifications. For example:

As your first reading of this page would be different from a second reading if you tried again, he proposed to *index* certain words when necessary, using *dates* to show how things change over time:

New York $_{2000}$	is different from	New York $_{2007}$
I $_{2006}$	am not	I $_{1984}$
Seminar $_{1997}$	is different from	Seminar $_{2007}$
Bill Clinton $_{1999}$	had different views from	Bill Clinton $_{2004}$
John $_{1988}$	is not	John $_{2006}$

Not only did Korzybski suggest modulating our perception of time through the use of indexes, some of his disciples[3] also suggested the use of an anxiety rating on a scale 1-10 for certain emotional experiences so as to help modulate our perception of pain. This has become common practice these days in several psychological techniques aimed at enabling patients to better assess their own state. At the *extensional* level, variations are personal, individual and infinite.

To show the shift from the innumerable experiences available to us to the ways in which we structure them, let us first take the example of sounds. Of the thousands of sounds a

---

2 *Polish American writer (1879-1950) author of* Science and Sanity, *Institute of General Semantics, 1933.*

3 *Susan Presby Kodish and Bruce Kodish,* Drive Yourself Sane. *Foreword by Albert Ellis. Pasadena, Extensional Publishing, 2001.*

human throat can produce, a few are enough in every language for the purposes of verbal communication. Out of the multiple personal variations for any one sound, a *phoneme* will represent the abstracted set of smallest distinctive features which will enable us to distinguish one word from another. For example: the /s/ sound in *sip* and the /z/ sound in *zip* represent two different phonemes in English. When two words are distinguished by just *one* different sound, they are said to form a *minimal pair*. In contrast, although an initial /p/ sound is aspirated before a vowel but not before a consonant (try saying *pay* and then *play*, holding a sheet of paper in front of your mouth) there are no minimal pairs in English whose meaning depends only on whether the /p/ sound is aspirated or not.[4]

The wide variety of accents and pronunciations is one of the main difficulties encountered by interpreters. In the UK, for example, we have British English with its received pronunciation (the cultivated accent spoken on the BBC), but also Scottish English, Gaelic, Irish, Cockney and so many other regional varieties. American English also offers big differences between, say, the English spoken by a Texan farmer and a New Yorker. But then English is also spoken in Australia, New Zealand, Canada, South Africa, Nigeria, India, etc. It is also spoken by millions of people who have learnt it as a second language. The same thing happens in Spanish – 3rd language in the world today spoken by over 400.000.000 people with a wide range of varieties and accents: Castilian, Andaluz, and the accents from Extremadura, Valencia, Burgos or Asturias. (Basque, Catalan and Gallego being consid-

---

4 *In River Plate Spanish, although* **suela** *and* **zapato** *are spelled differently, from the point of view of sounds, there is no significant difference between the /s/ sound in* **suela** *and the /s/ sound in* **zapato***. There is just one phoneme /s/. Contrastingly, there are two phonemes in Spain where a distinctive difference is made between them. Although most speakers are unaware, in Rioplatense Spanish, the /s/ phoneme in* **suela** *is not the same as in* **mosca** *where the allophone /h/ takes its place.*

ered as separate languages. There is the Rioplatense accent, and the Spanish from Chile, from Peru, Ecuador, Venezuela, Central America, the Caribbean Islands, Colombian Spanish (considered the best among those in the Americas) and the mixed version spoken by millions of Hispanics in the United States. The same holds good for other languages which also show variations depending on the regions where they are spoken.

How do interpreters manage to interpret from such a variety of different accents? How can they translate almost with equal ease, the speech of a physician from India, of a Texan manager or of the English-speaking Chinese finance director of an international organization? The truth is that we often feel at ease with some varieties but not with others. The "accommodation" necessary for our acoustic system to identify certain phonemes when the speaker has an unfamiliar accent may take some extra milliseconds, which, in the case of simultaneous interpretation, may prove too long to ensure the flow of simultaneous understanding. So, it may prove healthier from the point of view of communication to slow down a bit if you are speaking to an international audience even if all members are supposed to speak the same language.

Now, the question of how we perceive objects as being the *same* when input is always changing goes well beyond the realms of sounds, phonemes and interpreting. We shall come back to this question again at the end of this chapter. We dealt with it already in chapter 20 where, through Saussure's concept of the *sign* and Pergnier's studies on *polysemy*, we managed to discriminate between individual utterances or uses of a word and the unifying concept underlying them; and between the different *referents* of a given noun and their linguistic invariant or core.

In a world of infinitely flowing various forms and ever-shifting sensations, the stability of invariants proves fundamental. Let us take another case now to see what invariance is and how it works.

On Invariance

Let us shift from the oral to the written language and take letters – not sounds – as references.

Let's consider letter A and some of its possible variations.

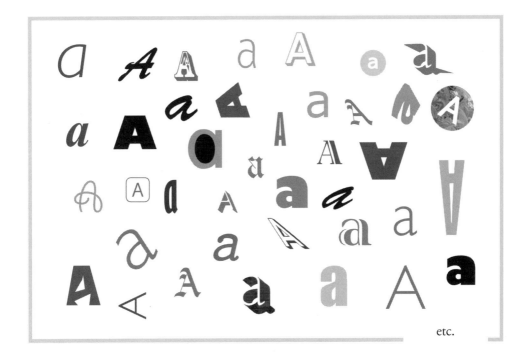

etc.

The reason why we can identify all the previous signs as the letter **A** in spite of the obvious or slight differences in design, size, texture, width, colour, etc., is because we are able to go up one abstraction step and recognize that they all relate back to the abstract unit "A", first element of a closed system called *alphabet*, set of letters or symbols in a fixed order, used when writing a language. In English there are 26 letters, each of which has certain distinctive traits which permit to distinguish each one of them from the rest. No graphic difference among the previous signs constitutes a distinctive trait as there can be between A and say, B.

etc.

In chapter 3, The Implied, I evoked Aristotle's famous example:

$$A = A$$

A equals A, if we accept that both elements, first A and second A point to an abstract third entity A (as opposed to B, C, D, E, etc.) It seems also unquestionable, though, that the first A cannot be considered identical to the second one if we take into account their positioning regarding the symbol =, since one appears before and the other after it.

I said in one of the opening pages of this chapter that the abstracting process thanks to which we select and combine elements permitting us to reach the invariant representations is difficult to describe. Alfred Korzybski did so towards 1930. More recently, neurobiologist and palmpilot inventor Jeff Hawkins made a fascinating new attempt which seems to overlap some of Korzybski's earlier work and even some of my own rather crude attempts at describing the interpreter's job.

"Nature, says Hawkins, solved the problem of variation in a clever way: the cortex creates what are called invariant representations, which handle variations in the world automatically."
The question is how.

Looking for 'Invariants' in Sciences

Roman Jakobson, the Russian linguist – founder of the Prague School of Linguistics and one of the true fathers of structuralism according to Levi-Strauss – was the first to demonstrate how *"among the infinite number of sounds voice can produce, every language chooses a very small number of them to set up a system through which meanings can be differentiated"*. Systems imply structuring.

Throughout the 20th century, researchers in different disciplines looked for invariants or universals in several fields: Chomsky in language, Levi-Strauss in social behaviour, Korzybski in systems and structures of different types.

We saw that looking for *similarities* and *differences* is a basic brain activity and perhaps one of the first that babies engage in. Distinguishing what remains permanent from what changes allows us to understand the world better and to get closer to the essence or the structure of things. We navigate then in an ocean of differences, trying to abstract from them an *invariant core*, something that remains stable, unchanging.

Levi-Strauss' art consisted of detecting analog mental constraints in modern and primitive societies. The myths and rules of social life are the raw material in which he detects the "structural invariants". He says:[5]

"Behind the enormous variety of cultures, there exists a psychic unity of mankind … Everything is in the language. By that I mean, structures, essence, functioning, dimensions, references, and planes are a mere reflection of the world at large".

5 *Claude Levi-Strauss, famous social anthropologist, from an interview with Guy Sorman.* Les vrais penseurs de notre temps. *Paris, Fayard, 1989.*

CHAPTER 23

On Understanding

Of time and the process of understanding. What is understanding after all?

V isitors to the magnificent Topkapi Palace in Istanbul may be surprised to find a beautiful waiting room only for interpreters. It is right next to the Ambassadors' Hall, where diplomats, emissaries, and officials once waited for the Sultan to receive them. From times immemorial, interpreters have been at the centre of international affairs, or rather next to it. *Space* was specifically established for them. In ancient times, though, *time* did not seem to press – not at least, when *understanding* was at stake.

Authorities would speak and then wait for interpreters to calmly render their versions. *Presence, focus* and *memory* were recognized as essential for the interpreter to do a good job. Since then, technological progress has opened up new possibilities but with it the urge to gain time has increased. After World War II, a new type of interpretation was officially born at the Nuremberg Trials. In November 1945, while the International Military Court was preparing to bring ex-Nazi leaders to trial, the decision was made to use *simultaneous interpretation* in order to save time during the hearings: interpreters would translate *during* the depositions, not *after* them.

Those pioneers amazed and stupefied the public. Interpreters in those days were often compared to "prima donnas" although they were unable to explain how they divided their attention in order to hear and speak at the same time. Simultaneous translating retained an aura of magic for many years. *"Had they lived in the Middle Ages, these interpreters would have gone directly to the stake"* a UN officer in Geneva supposedly said one day, amazed by an interpreter's gesticulations. *"He looks possessed".*

For years afterwards, indian chiefs, kings, Heads of State, ministers, diplomats, Heads of different religions, the military, scholars, researchers, adventurers, entrepreneurs, scientists, artists, etc. turned to the interpreter to check – through their eyes or through some words – whether the rhythm and the speed was correct. Participants seemed especially aware of the difficulties and subtleties involved in this "strange exchange". Speakers seemed more aware of – and awed sometimes by – the importance of *time* and *memory* – and this awkwardness was sometimes noticeable in their body posture and in the way they spoke.

Little by little, as with so many other things, the need for speed got the upper hand. Not only did speakers get used to being interpreted, and to being interpreted on the spot, they also began to deliver their lines faster. Not only did they get used to simultaneous interpreting, they also got used to increased pressure, shorter spans of time for their presentations, greater speed, more shortcuts, more acronyms, and also more interferences. Not only did they take for granted that interpretation was simultaneous, they also took for granted that *understanding* was. This was a big mistake. It takes time for the "penny to drop" as the British say – an image taken from the old public telephones.

Time is necessary for *understanding* since connections and associations have to be made, sometimes in a sequential order. It is true, though, that *understanding* can also happen in an instant, with the sudden perception of the true nature of things; and when true "insight" occurs, the pennies seem to drop all together like in a gambling device. Paradoxically, the deeper the understanding, the more quickly it occurs. Life would be magnificent if we could manage to shorten the intervals between moments of insight – or illumination as Aristotle called them.

But what does it mean to *understand*?

How can we approach *understanding*, detect, test or confirm it?

Understanding is, after all, the most fundamental operation; without it transmitting sense would no longer be feasible and translations would hardly get beyond the nonsense of word-by-word translation.

On Understanding

We understand with our intellect, with our mind; but also with our heart, with our emotions, and with our body, with our instincts.

We have all experienced a warm hand and *understood* that somebody was there to help; that somebody loved us; we may also have understood 'danger' at some point and developed a spontaneous chain of reactions that saved our life. This short-cut bypasses the normal logical paths that we use to solve problems intellectually.

So there seem to be different levels of *understanding:* sometimes it is our instincts that propel us to act; at other times we seem to be moved by our emotions; often it is our rational mind that seems in command.

The first striking thing about *understanding* is that once a set of data is organized and understood in a certain way, *adding* a new element or casting the existing elements in a new light may bring about a reorganization of the information and thus *a new understanding* of the situation. Our brains, and our bodies, seem capable of an infinite re-ordering of information.

It is even more awesome to realize that in certain cases the seemingly *same* situation or concept can be understood differently by the *same* person as time goes by, as if *understanding* grew deeper and wiser. Even with no external changes, a new configuration can pop up.

Another striking thing about understanding is that there need not be external signs to prove it occurred. Understanding occurs inside; more precisely in the brain.

In certain cases, proof that something has been *understood* is easy to obtain. We ask somebody to do something and he or she does so. Suppose we are in a room where all the windows are closed and we ask somebody to open one of them. If they get up and open it, we will clearly see that our wish – order or instruction – was understood.

Very often though, there are no external proofs since humans do not need to "do" anything to understand a story although emotional reactions may sometimes speak for themselves. On the other hand, *output* of some kind is mandatory to prove that a computer has "understood" instructions. But as Jeff Hawkins[1] reminds us, although Deep Blue beat Gary Kasparov playing chess, the big IBM computer does not necessarily *understand* chess.

"A calculator performs arithmetic but does not understand math. No computer can understand language as well as a three year old or see as well as a mouse".

Linguist and philosophy professor John Searle's experiment with the Chinese Room proves that *behavioural equivalence* is not enough to prove intelligence: as you will see in the case that follows no *understanding* occurs.

Searle's thought experiment:

Suppose you have a room with a slot in one wall, and inside is an English-speaking person sitting at a desk. He has a big book of instructions and all the pencils and scratch paper he could ever need. Flipping through the book, he sees that the instructions, written in English, dictate ways to manipulate, sort and compare Chinese characters. Mind you, the directions say nothing about the meanings of the Chinese characters; they only deal with how the characters are to be copied, erased, reordered, transcribed, and so forth.

Someone outside the room slips a piece of paper through the slot. On it is written a story and questions about the story, all in Chinese. The man inside doesn't speak or read a word of Chinese, but he picks up the paper and goes to

1 *Jeff Hawkins,* On Intelligence, *New York: Times Books, 2004.*

work with the rulebook. He toils and toils, rotely following the instructions in the book. At times the instructions tell him to write characters on scrap paper, and at other times to move and erase characters. Applying rule after rule, writing and erasing characters, the man works until the book's instructions tell him he is done. When he is finished at last he has written a new page of characters, which unbeknownst to him are the answers to the questions. The book tells him to pass his paper back through the slot. He does it and wonders what this whole tedious exercise has been about.

Outside a Chinese speaker reads the page. The answers are all correct, she notes – even insightful. If she is asked whether those answers came from an intelligent mind that had understood the story, she will definitely say yes.

But can she be right? Who understood the story? It wasn't the fellow inside, certainly; he is ignorant of Chinese and has no idea what the story was about. It wasn't the book, which is just, well, a book, sitting inertly on the writing desk amid piles of paper. So where did the understanding occur? Searle's answer is that no understanding did occur; it was just a bunch of mindless page flipping and pencil scratching. And now the bait-and-switch: the Chinese Room is exactly analogous to a digital computer. The person is the CPU, mindlessly executing instructions, the book is the software program feeding instructions to the CPU, and the scratch paper is the memory. Thus no matter how cleverly a computer is designed to simulate intelligence by producing the same behavior as a human, it has no understanding and it is not intelligent. Searle made it clear he didn't know what intelligence is; he was only saying that whatever it is, computers don't have it.

Quoted from J. Hawkins in *On Intelligence*.

This comparison with computers allows us to find the intrinsic characteristics of *understanding* we will now try to define.

Understanding is a dynamic internal process of associations and connections, sometimes at different levels, which establishes relationships and produces syntheses from time to time.

When we *understand* something – each other, a poem, a situation – we establish an internal relationship within ourselves and with something "outside of ourselves": other people, the poet who wrote the poem, etc. An intangible bridge is built between us and others. Communication takes place. *Communion, communication* come from Greek *koinônia* and Latin *communicare,* to have in common, be in a relationship, relate. Such a process can take place at different levels, physical, emotional, intellectual, etc. It may produce external behaviour; but this is not the inevitable result for successful understanding or successful communication.

Some non-conventional observers who have developed special capacities of attention claim that, even in those cases when nothing seems to happen outside, many things are *visible.* Signs that go un-noticed for the untrained eye are easily perceptible and obvious to them. Let us think of hypnosis expert, Milton H. Erickson, who astounded everybody with his incredible sense of observation; of his disciple, Ernest Rossi. Of Thérèse Berthérat, the anti-gymnastics initiator, who, in the completely different field of physical therapy developed similar powers of observation. The three of them, as well as many other physical and psychological therapists literally perceive lots of telling details through subtle changes in the colour or texture of a person's skin, a sudden blush or change in breathing, imperceptible eye movements. Are these extremely subtle changes and almost imperceptible muscular movements involuntarily mirroring the movements inside?

American psychologist Paul Elkman[2] has no doubts about it. He even goes further. To him, the information on our face,

---

2 *Quoted by Malcolm Gladwell in* Blink, The Power of Thinking without Thinking, *New York, Little, Brown and company, 2005.*

for example, is not just a signal of what is going on inside our mind. In a certain sense, "it *is* what is going on inside our mind". Fascinated by the abundance of information about emotion the human face provides, Elkman (together with Friesen and others) created a taxonomy of facial expressions, identifying distinct muscular movements as in a sort of universal anatomical emotional alphabet.

Time is necessary to observe, and to observe very minute details. Time is necessary to become aware of the process that is taking place while observing and to let information sink in. In the environment of physical movements and therapy, Berthérat stresses the importance of allowing time to feed information back to the system. The most important moment during her anti-gymnastics workshops is not when participants make movements but rather when they stop making them, and are flooded by the aftermath of sensations. It is fundamental to accept the sensations and allow them to flow so that information can complete the cycle and go up or get back to the starting point: this feedback loop of information turns out fundamental for our well-being. Berthérat insists on giving time and attention to this process because we often tend to interrupt it. When we do not, we start listening again to what our organism is telling us here and now.

While describing brain functioning, Hawkins stresses the importance of feedback as well:

> "For years, scientists ignored the feedback connections. But information flowing back is as important for correct prediction as information going forward. "The same feedforward-feedback process is occurring in all your cortical areas involving all your senses."[3]

Feedback is then a fundamental step in the process of *understanding*. Beware! Skipping it prevents us from learning from our previous errors.

----

3 Jeff Hawkins, On Intelligence, *New York: Times Books, 2004.*

As good communication experts know, the quality of the communication circuits in any organization today is measured not according to the way information gets *down* (orders, instructions, etc.) but rather according to how far, how correctly and how fast it travels *up* the organization. This is the "feedback loop" – an incredibly important mechanism.[4] If we compare the frequency of use of the expression in English and in Spanish, we shall easily infer that this concept is much more widely used in the AngloSaxon world than in the Spanish or Latin American contexts where *retrolimentación, devolución, restitución* are not very frequently used. Neither is *recurrencia* – the technical term used for military strategic planning in its latest phases.

Time is necessary for *understanding* as we said at the outset. But then it is equally true that *understanding* may come at lightning speed when we have an insight. And in those wonderful "aha" moments, external muscular signs are even easier to perceive since often jaws let go, mouths fall open, eyebrows go up, we relax, something comes in. There is acceptance, tension recedes.

Memory, attention, prediction seem to have a lot to do with *understanding*. *Understanding* implies listening, seeing, feeling, abstracting, making comparisons, associations, connections and sometimes synthesis.

We saw how important *prediction* was for *understanding* in our interpreting examples. As we saw in chapter 11, we use our previous experiences to anticipate events. It would be interesting to learn in detail how the confirmation of a forecast at one level triggers forecasts at other levels and how the layers of this complex system interweave with one another.

But Hawkins goes much farther since he equates *understanding* with *predicting*.

---

4 *It was thanks to well-known French crisis management expert Patrick Lagadec that I learnt how to carry out "experiential debriefings" ("restitución de experiencias") and carry them out in the corporate world.*

We saw that our capacity to abstract and produce *invariant representations* also turns out to be fundamental for understanding.

Phonemes are the invariant representation at the sound level, *signs* at the semantic level where we also found (with Pergnier) some smaller intrinsic *semantic knots* or linguistic invariants. Stereotyped storylines may be considered to constitute some kind of *pragmatic invariants.* Invariants are necessary to avoid getting lost in an ocean of diversity.

As also mentioned before, priorities, levels and categories must be set, concepts classified, levels of abstraction determined. It is this *structuring* which facilitates *understanding.*

Merleau-Ponty[5] says,

"To see is to dominate simultaneous multiplicities".

So is *understanding,* we may now add.

In a world of infinitely various forms and ever-shifting sensations, the stability of certain forms or patterns fosters and speeds up *understanding.* Our brain rapidly scans the whole in search of meaningful differences.

Let us reverse the question now and see what blocks, prevents or delays *understanding.*

Either too much or too little information. Not knowing the answers to the following: Who? To whom? Where? When? How? For what purpose? Erroneous attribution of motive and intent; lack of background information or failure to retrieve it; wrong or stereotyped scenarios; reversal of the natural orders of abstraction; taking the map for the territory; confusion, identification, jumping to conclusions; interference; contradictory signals; double binds; dispersion, fixation.

Although *understanding* implies certainty (about something at a given place and time), it is not something definitive and

---

5 *In* La fenomenología de la percepción, *México, Fondo de cultura Económica, 1957.*

fixed; it is a process susceptible to change and transformation. *Understanding* takes time, even if we can compress it while interpreting simultaneously. Time necessary to follow the rational path in linear sequence or to allow for information, for emotions and sensations to feed back to us. Feed-forward and feed-back are necessary for understanding in a process that needs "checking" or "confirmation". Quality in the slow processes may perhaps support quality in the faster ones.

When integration at different levels occurs, insights may happen independently of our will. Moments of illumination and blissful deep connection belong here as well as fast decisions that can save lives or "blink" snap judgments of dubious results.

If with our rational mind we track ideas from point to point, cabling chunks of thought, linking A to B and B to C, etc. some natural non-linear processes produce instantaneous A-Z connections and exhilarating semantic jumps.

It is important to be aware of and to use both types of *understanding*.

As with so many other things, something paradoxical emerges when trying to understand *understanding* since something seems to be and not be at the same time.

❖   ❖   ❖

CHAPTER 24

Delving into our Brain

Of what
the brain's
architecture has
to tell us about
how the
brain works.
Of what that
knowledge may
bring about.

Our "Three" Brains

It may be interesting to recall the evolution of our nervous system and of our brain.

We know as from Mac Lean in 1964[1] that as humans evolved over millions of years, they developed three brains, each enveloping the previous one. Our reptile cortex goes back about two hundred million years and it is our oldest phylogenetic acquisition. It is responsible still today for some of our most primitive reactions.[2]

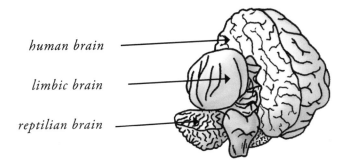

In the next evolutionary stage, mammals' reptilian brain was enveloped by what Broca (1878) called the "limbic lobe". The limbic system refers today to the limbic cortex and all

---

1 Paul D. MacLean (from the National Institute of Mental health, Bethesda, Maryland, USA) developed the theory of the three brains. Human beings are thus conceived as pluralistic beings whose coherence and harmony are to build.

2 See Henri Laborit, L'agressivité détournée. Paris, Union Générale d'Editions, 1970. And Alain Resnais' film Mon Oncle d' Amérique.

the subcortical structures. In a third evolutionary stage, the "neo-cortex" enveloped the other two in the most evolved mammals which, contrary to plants, need a nervous system to move around so as to get food and avoid danger.

Like Mac Lean, Laborit also speaks of "three brains": 1) the reptilian, 2) the paleocephalic, and 3) the neo-cortex, each with specific functions linking us to the remote past and to the open future.

A brain's main task is to preserve life through four basic mechanisms: 1) consumption, 2) reward, 3) punishment and 4) inhibition. *Consumption* means: food, sleep, copulation and structural upkeep; *reward* implies pleasure and gratification; *punishment* involves fear and triggers a "fight or flight" response; and *inhibition* will either postpone or cancel the output.

The theory of the three brains seems to provide a *reasonable* explanation to some of the most *unreasonable* human acts, such as sudden fits of temper, disproportionate violent reactions, etc. If this theory holds good, it is as fundamental for humans to exert neocortical control over our most "primitive brains" as it is to bridge those three brains and find an integrated harmonious coordination. Coordination and integration equally should be advocated for the optimized functioning of the two hemispheres.

After this extremely brief diachronic view of the development of the human brain, let us now concentrate on its latest development: our neocortex. Being no neuroscientist myself, and sure as I am that readers can easily find the latest anatomical descriptions in books or the Internet, I decided to pick just one neuroscientist among many others and follow his path. Stunned as I am at the coincidences in our way of describing some "events" (an interpreter's error in my case, the information circuitry in the neocortex in his), I will quote Jeff Hawkins' descriptions of the neocortex taken from his book *On Intelligence* as the basis for this chapter.

Our Neocortex

Astoundingly, as Hawkins states, everything we know about the world and about ourselves is stored in this two-millimeter-thick surface with the size of a big handkerchief.

"Almost everything we think of as intelligence – perception, language, imagination, mathematics, art, music, and planning – occurs here. Your neocortex is reading this book. (…)

Get six business cards or six playing cards – either will do – and put them in a stack. (It will help if you do this instead of just imagining it). You are now holding a model of the cortex. Your six business cards are about 2 millimeters thick and should give you a sense of how thin the cortical sheet is. Just like your stack of cards, the neocortex is about 2 millimeters thick and has six layers, each approximately by one card.

To accommodate our large brain, nature had to modify our general anatomy and evolution folded up the neocortex, stuffing it into our skulls like a sheet of paper crumpled into a brandy snifter. … Nerve cells or neurons are so tightly packed that no one knows exactly how many there are. … Some anatomists estimate there are about thirty billion neurons.

After twenty-five years of thinking about brains – *says Hawkins* – I still find this fact astounding. That a thin sheet of cells sees, feels, and creates our worldview is just short of incredible."

Hawkins[3] confirms Francis Crick's Astonishing Hypothesis: the mind is the creation of the cells in the brain.

"Only neurons and a dance of information. There appears to be a large philosophical gulf between a collection of cells and our conscious experience, yet mind and brain are one and the same".

---

3 *Jeff Hawkins*, On Intelligence, *New York: Times Books, 2004.*

Such a line of research is confirmed at present by authors of different origins; neurobiologist Robert Doty (1998) argues for example that the puzzle of how patterns of neuronal activity become transformed into subjective awareness "remains the cardinal mystery of human existence". Neurologist Jeffrey Schwartz says:[4]

> "We now know that the circuits of our minds change when our fingers fly over the strings of a violin; they change when we suffer an amputation, or a stroke; they change when our ears become tuned to the sounds of our native language and deaf to the phonemes of a foreign one. Neuronal circuits also change when something as gossamer as our thoughts changes, when something as inchoate as mental effort becomes engaged – when in short, we choose to attend with mindfulness. It allows us, by actively focusing attention on one rivulet in the stream of consciousness, to change – in scientifically demonstrable ways – the systematic functioning of our own neural circuitry."

This faculty our brains have to shape or reshape themselves has been called "neuroplasticity". It seems to prove that we have the power to shape our brains and consequently to sculpt our own selves and our destiny. Part of the aim of this book, as I stated on page 11 of the introduction, is to show the role *language* has – or may have – in this reshuffling or reshaping of our mind.

But let us go back to the neorcortex and look more closely at it following Hawkins' model. The cortex presents few landmarks: the giant fissure separating the two cerebral hemispheres and the sulcus that divides the back and front regions. There are, to the naked eye, no lines or colours demarcating the different areas. Yet, it has been known for a long time that some

---

4 *J. Schwartz, S. Begley,* The Mind and the Brain, *Reagan Books, New York, 2002.*

mental functions are located in specific regions of the brain, (for example, language is partly located in Broca's area) and that these areas are *arranged like an irregular patchwork quilt.*

(…) "Functions are not clearly delineated, they are mostly arranged in a branching hierarchy. Some elements are in an abstract sense, "above" and "below" others – not physically though, hierarchically. What makes one region "higher" or "lower" than another is how they are connected to one another. In the cortex, lower areas feed information up to higher areas by way of a certain neural pattern of connectivity, while higher areas send feedback down to lower areas using a different connection pattern. There are lateral connections as well. (…) The lowest of the functional regions, the primary sensory areas, are where sensory information first arrives in the cortex. These regions process the information at its rawest, most basic level".[5]

The cortex is made up of nerve cells or neurons. The six layers in the cortex are formed by variations in the density or type of cells and their connections. Each cell has branching wirelike structures called axons and dendrites. When the axon from one neuron touches the dendrite of another, they form small connections called synapses. In fact, they do not touch each other. What apparently happens when they connect is that one opens up and lets loose minute chemical substances known as *neurotransmitters* that attach themselves to receptors on the other neuron, either stimulating it – causing it to "fire" – or inhibiting it – causing it *not* to "fire".

---

5 For example, "… *visual information enters the cortex through the primary visual area, called V1 for short. V1 is concerned with low-level visual features such as tiny edge-segments, small-scale components of motion, binocular disparity (for stereovision), and basic color and contrast information. V1 feeds information up to other areas, such as V2, V4 and IT, and a bunch of other areas besides. Each of these areas is concerned with more specialized or abstract aspects of the information. Your other senses have similar hierarchies".*

Hawkins recalls neuroscientist Mountcastle and compares his and Darwin's ways of considering certain facts. For many years biologists had been looking for *differences* between species and Darwin had done likewise. But eventually Darwin had the insight to ask what all those species had *in common*. Mountcastle made similar observations regarding the neocortex. Anatomists had been looking for minute *differences* in cortical regions while Mountcastle focused on the remarkable uniformity of the neocortex and concluded that all regions were performing the *same* operation. *If there are **slight differences** between the regions, it is because of **what they are connected to** and not because of a difference in their functions.*

Coming back to our six-layered cortex, we can see how information flows both horizontally and vertically within this narrow space. Of course there is no point in reproducing here what you can read for yourselves in Hawkins' book but, with his permission, I will reproduce some of his diagrams and try to convey the best I can a "feel" of the infinitesimal movements he describes within that tiny space.

> "The neocortex is assumed to consist of a large number of columns (as surmised also by Mountcastle from anatomical and theoretical considerations). Each column is attuned to a particular feature at a given level in a hierarchy. It receives bottom-up inputs from lower levels, and top-down inputs from higher levels. (Other columns at the same level also feed into a given column, and serve mostly to inhibit the activation of exclusive representations.) When an input is recognized – that is, acceptable agreement is obtained between the bottom-up and top-down sources – a column generates outputs which in turn propagate to both lower and higher levels".

A complex internal hierarchical organization seems to preside over brain functioning. In a width of barely two millimeters we find: six layers, with columns of cells that run perpendicular to those layers; layers within each column connected via axons that run up and down; regions dealing with streams of patterns, billions of neurons, trillions of synapses.

"Our brain has an estimated several hundred million microcolumns; activity spreads up and down within every column of cells; in this columnar structure, information flows mostly horizontally in layer 1 and vertically layers 2 to 6."

Hawkins goes into minute descriptions to show how the cortex works and "how these coin-size cortical regions and their columns send and receive information up and down the cortical hierarchy".

"There are four things we know the neocortex does:

1. It stores sequences of patterns.
2. It recalls patterns auto-associatively.
3. It stores patterns in an invariant form.
4. It stores patterns in a hierarchy".

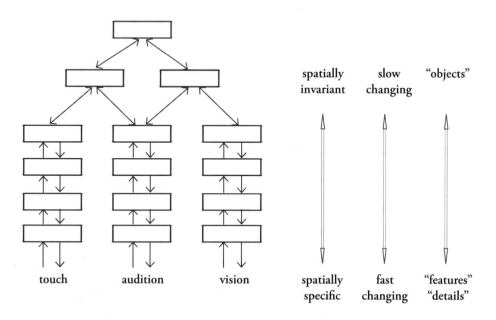

This is a purely conceptual diagram used by Hawkins in On Intelligence *(page 114) to show invariant representations formation in hearing, vision and touch. Reproduced with the author's consent.*

As anybody can read in *Wikipedia* in the Internet, it seems to be accepted today that "*the human brain appears to have no localized center of conscious control. The brain seems to derive consciousness from interaction among numerous systems within the brain. Executive functions rely on cerebral activities, especially those of the frontal lobes, but redundant and complementary processes within the brain result in a diffuse assignment of executive control that can be difficult to attribute to any single locale*".

Why did I think it necessary at this point to include information about the brain?

For several reasons. On the one hand, as management expert Michel Saloff-Lacoste mentions in his book *Management for the 3rd Millennium*,[6] inventions and developments are often the result of our *understanding* of our own body, or "extensions" of those parts of our body humanity has come to "know" better at a certain time in history. Let us take an example to make this clear: man's first tools or weapons can be considered a prolongation of their teeth or nails and some agricultural tools like the wheel or the plough, extensions of their arms, legs and feet. With the Industrial Revolution, it was the internal organs like the viscera or the intestines which were "cloned" or "reproduced" in factories and plants processing food or transforming raw materials. In the Information Age, with computers and electronic devices, it is the brain which information technology researchers seek to understand and imitate.

On the other hand, because I am convinced, along with many scientists and therapists, that greater knowledge of how our brain works will help us use it better, develop more appropriate behaviour, avoid bad habits, and consequently evolve more positively and happily. **The discoveries of how we – humans – function and how our brains work may also have an**

----

6 Michel Saloff-Lacoste, Le management du troisième millénaire. Holistique Systémique, *Paris, Editions de la Maisnie, 1991, Guy Trédaniel Editeur.*

impact on our behaviour and, we can hope, speed up social transformation and human evolution.

Finally, it was my own research that led me into this fascinating territory: in order to understand some of the processes I described and some of my early intuitions, a clearer picture of what happens – or may be happening – within the brain proves particularly useful.

Our Converging Hypotheses

For example, let's recall what happened to me while interpreting for the Bishops' Conference in Mar del Plata. I was very young in those days and as I explained before (chapter 3, page 68), perhaps shocked at hearing bishops talk about prostitution, I literally "missed" the word. Stunned by the awkwardness of my experience – it was in fact one of my first big international conferences – I stopped to observe. Although on that occasion, listeners did not notice my trouble, since I managed to "hide" it behind formal structures while getting help from my colleague, the intensity of *feeling at a loss* due to the "breach" of meaning was so strong that I still keep its memory vivid and intact. I did not want that to happen again. I wanted to *understand* what had happened so as to make sure it would not happen again.

Three things proved fundamental then, as seen from today:

1. My decision *to go back* to the trouble spot and not let it go by even if no breach had occurred "outside".

2. The exchange I had with my therapist regarding the incident which helped to isolate it and understand it better.

3. The realization that it was an emotion (of anguish or fear) that had led me into action.

The debriefing of my mistake in those early days of my career permitted me, as time went by and my knowledge of psycholinguistics improved, to analyse the incident from different perspectives. I delved inside and, with the tools provided by psycholinguistics, I managed to describe the process that might have taken place on that occasion and from which different paths opened up for research. (See page 68).

It would seem then that not only had I heard the word correctly at several levels – phonological, prosodic, lexical, syntactic (...) but that I rejected it precisely because I understood it. The speed of the response is staggering. All this suggests that there is a processing of information at a deep level, which happens simultaneously with acoustic processing and other operations. (...) This suggests the existence of a sort of scanning mechanism with very rapid to-and-fro or up-and-down movements between the various levels.

Now, years later, when falling upon Hawkins' descriptions of the information flow in our neocortex, *up-and-down, to-and-fro,* I feel astounded at the overlapping of some of them – infinitely more detailed than mine – and my own. The correspondence seems awesome since our starting points, fields of study and purpose of research differ so much.

His inferences seem to corroborate mine and, I would dare say, my inferences might be corroborating his. This allows for yet another inference: when *different* lines of reasoning, stemming from *different* fields, seem to lead to the *same* or similar inferences, attention should be paid to them and research encouraged along those lines.

Talking about the neocortex again, Hawkins says:

"When input is ambiguous (semi garbled word or confusing visual image) a bottom-up/top down matching mechanism enables you to decide between two or more interpretations. Every movement in your waking life, each region of your neocortex is comparing a set of expected columns driven from above with the set of observed columns driven from below. Where the two sets intersect is what we perceive".

The intersection of these two sets seems equivalent to the "here-and-now" intersection where the two axes introduced in chapter 6 meet: the *synchronic axis* and the *diachronic axis*. (See page 127).

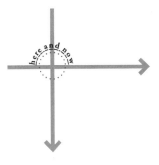

There is yet another coincidence. From the very first chapter of this book I drew a parallel between the mental mechanisms needed to organize visual images, figures and forms and those needed to make sense out of sounds and phonemes, signs and structures. I also remember how awed I felt when the first glimpse of this crossed my mind. I dared verbalize it only metaphorically then:

Seeing and speaking are probably more than just good friends.

Hawkins states that our brain processes inputs from our *different* senses in exactly the *same* way in an assertive manner. He will even say – quoting Vernon Mountcastle – that just one algorithm is enough to describe all those processes.

The consequences of this may be far-reaching. Technological research is Hawkins' field. Knowledge about how our brains function will surely help him and others to reproduce *outside* what happens *inside*. He will most probably add to the palmpilot the invention of some other fabulous devices. He is lucky enough to work in a sphere where processes yield materialized results: concrete "objects" or "products" can be touched, sensed, felt, seen or heard.

But there is yet another field, closer to my own humanistic domain, where consequences may be even farther reaching: education. At the crossroads of our converging inferences, and on the sound bases of physical data about the nature and characteristics of our nervous systems, a thousand burbling ideas come out pointing to the development of our human potential. A true transformation in our approach to education could thus be geared in such a way so that our capacities of observation, attention, memory, association, prediction, etc. occupy the centre of the stage. It is true that the initial results may be not so easily perceivable as a product you can touch. Yet, a revolution in thinking techniques, abstracting exercises, imagination training, creative thinking, emotion management, team-work, etc. could thus be brought about.

In fact, many of these things have already been successively tested and applied. Some of their results are the intangible positive forces at work in some human groups today.

Our thrust should contribute to disseminate them throughout, to make them accessible and available to the very many. One more right should then be added to the universal human rights' list, according to the presently prevailing Western logic: the right to develop one's own intelligence – both rational and emotional.

Why then not share – and contribute to – other people's dreams? If we changed our way of conceiving learning, paraphrasing Aldous Huxley, we could seek social transformation through the simultaneous attack on all fronts: economic, political, educational, psychological, etc.

❖ ❖ ❖

Synthesis and Conclusions

In ancient times, a Chinese wise man was asked by some of his disciples what would be the first thing he would do if given the power to settle the nation's affairs. He answered: "I would, of course, insist on making everybody speak correctly."

"But Master", they told him, "that seems without importance. Why should you attribute to it so much?"

And the old Master answered: "When one does not speak correctly, what one says is not what one intends. If what one says is not what one means, what should be done is left undone. If this is left undone, values and art get corrupted. If values and art get corrupted, Justice sails adrift. And if Justice sails adrift, the whole nation falls in utter confusion."

Attributed to Confucius

Part V

RECONSTRUCTING BABEL
FROM WITHIN

La Tour Babel by Lucas van Valckenborch (before 1535-1597). The Louvre Museum.

BABEL – Genesis 11: 1-9

After the deluge and after the earth was repopulated, Genesis tells the strange story of the Tower of Babel.

"And the whole earth was of one language, and of one speech. And it came to pass, as they journeyed from the east, that they found a plain in the land of Shinar; and they dwelt there. And they said one to another, Go to, let us make brick, and burn them thoroughly. And they had brick for stone, and slime had they for mortar. And they said, Go to, let us build us a city, and a tower, whose top may reach unto heaven; and let us make us a name, lest we be scattered abroad upon the face of the whole earth."

"And the LORD came down to see the city and the tower, which the children of men builded. And the LORD said, Behold, the people is one, and they have all one language; and this they begin to do: and now nothing will be restrained from them, which they have imagined to do.[1] Go to, let us go down, and there confound their language, that they may not understand one another's speech. So the LORD scattered them abroad from thence upon the face of all the earth: and they left off to build the city. Therefore is the name of it called Babel; because the LORD did there confound the language of all the earth: and from thence did the LORD scatter them abroad upon the face of all the earth."

----

1 The Bible, King James Version. Genesis, XI, 1 to 9.

CHAPTER 25

Babel Crumbling Down

Of how language itself may constitute a trap to impede good communication.

B efore concluding, I would like to revert to one of the myths that have profoundly marked Western civilization: that of the Tower of Babel. Myths are condensed stories, expressing symbolically something we should learn. As in all myths – with their fabulous accounts about gods, superhuman beings and extraordinary events and circumstances – there is something for us to learn in this one. According to Genesis, the Babylonians wanted to make a name for themselves by building a mighty city and a tower "with its top in the heavens". God disrupted the work by so confusing the language of the workers that they could no longer understand one another.

Babel has become the symbol of confusion and disorder imposed on men as punishment for their errors. Ancient Babel, near Babylonia, seems far away from us both in space and time. Awkwardly, present-day Iraq, where ancient Babel was geographically situated, appears to be one of the emerging signs of generalized confusion, disorder and war in a globalized world. We seem to have collectively taken some wrong "turns", and it would seem we should collectively undo our way and start again.

But confusion today seems no longer to stem from the variety of languages and the difficulty to translate. It is *language itself* which constitutes the trap, not *languageS*. The problem is not to find bridges between one language and the next; the problem is to find a common ground for understanding *no matter what the language*. The problem is the upheaval, the reversal of the orders of abstraction within any language. As if we were in need of an English-English – or Spanish-Spanish – interpreter to understand what people mean. Something seems to have got disrupted in the use of language itself. Orders of abstraction overturned, hierarchies flattened, bridges collapsed, maps and territories disconnected, false-to-fact statements presented as true-to-fact, systematic symbol destruction, loss of common referents, motives misinterpreted.

In spite of the efforts of many to reach understanding and peace, the Biblical curse of dissipation and confusion seems to hold good today.

But while myths tell the story of heroes and gods, semigods and goddesses, our interaction today has to do not with them, nor with dragons and monsters, armies of a thousand warriors or Herculean tasks but rather with *ordinary* men and women who lead *normal* lives according to the different standards of living both in the Western world and in the East, both in the North and the South. We are not expected – and we do not expect others – to carry out extraordinary deeds any more. There is no kingdom or county or prince by way of reward. Therein lies perhaps our challenge: as no great deeds are expected, we tend to disregard many things. It is through lack of attention, or care for small details that we may often get off the right track. We wish to go fast and finish whatever we are doing quickly. Here is the trap, as dangerous as the fiery tongue of dragons once was, although much more disguised. Here lies our challenge, too: pay attention and take time. Contrary to mythical heroes, it is perhaps the challenge of present men and women to care for little things and make through them a difference. No heroes or heroines individually standing out, but millions of human beings more and more consciously aware that what they think, do and say, counts. No exceptional deed, no massive war, no acclamation but the exceptional personal battle we fight day in day out against the genetic weight and customs of the past.

The trouble is that there seems to be an immense disproportion between the calamities that may ensue as a consequence of the misuse of our language abilities and the often simple insignificant deviations and everyday habits that pave their way. Far from the heroic deeds and characters that courageously managed to set things straight, it is through very simple gestures and careful attitudes that we can manage to bring about change in our lives – right away.

Let a few examples show how deeply we can get entangled in words and how swiftly and imperceptibly the words we use can lead us to drift away from our aim, motive, intention or wishes.

A Few Contemporary Instances of Disruption and Collapse

1. Mexican president Fox was publicly accused of discriminating against AfroAmericans when, in order to defend Mexican citizens working in the United States, he said that not even AfroAmericans would accept certain jobs Mexicans normally do in the United States. He surely meant to defend his own people, not to hurt others, and refused to apologize. His words, nevertheless, caught him in a politically incorrect cross-cultural trap.

2. A *Newsweek* article published in early 2005 on the alleged Koran denigration in Guantanamo triggered violence and deaths in the Middle East. This is a frightening example of words having lethal effects thousands of miles away from their place of origin. The veracity of the information was later denied.

3. Members of the Argentine government seemed proud of organizing the IV Summit Meeting of the Americas in Mar del Plata in November 2005 and of welcoming American presidents and heads of government to their often crisis-stricken soil. Foreign leaders took some time to realize that some members of the Argentine government had also taken part in the organization of the Counter Summit Meeting being held at the same place at the same time as an act of protest against the first.

4. General-semanticist Kate Gladwell reports the following incident: A college junior at a charity-sale, adding prices by hand because the computerized cash-register had broken down, objected when she pointed out that 3 times $1.95 did not equal $3.70 which he had somehow arrived at. "Do you mean I did it wrong?" he objected. "There is no right or wrong. It's just opinion! You do things your way, I do them my own, so what?" Kate later learnt from the charity-sale operator that she had not succeeded in making the student understand why she had to dismiss him after this and similar errors. Some people seem to lack the notion

that certain codes are universally shared and that there are "right and wrong answers" according to them.

References give way, certainties collapse, whole chunks of reality break up, mental disorders abound. Language disorders reveal disorders of other types. Language traps catch us up in their grids and make us their prisoners. Confusion often prevails.

The following examples – taken from the conference world again – show how certain unimportant mechanisms may prove useful in isolation but they may end up producing increasingly undesired effects when used in excess.

Let us consider the use of acronyms, meant as shortcuts to gain time. The following example was taken from a conference on human rights in Buenos Aires, June 2005.

1st Case – Compression of information

Original speaker	Interpreter's version	
The CF will modify its own T of R in cooperation with the IEC or in case of disagreement, refer them to the next ICM.	*El Foro de Presidentes modificará su mandato conjuntamente con el Comité Ejecutivo Internacional o, en caso de desacuerdo, lo remitirá a la próxima reunión del Consejo Internacional.*	The Chairs' Forum will modify its own terms of reference in cooperation with the International Executive Committee or in case of disagreement, will refer them to the next International Council Meeting.

Of course, if the interpreter did not know beforehand what the acronyms stood for, he would not manage to interpret them correctly. What he could have done is follow the speaker closely and use the correct equivalence of acronyms to produce something like:

> *El FP modificará su T de R junto con el CEI o en caso de disputa, los remitirá a la próxima reunión del RCI.*

> The CF will modify its own T of R in cooperation with the IEC or in case of disagreement, refer them to the next ICM.

Another example taken from a data-processing conference:

> "Tuxedo is an OLTP giving good results. X/Open has determined the DTP but we are waiting for the IEEE final evaluation. The TPS of the 4GL will be decisive."

The list of acronyms the Swedish speaker took the trouble to take to the interpreters' booth makes his concern about the difficulties involved evident. It is indeed better to have the list of acronyms before one's eyes when interpreting, at least not to mistake one phoneme for another. But unless interpreters can link those letters to *something else* – a concept, a trade-mark, a program, an institution, etc. – they will hardly *understand* what they are hearing!

Delegates or executives sharing the same environment tend to use more and more acronyms forgetting these seem to be babbling to the majority. If this triggers a feeling of "belonging in the group" for some, others even within the group may experience a feeling of disconnection, let alone those alien to the group.

I like the case of acronyms because it shows in a nutshell how insignificant little habits may end up producing increasingly undesired effects.

There is a principle from which disorder may be ordered. We should find the inner thread connecting the variables of the different examples.

It is easy in the case of acronyms. We shorten sounds to explain and understand things faster. The mechanism works nicely when used with moderation; excess produces opposite results.

Qualifiers are used to give precision, subtlety and richness to something being described. If they are used to keep the microphone longer (or to "sound" precise and subtle) they produce the opposite effect. Interpreters seem to perceive these difficulties in both cases right away.

2nd Case – Laxity of expression

As readers know, adjectives in English precede the noun; not so in Spanish where we generally need to identify the noun first. If the number of adjectives is great, interpreters may experience some difficulty in remembering them all, especially if not much meaning is conveyed through them.

Let us see what writer E. Goldsmith[1] has to say about what he calls "the language of development", i.e. the language used, according to him, by some international experts, members of UN organizations, government officials and some supranational institutions.

> The "Development Industry" has mastered the techniques of saying much and meaning nothing. Consider the following extract from a 1984 speech by the then Assistant Director-General of a well-known international organization:
>
> "This programme is based on an integrated approach to the development of small-scale fisheries and the improvement of the socio-economic conditions of communities of artisanal fishermen and their families. It will promote the skills, capacities and potentials of fishing communities, through the active involvement and participation of the fishing villagers in the planning and implementation of management and development activities."
>
> To the uninitiated it sounds wonderful. In reality none of it stands up to a critical analysis.
>
> ...

1 In The Ecologist, *London, Vol. 21, Nº 2, March / April, 1991.*

The techniques used by the development industry's sophisticated propaganda machine have been analyzed by A.F. Robertson. He highlights the language used for selling its policies and stresses that much of its value rests in "its imprecision of meaning". He points out that the "buzz words" which it uses can be "combined into almost infinite permutations and still "mean" something".

Robertson illustrates his point by listing the 56 words which occurred the most frequently in a planner's lexicon. These are arranged in four different columns of 14 words.

	A	B	C	D
1	Centrally	Motivated	Grass-roots	Involvement
2	Rationally	Positive	Sectorial	Incentive
3	Systematically	Structured	Institutional	Participation
4	Formally	Controlled	Urban	Attack
5	Totally	Integrated	Organizational	Process
6	Strategically	Balanced	Rural	Package
7	Dynamically	Functional	Growth-Oriented	Dialogue
8	Democratically	Programmed	Development	Initiative
9	Situationally	Mobilized	Cooperative	Scheme
10	Moderately	Limited	On-Going	Approach
11	Intensively	Phased	Technical	Project
12	Comprehensively	Delegated	Leadership	Action
13	Radically	Maximized	Agrarian	Collaboration
14	Optimally	Consistent	Planning	Objective

One word can be selected at random from each column to compose a four word, typical development phrase. For example, A3, B6, C9 and D12 make "systematically balanced cooperative action." A12, B9, C6 and D3 construct another fine sounding phrase, *comprehensively mobilized rural participation*. None of these phrases mean anything yet they are typical of the seductive language which fills the countless speeches, plans, project proposals and glossy pamphlets of the development industry".[1]

---

1 *My thanks to colleague Malcolm McFarlane for having provided me with this text.*

I have the feeling of having interpreted much "worse" speeches than the one quoted here. Colleagues will agree, I am sure, that there are cases in which speakers do not seem to value or respect the power of words, where blabla prevails and the chance is missed to really communicate and act. In such cases, speakers do not seem aware of their own responsibility when taking the floor. They seem to believe they are filling a blank in a roster of actors nobody pays much attention to.[2] Fortunately, there are as many cases of speakers responsibly making use of their chance.

Compression of information takes place, often for the sake of gaining *time*.

Shortcuts – like acronyms – certainly allow us to go faster but when used in excess they hinder communication. At the opposite extreme, laxity of expression takes place, often for the sake of gaining *space*. An abundant number of qualifiers does not guarantee clarity; it often produces the opposite effect.

Language can become the most frightening labyrinth from which it seems almost impossible to escape. Language becomes, in certain cases, one of the worst possible barriers to actual communication itself.

Let us review again some of the problems we may face.

When there is a tremendous information overload, the filters helping to select and abstract data can break down: anything can get in. No appropriate selection or filtering takes place. The same thing happens to our liver for example, or other organs, when too much of an unwholesome substance is ingested. The immune system breaks down, anything can get in, the person accepts everything as "okay".

But the opposite can happen too. When information gets blocked, nothing *new* can get in. People get stuck in their old paradigms and reject any new idea. This was what communication expert Irving I. Lee. called the "allness disease" for

---

2 *Cognitive neurologist Marsel Mersulam (Northwestern University) openly states that boredom is the worst possible thing to keep a brain sane and alert.*

which he proposed a number of clever exercises[3] and recipes to open a "closed mind". When people close their mind, jaws get stuck, breathing is short, contraction ensues, no learning can occur. Paralysis or involution is on the way.

Memory problems and association difficulties take place as well as trouble in focusing, in paying attention and staying connected to a certain subject or in assigning priorities. And so do the "opposite" difficulties: the apparent impossibility to "forget" certain things, to let go of a certain subject and pass on to something else so as not to stay obsessively fixed with the same idea. Some cannot "focus", others exclude from their visual field the rich peripheral environment, as if the *scanning*

3 Irving and Laura Lee, Handling Barriers in Communication, *International Society for General Semantics, & Harper & Row Publisher, San Francisco, 1956, 1957.*

mechanism allowing for a general view of the situation at large were blocked.

Some people seem not to perceive certain *differences* or pretend they do not exist. They flatten what looks multidimensional or reverse the natural order of things. They seem unable or unwilling to discriminate among different levels of classification as the lyrics of a well-known Argentine tango, *Cambalache*, cynically showed: "everything is the same, nothing makes any difference, the honest man is on a level with the thief". Its author, Discepolo, must surely have meant it as a criticism of 20th century Argentine confusion but ended up producing a self-fulfilling prophecy.

Other people find it extremely difficult to recognize the *similarity* of certain patterns. Patterns to classify and give priorities to functions, subjects and roles seem to have got lost somewhere along the way.

Nevertheless, and as suggested at the outset, language provides us with a wonderful set of tools with which to build solid understanding, favour critical and creative thinking, develop our intelligence and wisdom and encourage evolution. Our challenge is to learn how to best use these tools.

❖ ❖ ❖

CHAPTER **26**

A New Horizon

Synthesis and

Conclusions.

Mental Organizers.

The Sky is the Limit.

*S*ynthesis is a good way to counterbalance and overcome *confusion*. Summing up enables us to abandon Babel in ruins – to abandon confusion, debris and pride – and help build a new Babel. Babel, symbol of what this time? Not of confusion and punishment, certainly! But of mankind's ancient aspiration to evolve, to grow up, to reach Heavens – if you will – but through no physical or external means this time.

Whereas *confusion* tangles, mixes, dispels, reverts and flattens hierarchies and priorities, *synthesis* helps integration and paves the way for order, hierarchies, priorities and levels.

Now we shall briefly look back at what we have been doing throughout these pages and attempt to sum it up.

Synthesis

In order to work "in simultaneous", interpreters must elaborate *wholes* or *ensembles* characterised by the elements of varying nature which make them up and come from different levels. To cope with the unexpected, they learn to anticipate and predict, to contrast expectations with facts, to look for feedback information in order to verify, cancel out or let hypotheses stand. Much more than *experts on words*, interpreters are therefore *experts on hypotheses*, specialists in the relationships which can exist between various "wholes". To explain the work of interpreters we have had, like them, to put together in one "whole" elements of differing natures. In the words of ethologist Lorenz:[1]

----

1 *Lorenz*, Consideraciones sobre las conductas animal y humana, *Barcelona, Plaza y Janes, 1980.*

"... the more complex the system, the greater the need for an analysis of its totality".

We began this book by comparing the interpreter's words with those of the speaker and soon realised that beyond the description of the *façade* of words and the stone by stone construction, it was necessary to seek the relationships of force and balance which make up the scaffolding and keep the building erect; in this way we passed on from the analysis of words to the consideration of the logical, social and emotional structure underlying them.

The unfolded vision of an interpreted *speech act* allowed us to deconstruct the work of interpreters and detect the various levels at which they operate. The stereoscopic vision of a single *speech act* then permitted us to grasp it in its entirety. But in order to grasp a *speech act* integrally we had to transfer emphasis from *speech* to *action*. It was not easy to cross this border for doing so required including in the analysis very difficult elements to apprehend theoretically, such as feelings or tone of voice. Studying an act implies the demarcation of sequences and perceiving what is momentary as an integral part of a larger "whole", distinguishing the elements that "travel together" from those that do not.

Movement seems to characterize our mental life – from the intangible up-and-down, to-and-fro microscopic movements in our minds that escape our control, to the controllable movements in discourse which facilitate understanding. Movements are necessary for perception and association. *Understanding* implies connections and movement as well.

Analysing an act entails the detection of its component layers (phonologic, semantic, psychological, etc.) whereas it is in the ever-changing breakdown and different integration of these levels that it is finally understood and defined. It also presupposes bringing up the *role* of the main players, of the relationships which bring them together and the social laws that govern them, all of which means, in other words, starting to unmask social *competence* (as opposed to social *performance*) and the entire array of rules governing our behaviour in society.

Problems of perception lead to reflection on the simultaneous and reciprocal translation of our senses and to the multi-levelled image they give us of the "here-and-now", which amounts to bringing up again the subject of *space* and *time*.

The study of *interferences* from a multiplicity of viewpoints sheds light on the crossroads and places its finger on the pulse of the *relationship* between what is conscious and what is not, between what is individual and what is social, between the part and the whole, between what is present now and what was present before.

Like the first letter of the Hebrew alphabet, the *Aleph,* which in Hebrew tradition represents the mysterious gate between the Absolute and the Relative, the intersection of the two axes stands for the "here-and-now" from where interpreters, and speakers, can handle "simultaneous multiplicities" and facilitate *understanding*.

"*So small it has no interior, so vast it has no limits*" – as the Taoist saying goes.

The notions of *implicature* and of *direct and indirect acts* give a new perspective to the way in which the concept of *truth* may be approached. What is said may be true and what is implied may be false, for an isolated sentence cannot be either true or false. And though it may be true that the linearity of a speech precludes saying one thing and then its contrary, it is also true that it can be done by generating meaning through changes in context, level, or framework.

In a world of infinitely flowing varied forms and ever-shifting sensations, the stability of *invariants* proves fundamental. Looking for similarities and differences seems to be one of the first mental activities babies do. Introspection is important since we can infer part of the activities our brain carries out, although not others. But the possibility exists that the more carefully and attentively we consciously perform certain processes, the more accurate and precise our non conscious, automatic responses will be. Attention and what we do with it, how we *choose* to use it, is fundamental, as well as how we use and train our memory.

Interpreters interpret what they *think* speakers mean. Along similar lines, philosopher Cassius Jackson Keyser[2] had long before remarked:

> "The character of human history, the character of human conduct, and the character of all our human institutions depend both upon what man *is* and in equal or greater measure upon what we humans *think* man is"

It is fundamental then to bring together, synthesize, update and make available the latest research on different disciplines. What we end up *thinking* about our own nature, about what we are and how our brain works will certainly end up having a tremendous impact on what we do and how we do it. Our beliefs condition our actions.

At the end of the road we have travelled, all this makes us take a double turn to conclude: at the "theorical" level and at the "pragmatic" one.

From a theoretical point of view, we conclude on the necessity to detach language problems from the exclusively linguistic environment so as to study them from a multiple transdisciplinary perspective within the Cognitive Sciences and/or within a theory of actions.

From a pragmatic point of view, we conclude on the necessity of getting trained so as to use both our brain and our language capacity to the best of our human possibilities. There are certain things we could – and should – start doing right away.

---

2 *Cassius Jackson Keyser,* Lecture XX from Mathematical Philosophy, *New York, 1922.*

Mental Organizers

The tools to change our vision of the world and what we say and how are at our disposal. They do not belong to any one person or group. Nor are they my own invention. They are the result of research, conscious efforts and time devoted by many; they are the result of many people's insights and the fruit of the combined rich work of hundreds, or thousands, of people throughout the ages. Man wanted to fly and did not manage to do so by himself but ended up flying thanks to the combined efforts of many individuals. I trust our enormous capacity to evolve together.

A few years ago, based on this research and on the premises of General Semantics, I designed what I called "mental organizers" to help us clean up our perceptions and – our thoughts. In my experience they facilitate our way from:

confusion   to **ordering**   to **creativity**

Synthesis is necessary to evolve. To evolve, we should set our priorities straight.

There are four operations we need to carry out to set our priorities right:[3] observe, evaluate, decide and do. And then, observe the results, evaluate them, go on or change the orien-

----

3 Rachel Lauer, *A Meta Curriculum Based Upon Critical Thinking.* Et cetera. A Review of General Semantics. *Volume 53. Winter 96-97.*

tation, etc ... While doing this, we are already applying some kind of scientific orientation in our daily lives. Consequences will include, inter alia, a feeling of better integration within ourselves, with others and with the environment.

These "mental organizers" can help us clean up some of our perceptual or cognitive disturbances. They can help us select the data and combine them. They can help us think critically and creatively. There are exercises to be done, experiences to go through, syntheses to be personally made. It is hands on.

This is practical and it requires going through the actual experience, not just describing it or reading about it.

Our "two axes" will help us perform a number of actions such as:

abstract, select,
integrate,
associate, assimilate,
dissociate,
compare, contrast,
distinguish, differentiate,
induce,
deduce,
structure in wholes,
de-structure,
classify,
prioritize, evaluate, etc.

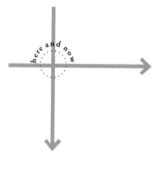

And there is also our "basic kit of thinking tools" to help build *understanding*.

Maps (to represent), scales (to weigh and compare), classifiers (to organize), chains (to associate), scissors (to separate and discriminate), glue (to blend), ladders (to abstract), etc.

We can thus train ourselves to perceive and think better, to manage our emotions and thoughts, to shape and remodel our neocortex over and over again creating new connections between neurons. To bridge our two hemispheres and our three brains. Just as we engage in personal physical training to keep active and young, we should also do something to keep our neurons going.

The Sky is the Limit

I said in the introduction to this work that even in the very early days of this research it was absolutely clear in my mind that some of the insights revealed by this method of research could be of interest beyond the interpreting world itself.

I was – and I am – convinced that language provides us with a wonderful set of tools with which we can transform ourselves and, thus, the world. I know today that to use language in this conscious manner implies an enormous personal challenge since our margin for manoeuvring is not big; I also know that we can help each other out: the more some of us try, the less difficult it will become for all.

We are not accustomed to using language creatively at every instant; perhaps only poets are. Nothing, though, should prevent us from doing so. Or perhaps something does: the weight of the past, comfort of what is already known and accepted, tradition, habits and customs. Our foes lie inside. They are old acquaintances. Paradoxically, in order to surmount them we need as much energy, strength and perseverance as mythical heroes did to decapitate many headed monsters. And the trophy – if any – is just a wider inch of inner space. It is an enormously big – incredibly insignificant task.

To start using language in a creative, powerfully transforming manner, we needed first to become aware of the way language works, of its limitations and possible traps as well as its potential. It was necessary to unveil some of the hidden operations behind.

It is my humble hope that these pages may contribute towards this end.

The sense of a book goes well beyond its chapters, paragraphs and letters. It would make me happy to learn that something of that breath still accompanies you as you now close this one.

❖   ❖   ❖

A Final Word

I n my personal quest for *understanding* and *making sense*, I borrowed many ideas from others. I am indebted to all of them, as well as to my spiritual masters, family and friends, therapists, teachers, colleagues in different disciplines and students.

Most of the authors and researchers quoted – and many others not mentioned – offer much more refined and detailed descriptions about their own fields of research, with more precise terminology in their native languages, in a loftier style, in a dynamic and often academic manner that keeps aggregating research results and newer data. I highly recommend visiting them to those interested in particular areas or aspects of research.

Like a detective on a special mission, or like a hound in search of its prey, what I did was to sniff around looking for the elements I instinctively thought useful in a number of different fields. I combined them in a certain manner, made a life-long research of my own and integrated them in what became a personal synthesis that, like a virtual compass, helps me navigate in life's turbulent waters without getting lost.

It is the *implementation* of the synthesis of that experience that matters to me here and now.

Knowing what we know about how we function, and with the personal matrix of the acquired knowledge at hand, my feeling is we should act … NOW.

GLOSSARY

The terms in the following alphabetical list make up the glossary, which was organized according to different concepts and dichotomies following different authors.

Abstract, abstraction
Diachrony
Enunciation
Illocutionary Act
Indexes
Intensional
Locutionary act
Paradigm
Phatic act
Phonetic act
Register
Speech Act
Syntagm

Conversational maxims
Direct and indirect speech acts
Extensional
Implicature
Indirect act
Lexeme
Morpheme
Perlocutionary Act
Phoneme
Principles of cooperation
Rhetic/al act
Synchrony

*language and speech (langue et parole)

Language = system, code of signs permitting communication.

Speech = use of the system in specific and individual ways.

The basic distinction made by **F. De Saussure** between the abstract entity of rules and laws – the system – shared by a linguistic community, and the personal instances of its specific use (what can be actually observed in speech) can also be applied to other disciplines. The opposition between the virtual system versus an instance of it will be fundamental from a semiological point of view. Systems of rules governing the behaviour of man in society can thus be contrasted to its members' concrete instances of action and reaction; *mental structures* or thought patterns of a given culture can be confronted with the specific thinking of a member of that culture at a given point in time and space. Contrasting such concepts in this way, Saussure puts his finger on the pulse of the matter: man is inserted in a double space-time game which defines him here-and-now as a unique being with unique experiences and also as someone immersed in a community whose rules he learns, shares and modifies while simultaneously being irretrievably moulded by them.

In the Anglo-Saxon context, **Chomsky** will give greater thoroughness to this dichotomy, which he will exclusively focus on the individual restricting it to "**competence** and **performance**". **Alfred Korzybski** will also deal with it, changing focus again, in other terms: **intensionality** and **extensionality**.

In all three cases, though, the first term of the dichotomy stands for what is abstract, or the result of a long series of abstractions; while the second term stands for what is being produced and can be perceived here and now, experientially.

*signifier and signified (meaning)

Signifier = the acoustic image, the sensorial part of the sign

Signified = the concept.

Signifier and *signified* make up the *sign*, a fundamental notion in linguistics. What the sign unites is not a thing and a name but rather an acoustic concept and an image. In **Saussure**'s classical definition there must be a relationship of balance or symmetry between both phases. The relationship between them creates *meaning*.

*synchrony and diachrony

Synchronicity = at the same time

Diachronicity = along any length of time

A language phenomenom is said to be *synchronic* when the elements and factors it brings into play correspond to a single moment in a single language. It is *diachronic* when there is intervention of elements which belong to different moments in the development of a given language.

Saussure was the first to draw our attention to the importance of the *synchrony-diachrony distinction* with which he reoriented modern linguistics from historical insights to contemporary studies of the language. "The synchronic law establishes a state of things." Diachrony assumes, on the contrary, the dynamic factor with which an effect is achieved. I have used these terms in this book not in reference to an entire discipline but to the everyday use of words or phonemes.

*syntagm and paradigm

Syntagm = linear association of various consecutive units; horizontal linkage of elements based on the linear nature of language, which precludes the pronunciation of two elements simultaneously.

paradigm = all types of linguistic elements regardless of the principles grouping them; associative group, list or set of elements which could be located in a given place in a syntagm and replace the unit found therein.

Syntagmatic connections happen *in praesentia*; paradigmatic ones *in absentia*. They are two different orders of coordination.

A syntagmatic relationship is one where signs occur in sequence or are parallel and operate together to create meaning.

A paradigmatic relationship is one where an individual sign may be replaced by another.

Syntagms and *paradigms* provide a structural context within which *signs* make sense; they are the structural forms through which signs are organized into codes.

Ferdinand de Saussure. *Cours de Linguistique Générale*. Paris. Payot, 1970.- Course on General linguistics.

*abstract, abstracting

These terms imply selecting, picking out, separating, summarizing, deducting, removing, omitting, taking away. As an adjective, not concrete.

*abstracting

A technical term in General Semantics that refers to a personal process, somewhat different for each person, involving:

a) structurally-determined selecting/filtering, including transducing.

b) functional selecting depending on past experiences, moods, needs, interests, etc.

c) integrating, summarizing, gestalting

d) self-reflexiveness – including reactions to reactions, etc.

The entire process is potentially self-corrective and produces results that can be communicated.

*intensional and extensional

Intensional and *extensional* could be defined as two semantic attitudes that have played an enormous role in the development of our forms of representation and our civilization.

Intensional relations are relations of "concepts", ascertainable *a priori*. An intensional orientation is characterized by an over-dependence on definitions, verbalizations, etc.

Extensional relations are relations for denoted facts, discoverable only by inspection of the existent, only discoverable by the enumeration of particulars.

An extensional orientation gives priority to non-verbal orders of abstracting. *Intension* covers the relations which hold good for all the possible individuals, while *extension* holds only for the existent.

The *extensional method* is in accordance with the structure of our nervous system and it ensures survival. The problems of *order* and *extension* are of paramount structural importance for sanity.

Some extensional devices – like indexing, dating, adding et cetera, etc. – increase the probability of acting appropriately in each situation.

*indexing

The use of indexing comes from mathematics, where variables are given subscripts, for example, $conservative_1$ is not $conservative_2$; $liberal_1$ is not $liberal_2$.

*dating

Following a similar procedure, we distinguish $Paris_{1989}$ from $Paris_{2007}$.

Alfred Korzybski, *Science and Sanity.* An introduction to Non-Aristotelian Systems and General Semantics. The International Non-Aristotelian Library Publishing Company distributed by the Institute of General Semantics. First edition, 1933.

Susan Presby Kodish and Bruce Kodishs. Foreword by Albert Ellis. *Drive Yourself Sane.* Extensional Publishing. Pasadena, California, 2001.

*enunciation

The act of enunciating, announcing, proclaiming, or making known; open attestation; declaration.

There are different possible definitions but it is the historical event which lets a phrase go from a virtual to an actual condition, materializing it, that interests us here. *Enunciation* as production of an utterance requires that certain conditions be considered: who, to whom, where, when, why and what for.

*speech act.

Specific instance; act during which a person begins to speak in a specific place and time to express something normally directed at somebody with some intention and purpose.

*speech act theory

Based on J. L. Austin's *How to do Things with Words*, its major premise is that language is as much, if not more, a mode of action as it is a means of conveying information. The basic emphasis of *speech act theory* is on what an utterer means by his utterance rather that what x means in a language. *Speech act theory* holds that the investigation of structure always presupposes something about meanings, language use, and extralinguistic functions.

From the standpoint of today's English analytical philosophy, Austin finds that there are enunciates which are neither true nor false; they are simply destined to "do something", and acknowledges the deep interplay of the utterance with the characteristics of enunciation.

"We must always consider", according to Austin, "the total situation in which the utterance is issued – the total **speech act** …" A speech act can be divided into three components:

*locutionary act = the act of saying something (with an abstract meaning to the extent that sounds are emitted and combined and to the extent that a syntactic relationship is established and represented by words).

*illocutionary act = the performance of an act in saying something as opposed to the performance of an act of saying something. (Taking into account the conditions of enunciation with illocutionary force, intention and purpose).

*perlocutionary act = saying something will normally produce certain consequential effects upon the feelings, thoughts or actions of the audience, of the speaker or of other persons.

From this point of view each time we speak we produce *locutionary, illocutionary and perlocutionary acts* at the same time. In other words, a *locutionary act* has meaning; it produces an understandable utterance. An *illocutionary act* has force; it is informed with a certain tone, attitude, feeling, motive, or intention. A *perlocutionary act* has consequence; it has an effect upon the addressee.

But the **locutionary act** itself is the combination of three types of acts:

*phonetic act … or the sound chain or linking of sounds (or association of phonemes in a given language)

*phatic act ... or prosodic act, which encompasses everything concerning melody and intonation. (Uttering words conforming to a grammar)

*rhetic act ... or the resulting combination of different meanings. The rhetic act reports subjects' meaning, not their words.

> Two interesting books to compare:
> J.L. Austin. How To Do Things with Words. Oxford. 1962.
> C. Minteer. Words and What They Do To You. Institute of General Semantics, Ridgefield Connecticut. (Beginning Lessons in General Semantics for Junior and Senior High School).

*direct and indirect speech acts.

We can perform a speech act 1) *direcly or indirectly*, by way of performing another speech act, 2) *literally or non literally*, depending on how we are using our words, and 3) *explicitly or inexplicitly*, depending on whether we fully spell out what we mean.

John Searle finds that there are utterances with two illocutionary forces instead of one. In these utterances, one of those forces is exerted indirectly through the other one. For example, we can make a request or give permission by way of making a statement, saying for instance, *I am getting thirsty*.

An *indirect act* is one in which the speaker conveys to the listener more than what he is really saying, thanks to their common baggage of shared linguistic and non linguistic information and to the listeners' rationalizing and inferential capacity.

Thus, *indirection* becomes evident in the following example:

"X": – Let us go the cinema tonight.

"Y": – I have to study for a test.

where we find that "Y" 's statement is a primary illocutionary act of refusal and a secondary illocutionary act of assertion.

The primary illocutionary act = the indirect act.

The second illocutionary act = the direct act.

> J. Searle The Background of Meaning. In Speech Acts. Theory and Pragmatics. Boston. D. Reidel. 1980.
> And Kent Bach, Routledge Encyclopedia of Philosophy entry.

*implicature

According to Grice, the creator of the theory of *conversational implicatures*, this is one of the conditions which rules conversation.

He gives the following example: A and B are talking about a common friend, C, who has just started working for a bank. A asks B how he is doing in his new job and B replies: – "Very well, I believe. He likes people and he hasn't been put in jail yet".

Whatever B implied, suggested or wanted to say in this example is different from what he said, which was merely that C had not yet been put in jail.

An *implicature* is a conclusion stemming from the conversation, its assumptions, constants and maxims. A *conversational implicature* is based on an addressee's assumption that the speaker is following the conversational maxims or at least the cooperative principle.

*the principle of cooperation.

The general principle of cooperation says that a contribution must be made as required at the time it happens and under the four following ***maxims of conversation:**

1) Amount. Give all the information necessary, but only that which is necessary.

2) Quality. Be truthful: do not say what you believe to be false and do not say something for which you have no proof.

3) Relevance. Say what needs to be said, something related to the subject and not dragged in artificially.

4) Modality. Avoid being ambiguous or obscure; be clear, brief and straightforward.

H.P. Grice. Logic and Conversation in Syntax and Semantics, Pragmatics. Edited by Peter Cole, New York, Academica Press, 1975.

See also David Gordon and George Lakoff. Conversational Postulates in Syntax and Semantics.

*register.

Range of vocabulary, grammar, etc. used by speakers in particular social circumstances or professional contexts. Each one of the styles with which an utterance is produced. (formal, informal, colloquial, familiar, vulgar, etc.). Set of particular characteristics.

*phoneme.

Of the many thousand of sounds, which the phonation apparatus can produce, approximately thirty phonemes belonging to a single language can be found. The ***allophones** are non-significant variations of a phoneme. In

River Plate Spanish, /h/ can replace the phoneme /s/ in certain sound positions as in, for instance, "mosca" /mohka/.

*morpheme.

Significant combinations of phonemes such as prefixes, suffixes, etc.

*lexeme.

Combinations of phonemes and morphemes in larger significant units or words.

Phonemes, morphemes and *lexemes* could be considered the *bricks* with which we build sentences following certain syntactic laws. We create/depict /transmit endlessly complex rich and fascinating worlds through them.

Oswald Ducrot, Tsvetan Todorov. Dictionnaire Encyclopédique des Sciences Sociales

BIBLIOGRAPHY

Linguistics-Philosophy of the Language-Semiology

AUSTIN, John L. *How To Do Things with Words.* Oxford, 1962.

AUSTIN, John L. *Le langage de la perception*, Paris, Armand Colin, 1971.

BENVENISTE, Emile. *Problèmes de Linguistique Générale*, París, Gallimard, 1966.

BERLITZ, Charles. *Native Tongues.* New York, Putnam, 1982.

BLOOMFIELD, L. *Language*, New York, Henry Colt & Cie, 1933.

CALVET, Louis J. *Pour et contre Saussure*, Paris, Payot, 1975.

CATFORD, J. C. *A Linguistic Theory of Translation*, London, Oxford University Press, 1969.

COTTERET. *57744 mots pour convaincre*, Paris, PUF, 1976.

CHOMSKY, Noam. *Syntactic Structures*, Paris, Seuil, 1957.

DUCROT, Oswald. *Dire et ne pas dire*, Paris, Hermann, 1972.

DUCROT, Oswald. "Le structuralisme en linguistique" in *Qu'est-ce que le structuralisme?*, Paris, Seuil, 1968.

DUCROT, Oswald. *El decir y lo dicho*, Buenos Aires, Hachette, 1984.

DUCROT, O.; TODOROV, Tzvetan. *Dictionnaire encyclopédique des sciences du langage,* Paris, Seuil, 1972.

FAUCONNIER, Gilles. "Comment contrôler la vérité. Remarques illustrées par des assertions dangereuses et pernicieuses en tout genre", in *Actes de la Recherche en sciences sociales*, Nº 25, Paris, Minuit, 1979.

FAUCONNIER, Gilles. "Is There a Linguistic Level of Logical Representation?" in *Theoretical Linguistics*, Vol. 5 Nº 1, Berlin, Walter de Gruyter, 1978.

FAUCONNIER, Gilles. "Remarque sur la théorie des phénomènes scalaires" in *Semantikos*, Vol. 1, Nº 3, Paris, The Semantikos Association, 1976.

FAUCONNIER, Gilles. *Espaces Mentaux*, Paris, Minuit, 1984.

FAUCONNIER, Gilles. "Questions et actes indirects" in *Langue Française*, Nº 52, Paris, Larousse, 1981.

FAUCONNIER, Gilles. "Pragmatic Entailment and Questions" in *Speech Act theory and Pragmatics*, edited by J. Searle, F. Kiefer and M. Bierwisch, Boston, D. Reidel, 1980.

FOUCAULT, Michel. *L'ordre du discours*, Paris, Gallimard, 1971.

GORDON, David; LAKOFF, G. "Conversational Postulates" in *Syntax and Semantics*, edited by Peter Cole, London, Academic Press, 1975.

GREIMAS, Algirdas J. *Du Sens*, Paris, Seuil, 1970.

GREIMAS, A. J.; COURTES, J. Sémiotique. *Dictionnaire raisonné de la théorie du langage*. Paris, Hachette, 1978.

GRICE, H. P. "Logic and Conversation" in *Syntax and Semantics,* Edited by Peter Cole, London, Academic Press, 1975.

GRICE, H. P. "Significado" in "Cuadernos de crítica Nº 1", México, UNAM, 1977.

HJEMSLEV, L. *Prolégomènes à une théorie du langage*, Paris, Minuit, 1968.

JAKOBSON, Roman. *Essais de linguistique générale*, Paris, Minuit, 1963.

JAKOBSON, Roman. *Selected Writings*, The Haye, Mouton, 1971.

JAKOBSON, Roman. *Six leçons sur le son et le sens*, Paris, Minuit, 1976.

LAKOFF, George; JOHNSON, Mark. *Metaphors We Live By*, The University of Chicago Press, Chicago, 1980.

KERBRAT-ORECCHIONI, Catherine. *La enunciación de la subjetividad en el lenguaje*, Buenos Aires, Hachette Universidad, 1986.

MAGARIÑOS DE MORENTIN, J. A. *Curso de Semiología Estructural*, Bs.As., ILAE, 1975.

MAGARIÑOS DE MORENTIN, J. A.; KIVILEVICH. *Semiología del pensamiento científico*, Bs.As. ILAE, 1976.

MAGARIÑOS DE MORENTIN, J. A. *El signo*, Bs.As., Hachette, 1983.

MARTINET, A. *Eléments de linguistique générale*, Paris, Armand Colin, 1970.

PARIENTE, J. C.; BES, G. *La Linguistique contemporaine*, Paris, PUF, 1973.

PECHEUX, M. *Les vérités de la palice*, Paris, Maspero, 1975.

RECANATI, François. "Qu'est-ce qu'un acte locutionnaire?" en *Communications*, Nº 32, Paris, Seuil, 1980.

RECANATI, François. "Some Remarks on Explicit Performatives, Indirect Speech Acts, Locutionary Meaning and Truth Value" in *Speech Act Theory and Pragmatics*, edited by J. Searle, F. Kiefer and M. Bierwisch, Boston, D. Reidel, 1980.

RECANATI, François. *La transparencia y la enunciación. Introducción a la Pragmática*. Buenos Aires, Hachette Universidad, 1981.

RICOEUR, Paul. *De l'interprétation*, Paris, Seuil, 1975.

RICOEUR, Paul. *La métaphore vive*, Paris, Seuil, 1975.

SAUSSURE, Ferdinand de. *Cours de Linguistique Générale*, 1916, Edition critique préparée par Tulio de Mauro, Paris, Payot, 1974.

SEARLE, John. *Speech Acts*, Cambridge University Press, 1969.

SEARLE, John. *The Philosophy of Language*, Oxford Readings, Oxford/Oxford University Press, 1979.

SEARLE, John. "The Background of Meaning" in *Speech Act Theory and Pragmatics*, Edited by J. Searle, F. Kiefer and M. Bierwisch. Boston, D. Reidel, 1980.

SEARLE, John. *Expression and Meaning*, U. K., Cambridge University Press, 1979.

SIMONIN-GRUMBACH, J. "Pour une topologie des discours" in *Langue, Discours, Société*, Paris, Seuil, 1975.

STEINER, G. *After Babel, Aspects of Language and Translation*, London & New York, Oxford University Press, 1975.

SPERBER, Dan. "Rudiments de Rhétorique Cognitive" in *Poétique* (revue), Paris, Seuil, 1975.

STRAWSON, P. *Etudes de logique et de linguistique*, Paris, Seuil, 1977.

ULLMANN, S. *Semantics: An Introduction to the Science of Meaning*, Oxford, Basil Blackwell, 1972.

WHORF, Benjamin Lee. *Language, Thought, and Reality,* Cambridge, Massachusetts, The MIT Press, !st edition, 1956, 21st edition, 1993.

YAGUELLO, Marina. *Alice au pays du langage: Pour comprendre la linguistique*, Editions du Seuil, Paris, 1981.

Psycholinguistics

BEAUVILLAIN, C. "Proyecto de investigación presentado para el ingreso al CNRS, 1981 y 1982. Etudes des processus de perception et de production linguistique dans la traduction simultanée".

DENHIERE, Guy. "Le rappel d'un récit par des enfants de 6 à 12 ans", Paris, Laboratoire de Psychologie de l' Université de Paris VIII, Documento N° 98, 1978.

DENHIERE, Guy. "Mémoire sémantique, conceptuelle ou lexicalle?", Paris, Laboratoire de Psychologie de l' Université de Paris VIII, Documento N° 48, 1975.

ERLICH, M. F. "Approche expérimentale des rapport entre compréhension et mémorisation d'un texte", Paris, Laboratoire de Psychologie Expérimentale de l'Université René Descartes, 1981.

FREDERIKSEN, C. "Representing Logical and Semantic Structure of Knowledge Acquired from Discourse" in *Cognitive Psychology 7*, Academic Press, Inc., 1975.

MEHLER, J. *The Role of Syllables in Speech Processing: Infant and Adult Data.* London, Phil. Trans. R. Soc. Lond. B. 295, 333-352, 1981.

MEHLER, J.; SEGUI, J.; PITTET, M.; BARRIERE, M. "Strategies for Sentence Perception" in *Journal of Psycholinguistic Research*, Vol. 7, N°1, 1978.

PYNTE, J.; DENHIERE, G. *Influence de la thématisation et du statut syntaxique des propositions sur les temps de lecture et la mémorisation de récits*, France: Laboratoire de Psychologie de l'Université de Provence et de Paris VIII, 1980.

PYNTE, J.; DO, Ph.; SCAMPA, P. "Lexical Decision Times during the Reading of Sentences with Polysemous Words". Aix-en-Provence, Laboratoire de Psychologie de l'Université de Provence.

FERRAND – GRAINGER. *Psycholinguistique Cognitive, Essais en l'Honneur de Juan SEGUI,* Bruxelles, De Boeck, 2004.

SEGUI, DOMMERGES; FRAUENFELDER; MEHLER. "L'intégration perceptive des phrases: aspects syntaxiques et sémantiques" in Bulletin de Psychologie N° 6.

SPERKLE, E.; HIRST, W.; NEISSER, U. "Skills of Divided Attention" in *Cognition*, 4 215-130, Lausanne, Elsevier Sequoia, 1976.

SWINNEY, D. "Lexical Access during Sentence Comprehension. Consideration of Context Effects", in *Journal of Verbal Learning and Verbal Behaviour*, London, Academic Press, 1979.

TANEHAUS, M.; LEIMAN, J.; SEIDENBERG, M. "Evidence for Multiple Stages in the Processing of Ambiguous Words in Syntactic Contexts" in *Journal of Verbal Learning and Verbal Behaviour*, 18, 1979.

WRIGHT, P. "Feeding the Information Eaters: Suggestions for Integrating Pure and Applied Research on Language Comprehension" in *Instructional Science 7*, 1978.

Translation and Interpretation Theory

ALEXIEV A, B.; CHERNOV, G. *Theory and Practice of Simultaneous Interpretations.* In Russian. Mezdunarodnyje Otnosenija 5/4, Moscú, 1983.

BARBIZET et al. *"Vouloir dire: intonation et structure des phrases"* in Folia Linguistica, XIII, Mouton, 1979.

BARIK, H. M. *"A Description of Various Types of Omissions, Additions and Errors Encountered in Simultaneous Interpretation"* in Meta, N° 16.

BERLITZ, Charles. *Native Tongues,* New York, Perigee Books, 1984.

BERMAN, Antoine. *L'épreuve de l'écrivain,* Paris, Le Seuil, 1984.

BERTONE, L. "On Simultaneous and Consecutive Interpretation" in *The English Language Journal* Vol. 7 N°3-4, Bs.As., 1976.

BERTONE, L. "Sur la Relativité du Sens", in the *AIIC Bulletin*, Geneva, March 1984.

BERTONE, L. "Plusieurs façons de dire non", in *La Négation, Etudes Contrastives, Travaux du Crelic*, Paris, Université de la Sorbonne Nouvelle, 1986.

BOWEN, D. & M. *Steps to Consecutive Interpretation*, Washington, Pen and Booth, 1984.

BRISLIN, R. W. *Translation, Applications and Research*, London, Oxford University Press, 1969.

CATFORD, J. C. *A Linguistic Theory of Translation*, London, Oxford University Press, 1969.

CHERNOV, G. "Semantic Aspects of Psycholinguistic Research in Simultaneous Interpretation" in *Language & Speech*, 22/3, 1979.

DESLILE, J. (ed.) *L'Enseignement de l'Interprétation et de la Traduction*, Ottawa, Presses Universitaires d' Ottawa, 1981.

DOLLERUP, Cay, and VIBEKE, Appel. (eds) *Teaching Translation and Interpreting 2 and 3*. Amsterdam/Philadelphia, John Benjamins, 1994 and 1996.

EKVALL, Robert. *Faithful Echo,* Twayne Publishers, New York 1960, Library of Congress Catalog N° 6015421.

GAMBIER, Yves; GILE, Daniel; TAYLOR, Christopher. *Conference Interpreting: Current Trends in Research.* Amsterdam/Philadelphia, John Benjamins, 1997.

GERVER, D. *"Simultaneous Listening and Speaking and Retention of Prose"* in "Quarterly Journal of Experimental Psychology", N° 126, London, 1974.

GERVER, D.; SINAIKO, W. *(eds.) Language Interpretations and Communication*, NewYork, Plenum Press, 1978.

GERVER, D.; LONGLEY P.; LONG J.; LAMBERT, S. "Selecting Trainee Conference Interpreters", *Journal of Occupational Psychology* N° 57, London, 1984.

GILE, Daniel. *Basic Concepts and Models for Interpreter and Translator Training*, Amsterdam/Philadelphia, John Benjamins, 1995.

HERBERT, J. *Manuel de l'interprète*, Geneva, Georg, 1975.

ILG, G. "L'interprétation consécutive" in *Parallèles* N° 3 and 5, Geneva, Cahiers de l'ETI, University of Geneva, 1980 and 1982.

KAHANE, E. "La interpretación de conferencias o el teatro como metáfora" en *Cuadernos Hispanoamericanos*, N° 431, Madrid, 1986.

LADMIRAL, J. R. *Traduire: théorèmes pour la traduction*, Paris, Payot, 1979.

LAMBERT, S., *Recognition and Recall in Conference Interpreters*, PhD thesis, University of Sterling, 1983.

LAMBERT, Sylvie; MOSER-MERCER, Barbara. (eds), *Bridging the Gap*, Amsterdam/Philadelphia, John Benjamins, 1994.

LEDERER, M. *La Traduction Simultanée – Expérience et Théorie*, Paris, Minard, Letrres Modernes, 1981.

LEDERER, M. *Interpréter pour traduire* (with D. Seleskovitch).

META (Special issue devoted to conference interpreting), E. Orleas-Gerstein (ed.), 30/1, Québec, 1985.

MOSER, B. *Simultaneous Translation: Linguistc, Psycholinguistic and Human Information Processing Aspects*, PhD thesis, University of Innsbruck.

MOSER-MERCER, B. "Screening Potencial Interpreters", in *Meta*, 30/1, 1985.

MOUNIN, G. *Les problèmes théoriques de la traduction*, Paris, Gallimard, 1963.

NOLAN James. *Interpretation. Techniques and Exercises,* Clevedon, Buffalo, Toronto, Multilingual Matters, 2005.

PERGNIER, M. *Les Fondements Sociolinguistiques de la traduction,* Paris, Thèse d' état diffusée par Honoré Champion, 1976.

SELESKOVITCH, D. *L'interprète dans les conférences internationales - problèmes de langage et de communication*, Paris, Lettres Modernes Minard, 1968.

SELESKOVITCH, D.; LEDERER, M. *A Systematic Approach to Teaching Interpretation.* Translated by Jacolyn Harmer. USA, Published by The Registry of Interpreters for the Deaf, 1995.

TAYLOR-BOULARDON, Valery, *Conference Interpreting. Principles and Practice.* Adelaide, Crawford House Publishing, 2001.

THIERY, Ch. "L'enseignement de la prise de notes en interprétation consécutive: un faux problème?", in *L'enseignement de l' interprétation et de la traduction*, Ottawa, Ed. Deslile, Univ. Of Ottawa Press, 1981.

VAN DAM, I. *"Strategies of Simultaneous Interpretation"* in Monterey Minutes, 1986.

WALTERS, V. *Services Discrets.* Paris, Plon, 1979. (Silent Missions)

WEBER, W.K. *Training translators and conference interpreters*, Orlando Florida: Harcourt Brace Jovanovich Inc., 1984.

Theatre

ARTAUD, A. *El teatro y su doble.* Bs. As., Sudamericana, 1973.

HETHMON, R. *El método del Actor's Studio*, Bs. As., Editorial Fundamentos, 1977.

STANISLAVSKI, C. *La construcción del personaje*. Madrid, Alianza, 1975. (*Creating a Role*, London, Theatre Arts Books, reprint edition, 1989).

STANISLAVSKI, C. *Building a Character*, London, Theatre Arts Books; reprint edition, 1989.

STANISLAVSKI, C. *El trabajo del actor sobre sí mismo*. Bs. As., Quetzal, 1974. (*An Actor Prepares*. London, Routledge, reprint edition, 1989).

TOPORKOV, V. *Stanislavski dirige*, Madrid, Fabril Editor.

Psychology-Sociology-Communication

ARNHEIM, Rudolf. *Arte y percepción visual*, Bs. As., Eudeba, 1962.

ARNHEIM, Rudolf. *El pensamiento visual*, Bs. As., Eudeba, 1971.

BANDLER, R.; GRINDER, J. *Patterns of the Hypnotic Techniques of Milton H. Erickson, M.D.*, Cupertino, Meta Publications, 1975.

BATESON, Gregory. *Steps to an Ecology of Mind. Vers une Ecologie de l'Esprit I y II*. París, Seuil, 1977 y 1980.

BATESON; BIRDWHISTELL; GOFFMAN; HALL; JACKSON; SCHE-FLEN; SIGMAN; WATZLAWICK. *La nouvelle communication*, Paris, Seuil, 1981. (*How Real Is Real ?*).

BLOCK, J. Richard; YUKER, Harold. *Can You Believe Your Eyes?*, New York, Brunner/Mazel Edition, 1992.

CHANGEUX, J. P. *L' homme neuronal*, Paris, Fayard, 1983.

DE BONO, Edward. *The Mechanism of Mind*, London, Penguin, 1971.

DE BONO, E. Po: *Beyond Yes & No*. London, Penguin, 1971.

DE BONO, Edward. *Practical Thinking*, Pelican Books, England, 1976.

DE BONO, Edward. *Future Positive*, Pelican Books, England, 1980.

DE BONO, Edward. *Handbook for the Positive Revolution*, Penguin Books, England, 1992.

GOFFMAN, Erving. *Strategic Interaction*, Oxford, Basil Blackwell, 1970.

GOFFMAN, E. *The Presentation of Self in Everyday Life*, London, Penguin, 1978.

GOFFMAN, E. *Forms of Talk*, Philadelphia, University of Pennsylvania Press, 1981.

GORDON, David; MEYERS-ANDERSON, M. *Therapeutic Patterns of Milton H. Erickson*, Cupertino, Meta Publications, 1981.

HALEY, Jay. (edited by), *Conversations with Milton H. Erickson, M.D.*, New York, Triangle Press, 1985.

HUXLEY, Aldous. *The Art of Seeing*, London, Chatto & Windus, 1977.

LABORIT, Henri. *L' agressivité détournée*, Paris, Union Générale d' Editions, 1970.

LABORIT, H. *L'homme imaginant*, Paris, Union Générale d'Editions.

LE NY, Jean F. *La sémantique psychologique*, Paris, PUF, 1979.

LORENZ, Konrad. *Consideraciones sobre la conducta animal y humana*, Barcelona, Plaza y Janés, 1982.

MALANDRO, Loretta; BARKER, Larry. *Nonverbal Communication*, Addison- Wesley, 1983.

MERLEU-PONTY, M. *Fenomenología de la percepción*, Méjico, Fondo de Cultura Económica, 1957.

PIAGET, J. *Epistémologie et sciences de l'homme*, Paris, Gallimard, 1972.

PIAGET, J. *Problèmes de psychologie génétique*, Paris, Denoel, 1972.

RIBOT, Théodule. *Psychologie de l'attention*, Paris, Alcan, 1916.

RIBOT, Th. *La vie inconsciente et les mouvements*, Paris, Alcan, 1916.

RIBOT, Th. *Problèmes de psychologie affective*, Paris, Alcan, 1914.

RIBOT, Th. *L' Evolution des idées générales*, Paris, Alcan, 1914.

ROSSI, Ernest; NIMMONDS, David. *The 20 Minute Break,* Jeremy Tarcher, Inc., Los Angeles, 1991.

ROSSI, Ernest. *The Psychobiology of Mind-Body Healing, New Concepts of Therapeutic Hypnosis.* N.Y. and London, Norton & Co., 1986.

SWENSON, L. *Teorías del aprendizaje*, Bs. As., Paidós, 1984.

TOMATIS, A. *L'Oreille et la vie*, Paris, Lafont, 1977.

VERNON, M. *Psicología de la percepción*, Bs. As., Hormé, 1979.

WATZLAWICK, Paul. *How real is real? Communication, Disinformation, Confusion*, Nueva York, Random House, 1976.

WILSON, Robert Anton. *Quantum Psychology. How Brain Software Programs You and Your World,* Tempe, Arizona, New Falcon Publications, 1990.

WOLINSKY, Stephen. *Hearts on Fire. The Tao of Meditation.* San Diego, Blue Dove Press, 1996.

WOLINSKY, S.; RYAN, M. *Trances People Live: Healing Approaches in Quantum Psychology,* The Bramble Company, USA, 1991.

Psychoanalysis

ANCELIN SCHÜTZENBERGER, Anne. *Aïe mes aïeux!*, Paris, Desclée de Brouwer, 1993.

DUPARC, François. *Le mal des idéologies*, Paris, PUF, 2004.

FREUD, Sigmund. *Psicopatología de la vida cotidiana*, Madrid, Alianza Editorial, 1970.

FREUD, S. *Introduction à la psychanalyse*, Paris, Payot.

FREUD, S. *Cinq leçons sur la psychanalyse*, Paris, Payot.

LACAN, Jacques. *Ecrits I e II*, Paris, Seuil, 1966 y 1971.

MORENO, J. L. *Psicodrama*, Nueva Cork, Beacon House.

MORENO, J. L. *Psicoterapia de grupo y psicodrama*, Méjico, Fondo de Cultura Económica, 1966.

General Semantics

ALVAREZ, Ramiro. *Pensándolo Bien … Serendipity*, Desclée de Brouwer, Bilbao, 1999.

BOIS, J. Samuel. *Explorations in Awareness,* Viewpoints Institute, USA.

BROOKFIELD, S.; BROWNE, M.; CHAFFEE,J.; KEELEY, S.; MAYFIELD, M.; PAU, R.; SERIVEN, N.;TRAVIS, C.; WADE, C. *Conversations wiht Critical Thinkers*, The Whitman Institute, San Francisco, 1993.

CARO, Isabel (University of Valencia, Spain) and Schuchardt READ, Charlotte, With Foreword by Albert Ellis. *General Semantics in Psychotherapy*, USA, Institute of General Semantics, 2003.

HAYAKAWA, S. I.; ALAN, R. *Language in Thought and Action,* 1941 Copyright by Harcourt Brace Jovanovich, Inc. 1990.

HOFFMANN, Greg. *Media Maps and Myths,* Wisconsin, M&T Communications,1993.

JOHNSON, Kenneth. With foreword by Steve Allen, *Thinking Creatically. Thinking critically. Thinking creatively.* Englewood, N. J., Institute of General Semantics, 1991.

JOHNSON, W. *People in Quandaries.* USA, Harper & Brothers, 1946.

KODISH, Bruce. *Dare to Inquire. Sanity and Survival for the 21st Century and Beyond,* Pasadena, Extensional Publishing, 2003.

KORZYBSKI, Alfred. *Manhood of Humanity*, USA, Institute of General Semantics, 1st edition, 1921.

KORZYBSKI, Alfred. *Science and Sanity*, The International Non-Aristotelian Library Publishing Company, Distributed by the Institute of General Semantics, 1933.

LEE, Irving J.; LAURA L. *Handling Barriers in Communication,* USA,

Harper and Row, Publishers, 1956. Reprinted by the International Society for General Semantics.

LEE, Irving J. *Language Habits in Human Affairs*, USA, Harper and Brothers, 1941, Second edition edited by Sanford Berman. Concord, California, International Society for General Semantics, 1994.

LEE, Irving J. *How To Talk with People,* Harper and Row, Publishers, 1952, International Society for General Semantics.

MINTEER, Catherine. *Words and What They Do to You*, Internacional Society for General Semantics, Concord, CA, 1952.

MORAIN, Mary. (Edited by) *Classroom Exercises in General Semantics*, San Francisco, International Society for General Semantics, 1980.

MORAIN, Mary. Edited by, *Teaching General Semantics – A Collection of Lesson Plans for College and Adult Classes*, San Francisco, International Society for General Semantics, 1969.

NIERENBERG, Gerard. *The Complete Negotiator.* Nierenberg & Zeif Publishers, 1986.

PEMBERTON, William. *Sanity for Survival. A Semantic Approach to Conflict Resolution,* San Francisco, Pemberton Publications, 1989, 1991.

POTTER, Robert. *Making Sense, Exploring Semantics and Critical Thinking,* USA, Globe Book Company, Inc. 1974.

PRESBY KODISH, Susan; KODISH, Bruce. With foreword by Albert Ellis. *Drive Yourself Sane,* Pasadena: Extensional Publishing, 2001.

PRESBY KODISH, Susan; HOLSTON, Robert. *Developing Sanity in Human Affairs.,* Greenwood Press, 1998.

SAUCET, Michel. *La sémantique générale aujourd'hui.* Paris, Le Courrier du Livre, 1987.

SAWIN, Gregory. Introduction by Alvin Toffler. *Thinking and Living Skills.* Concord: International Society for General Semantics, 1995.

WEINBERG, Harry. *Levels of Knowing and Existence,* Institute of General Semantics. Englewood, New Jersey, 1959.

Intercultural Studies

BENEDICT, Ruth. *The Chrysantheum and the Sword,* Boston, Houghton Mifflin, 1946.

CARROLL, Raymonde. *Evidences invisibles, Américains et Français au quotidien,* Paris: Seuil, 1987.

DAVEY, William. *Intercultural Theory and Practice: A Case Method Approach*, Washington: The Society for Intercultural Education, Training and Research, 1981.

FISHER, Glen. *Mindsets. The Role of Culture and Perception in International Relations.* Yarmouth, Intercultural Press, Inc., 1988.

FISHER, Glen. *International Negotiation. A Cross-Cultural Perspective,* Intercultural Press, 1980.

HALL, Edward. *An Anthropology of Everyday Life.* New York, Doubleday, 1992.

HALL, Edward. *The Hidden Dimension*, New York, Doubleday, 1966.

Neurosciences

FAUCONNIER, Gilles; TURNER, Mark. *The Way We Think. Conceptual Blending and the Mind's Hidden Complexities,* Basic Books, 2002.

GANASCIA, Jean Gabriel. *Les Sciences cognitives,* Paris, Dominos, Flammarion, 1996.

HAMPDEM-TURNER, Charles. *Maps of the Mind,* London, Mitchell Beazley Publishers Limited, 1981.

HAWKINS, Jeff; BLAKESLEE, Sandra. *On Intelligence,* New York, Times Books, 2004.

JASTROW, R. *Au-delà du cerveau*, Paris, Mazarine, 1982.

SCHWARTZ, Jeffrey M.; BEGLEY, Sharon. *The Mind and the Brain. Neuroplasticity and the Power of Mental Force,* New York, Harper Collins Publishers Inc., ReganBooks – 1st paperback edition, 2003.

TROCME-FABRE, Hélène. "La Pédagogie à l'écoute des neurosciences: enseigner à apprendre", in *Réussir par l'école. Comment?* ICEM Pédagogie Freinet, 1991.

Literature and Philosophy

BACHELARD, Gaston. La philosphie du non. Paris, PUF, 1940.

BORGES, Jorge Luis. *El tamaño de mi esperanza,* Seix Barral/ Biblioteca Breve, Argentina, 1995.

BORGES, Jorge Luis. *Obras completas*, Buenos Aires, Emecé,

GUILLEBAUD, Jean-Claude. *Le goût de l'avenir*, Paris, Seuil, 2003.

HEISENBERG, Werner. *Physics and Philosophy*, London, Penguin Books, 1962.

MORGAN, Marlo. *Mutant Message Down Under,* USA, Harper Collins Publishers, Inc. 1996.

SEARLE, John. *Minds, Brains and Science*, London, Penguin, 1984.

SCHURE, Edouard. *Les grands initiés,* Paris, Librairie Académique Perrin, 1960.

Management

BRABANDERE, Luc de. *The Forgotten Half of Change: Achieving Greater Creativity Through Changes in Perception,* Dearborn Trade Publishing, USA, 2005.

BRAIDOT, Nestor P. *Neuromarketing: Neuroeconomia y Negocios,* Editorial Puerto Norte- Sur S.L., Madrid, 2005.

ELDIN, Francois. *El management de la comunicación. De la comunicación personal a la comunicación empresaria.* Bs.As., Edicial, 1998.

GLADWELL, Malcolm. *The Tipping Point, How Little Things Can Make a Big Difference*, Boston, New York, London, Little, Brown and Co, 2000.

GLADWELL, Malcom. *Blink. The Power of Thinking without Thinking,* Back Bay Books, USA, 2005.

LAGADEC, Patrick; GHILOU, Xavier. *La fin du risqué zero.* Paris, Eyrolles, 2002.

ROHAN CHABOT, Henri-Pierre de. *Manager en vérité, des patrons et des hommes,* Office d'Edition Impression Librairie (O.E.I.L.), F.-X. de Guibert, Paris, 2001.

SALOFF-LACOSTE, Michel. *Le Management du Troisième Millénaire. Holistique Systémique,* Paris, Editions de la Maisnie, 1991, Guy Trédaniel Editeur.

SORMAN, Guy. *Les Vrais Penseurs de Notre Temps,* Le Livre de Poche, Libraire Artheme Fayard, 1989.

URY, William. *Supere el No! Cómo negociar con personas que adoptan posiciones obstinadas.* Grupo Editorial Norma, 1993.

Physical Awareness

BERTHERAT, Thérèse. *Le corps a ses raisons: auto-guérison et anti -gymnastique*, Editions du Seuil, Paris, 1976.

BERTHERAT, Thérèse. *Courrier du corps – Nouvelles voies de l'anti-gymnastique*, Editions du Seuil, Paris, 1981.

FELDENKRAIS, Moshe. *Awareness Through Movement,* Fefna, 1972.

FELDENKRAIS, Moshe. *The Case of Nora.* New York, Harper & Row, 1997.

HOFF, Ron. *I Can See You Naked.* Kansas City, Andrews and McMeel, 1992.

PEASE, Allan. *El lenguaje del Cuerpo*, Bs. As., Sudamericana Planeta, 1981.

PLANTE M.; PLANTE, Molly; ADAMS, S.; BLAY, N. *Ese cuerpo es suyo.* Buenos Aires, Hachette, 1983.

SELVER, Charlotte. *Sensory Awareness. The Rediscovering of Experiencing,* New York, Charles Brooks, 1974.

Video-films

Né pour Apprendre. Videogramme en 7 cassettes. Auteur: Hélène Trocmé-Fabre. Réalisateur: Daniel Garabédian. Coproduction Université de La Rochelle & Ecole Normale Supérieure Fontenay St-Cloud.

The Brain, Our Universe Within. 3 video films by Hatsuto Hachiya, Masakatsu Takao and Cathryn Garland. USA, Discovery Productions, 1994.

Powers of Ten. The films of Charles and Ray Eames. USA, Santa Monica, Pyramid Home Videos, 1968.

The Human Animal – A Personal View of the Human Species. Desmond Morris. BBC, 1994.

Talking Sense . Professor Irving Lee. From the 1952 Television Series *Of Men and Ideas.* DVD. USA, Fort Worth, Institute of General Semantics.

Films

HITCHCOCK, Alfred. *The Trouble with Harry (1955), Rear Window (1954), Family Plot (1976), The Man Who Knew Too Much (1934), Shadow of a Doubt (1943).*

LUMET, Sydney. *Twelve Angry Men (1957).*

LUMET, Sydney. *Fail Safe (1964).*

RESNAIS, Alain. *Mon Oncle d'Amérique (1980),* (With Gérard Depardieu, Nicole Garcia and Henry Laborit representing himself as a researcher).

Printed by *Artes Gráficas Papiros*

Castro Barros 1395, Buenos Aires, Argentina

October, 2006

Praise for the previous book by the same author on the same subject.

EN TORNO DE BABEL

Buenos Aires, Editorial Hachette, 1989.

« ... Now, here is an extremely unusual, intriguing and auspicious way of beginning a discussion of our subject ».

> SERGIO VIAGGIO, *former Chief of the Interpretation Section of the United Nations Office – Vienna.*

«Et voici que nous arrive, sur le vent austral, un cadeau magnifique, muni du viatique élogieux de Gilles Fauconnier, linguiste éminent et préfacier: Laura Bertone a consacré dix ans de réflexions à ce volume en cotillon simple, fait de courts chapitres substantiels mais limpides, et édifés sans prétention jargonneuse, contrairement à d'autres ... ».

> *Book review by* GÉRARD ILG. *Cahiers de l'Ecole de Traduction et d'Interprétation. Université de Genève.*

«A little gem of a book: short, interesting, insightful, informative, entertaining, serious and unpretentious ... ».

> *Book review by* SERGIO VIAGGIO *in The Interpreters' Newsletter, Università degli Studi di Trieste.*

«The book Laura Bertone offers us deals with simultaneous translation and is in itself an important contribution to the understanding of the discipline. The work has a greater scope, however: the rigorous study of a specific activity – interpretation – will reveal the cognitive operations of everyday life, those which are so difficult for us to understand directly, precisely, because they are universally distributed.
For this disclosure to come about we must act at two levels: first, destroying the simplistic social image of translation as an almost automatic transference from one code to another and, secondly, reconstituting the activity in depth attaching it to the more general cognitive schemes that it makes evident.
Herein lies the interest and originality of the work Laura Bertone has undertaken».

> *Prologue by* GILLES FAUCONNIER, *Professor and Chairman of the Cognitive Science Department at the University of California, San Diego.*